SA[illegible]
BETTER
DIVIDEND
INVESTING

IAN DUNCAN
MACDONALD

Informus Inc
Publishing Division

Library and Archives Canada Cataloguing in Publication
MacDonald, Ian D., author

SAFER BETTER DIVIDEND INVESTING
Ian Duncan MacDonald
828 US & Canadian Scored Dividend Stocks
Issued in print and electronic formats
ISBN 978-1-9991-980-2-2 (paperback)
ISBN 978-1-9991-980-3-9
1.Stocks 2.Dividends I Title. II Safer Better Dividend Investing
Published by
Informus Inc, Publishing Division,
2 Vista Humber Drive, Toronto, Ontario, Canada, M9P 3R7
sales@informus.ca
www.informus.ca
tel. 929-800-2397
Publisher: Informus Inc Cover Design: Ian D. MacDonald

Dedicated to my wife Carmen
who has made this book and
all the good things in my life possible.

Ian Duncan MacDonald

CHAPTERS

Other Books

By
Ian Duncan MacDonald

Non-Fiction

Income and Wealth from Self Directed-Investing

Fiction

Duel
Using Drought USA
Beware The Abandoned

7

CHAPTER 1
UNCOMMON STOCKS

Building a stock portfolio that will support you for the rest of your life is not difficult. The first step is being able to recognize which stocks are going to make you financially independent. All the information you need to identify such stocks is free and immediately available on the internet. This book is dedicated to showing you what information you need; where to find it and how to interpret it.

NOTE: Chapter 25 is an index of the book's contents. Items listed in the index are highlighted throughout the book. Within the book's chapters are sequentially numbered topic or question headings. Within these headings are the highlighted items. Anticipating that it will be used as a reference book, this format makes it easier to find answers whether the book is in an electronic or a printed format.

The following are two examples of listing in the index:

"3 years to fully recover.../CH 15/Q11"
"Board of Directors.../CH 1/T5"

CH = Chapter, Q = Question, T= Topic

This is not meant to be a dry textbook. It is a personal conversation in which I share with a friend what I have learned over the last 50 years about investing, business, and life. I have avoided the jargon and confusing technical concepts that the investment industry uses to

intimidate investors who would dare consider investing without the industry taking a bite out of your wealth.

(CH1/T1) **THE IDEAL STOCK**

The "good" dividends of financially strong companies provide a reliable income and a potential for a higher share price. There are 14,982 corporations in North America offering their common shares for purchase. For a strong portfolio you need to find 20 that come closest to matching the following "ideal criteria".

(1) A stock price greater than $100
(2) A stock price that was greater than $100 four years ago.
(3) A stock price that is now 99.50% greater than it was 4 years ago.
(4) A stock with a book value greater than $100.
(5) A current stock price greater than 49.5% of the book value
(6) Five or more analysts rating the stock a "buy".
(7) Five or more analysts rating the stock a "strong buy".
(8) A dividend yield percent between 7.50% and 10.49%.
(9) An operating margin greater than 79.50%
(10) An average daily volume of shares traded greater than 2,000,000.
(11) A stock's price-to-earnings ratio between 0.1x to 5.49x.

The reality is that in 20 years of reviewing thousands of stocks I have never found a perfect stock that met all eleven criteria. Since the ideal stock does not exist this means you must sort through those 14,982 stocks to find those 20 that come closest to matching these 11 criteria.

To help me sort out stocks I score them using the above 11 criteria. When the 11 scores are added they have the potential to reach a total of 100. After scoring thousands of stocks the highest score I have ever calculated is 78; the lowest score is 8. (I avoid buying stocks scoring under 50).

(CH 1/T2) **US & CANADA STOCKS**

In Chapters 18 to 21 you will find charts where I have scored for you all **628 US common stocks** paying a dividend of 6 % or greater. In Chapters 22 to 25 are all **199** scored Canadian common stocks paying a dividend of 3.5% or greater. Your 20 best stocks are in these two lists.

To help you easily find stocks to consider for your portfolio, all these stock lists were displayed and sorted four ways: (1) by descending stock score (2) share price (3) dividend yield percent (4) alphabetically. These sorts will help to shrink your search for the best 20 stocks to a reasonable number to evaluate.

(CH 1/T3) **STOCK SCORING**

A stock scoring system applies an objective, mathematically derived number to a stock. This number helps investors decide which of these dividend stocks will provide them with a reliable, generous dividend income plus show a substantial future increase in the value of their portfolio.

The stock scoring system was designed with the objective or providing an annual dividend income of at least 6% and a gain of 9% in their portfolio. Dividends get paid even during recessions and pandemics by financially strong companies. There are years, like 2020 and 2008 when portfolios do not increase. During years such as 2020 you live off your dividend income and wait for the stock market to rebound as it has after every downturn for the last 100 years. You do not sell the financially strong stocks that you have so carefully chosen and attempt to time your re-entry into the market. While the share price may have dropped you still own the same number of shares and 90% of your stocks should continue to pay the same dividends as they always have.

If you are buying financially strong dividend stocks for the first time during this downturn, you can look forward to good capital gains in the future. The stock prices of many strong companies are now at bargain prices compared to what you had to pay in 2019 and what you will pay in future years.

From Chapter 2 to Chapter 12 you will learn how each of the eleven factors that make up the total score are calculated. As well, you will learn why each factor was chosen and how it is an important consideration when selecting a stock for your portfolio. While the factors in these chapters could be used to manually calculate the total score for a stock***, everyone who buys my books can request a free copy of the stock scoring software which quickly calculates a stock's score on their personal computers***. *To receive the software send an emailed request to* ***imacd@informus.ca***. *If you have not received your software phone 929-800-2397 (a New York number) or (416-245-4994).*

While the scores for all 828 stocks appear in this book, investors are advised to recalculate the score immediately before buying a stock. As you can see in the Canadian dividend percent list, where last year's score and this year's score are displayed side-by-side, a few scores can change

Hermes
the parcel people

Receipt

Send, collect, return

This receipt is your proof of drop-off.

Date: 02 May 22
Webcam, Rhinocerse
- Micro USB, Jeans
MA Shorts

No. of parcels:

Thanks for using your local ParcelShop. Your parcel is in good hands.

Hermes

the parcel people

P1832326

- If you want to know what your parcel is up to, you can track it using the number above.
- If you've got a question about a return to a retailer, you'll need to contact them directly.
- Or, if you have any questions about any Hermes parcel, just visit our help section at **myhermes.co.uk**

significantly. Most of these scores are within 10 points of where they were last year. Those whose score changed more than 10 points from last year or did not qualify to appear last year have been high lighted.

(CH 1/T4) IMPORTANCE OF DIVIDENDS

The primary objective of the book is help investors select safe stocks for their portfolios. Dividends that are paid by financially strong companies almost guarantee that the stocks you invest in will be profitable and stable for many years to come. The generous, consistent dividend income from such stocks protects investors from ever being forced to sell shares at a loss in a market downturn. This is always the worst possible time to be selling stocks. With carefully chosen dividend stocks in your portfolio, the erratic daily fluctuations of the stock market remain interesting but largely irrelevant to your dividend income's well being.

I have been asked why so few of the financially strong dividend paying stocks have not reduced or canceled their dividend payments during the current recession? Anyone who has worked at a senior level in large public corporation understands why the last thing the executives of such companies ever do is cut dividends. They have too much to lose if they cut dividends.

(CH 1/T5) CORPORATE POWER

Technically a corporation's board of directors is elected by the shareholders. The directors hold the ultimate power in a corporation. They would have voted and approved the hiring of the chief executive.

Once a chief executive is in place, they quickly consolidate their power. Any strong competitors who were also considered for the chief executive's position are often terminated or removed from positions of power by the new chief executive. Their loyal supporters on the executive team are rewarded with key positions. The chief executive is often able to manipulate the adding of his or her "supporters" to the board of directors. The objective is to have a board of directors that will approve anything that the chief executive submits to them.

Everyone in the company receives salaries and incentives at the chief executive's discretion. Rewards are used to motivate and gain the loyalty of all employees, especially the senior executives who report directly to the chief executive.

Directors on the board are often regarded as a nuisance by chief executives, who see the board's ultimate power to fire him as a threat to his power. Corporations are not democracies.

The chief executive will see that the directors be given only as much information as is they are required to receive by law. A wall is built between the directors and the senior executives of the company to remove any possibility of collusion between the two and prevent "palace revolutions" by ambitious executives with an eye on the chief executive's job.

All the company's internal and external communication is also closely monitored by the chief executive to prevent any negative information reaching existing shareholders and the public who have the potential to become shareholders. Negative information can encourage shareholders to sell their common shares which can reduce the company's stock price. Disgruntled shareholders and a business' customers who complain to a company's board members or government regulatory bodies are always a potential threat.

The most sought-after executive incentive are stock options. At the beginning of each fiscal year, the number of shares the senior executives will receive in their stock option plan are presented. A stock option is an agreement that if the stock were currently trading at $10 a share, in one year from when they were granted, executives would be allowed to purchase their allotted number of company shares at that same $10 price, regardless of the current price.

An executive could be given 10,000 stock options at $10 a share. Without having to put up one penny, that executive could purchase the 10,000 shares at the $10 option price and sell them for their then current price of $20. This executive would have immediately realized $100,000 in additional income (over and above his salary).

If this executive chose to gamble, he might not exercise this option as soon as possible. He might choose to hold onto the options for years. In a strong, successful company over several decades these options could grow to be worth a million dollars or more. Companies often frown on those executives who make quick profits by selling their options as soon as it is possible. They think it displays disloyalty or a lack of commitment to the company's long-term objectives.

If a company has been paying an annual dividend of fifty cents per month per share to their shareholders for years, what do you think would happen if they cut the dividend? Typically, many shareholders would lose faith in the stock and sell it. An excess supply of stocks for sale on the market causes a share price drop.

A share price decline is certainly not what the company's executives want. They have been dreaming all year about how they will be spending their option money. Every employee working for them have been focused to do whatever is necessary to make sure the share price never drops. This means pushing for increased sales, cutting expenses to the bone, keeping salary increases for those below them as low as possible, reducing employee counts wherever possible, introducing new products, blocking the formation of unions, etc. They want the share price to increase steadily every year so they can always receive their stock option payout.

While there is an incentive for executives to push to increase share prices, there is no penalty if the share price should drop(other than not being able to benefit from the stock option incentive). This encourages risk taking in cutting corners for a short one gain rather than benefits that could be realized years in the future. Legal grey areas regarding environmental impacts, safety and employee welfare can be pushed to the limit.

Few financial advisors, who cater to speculators and have ever been executives in a large public corporation. They are often unaware of the tremendous impact stock options have upon profits and ultimately on share prices.

(CH 1/T6) **DIVIDEND PAYING COMPANIES**

Many analysts have prejudices against companies that pay dividends. While you may see the discipline and focus that paying dividends brings to a company, some analysts see paying dividends as a lame strategy to keep stock prices high when the company is no longer a "hot" speculative stock. The normal investment strategy advisors promote to speculators (who make up the bulk of investors) is to buy a stock and to sell it as soon as a significant price increase is realized and then repeat this practice over and over (until they lose all their money). Whether the company is stable, well run, and profitable is of little concern to speculators looking for the "quick buck". To them the stock market is a casino.

To pay a dividend a company must first be successful enough to show a profit. It is then up to the chief executive to make recommendations to the board of directors as to how profits should be spent. Money could be invested for future company development., to cut debt or reduce expenses by buying assets instead of renting or leasing, pay down debt, put in a reserve account for unexpected disasters like a pandemic, etc. . The executives of a dividend paying company will always recommend that a dividend be paid to their loyal shareholders. Not that the really care about the thousands of faceless shareholders but to preserve their stock options.

(CH 1/T7) **BUYBACKS**

Some large companies that do not pay dividends feel they can safely ignore the faceless mob of shareholders. Rather than pay dividends or strengthen the company, they spend millions of their profits to buy back shares in their own company on the open market. This usually massive buying action causes the share price-to-earnings ratio to increase in what may have been a falling market price. This positive change in the price-to-earnings ratio is perceived positively by many investors. It usually causes a temporary share price jump which can hide problems in the company that had caused the share price to drop. Since the price was increased unnaturally, there is little to stop it from dropping down again.

Buybacks do not boost earnings. For a corporation to suggest that it does, is meant to hide the truth. A company's growth in its bottom line can only be by its net income growth, not earnings-per-share. Similarly, top line sales growth can only be measured by its revenue figure.

Some companies buy back their own shares because their annual stock option bonuses are threatened. If a shareholder complains about not getting a dividend, the Chief Executive will assure them that they are only looking out for the welfare of the shareholders. They are sure investors would not want to see the value of their portfolios drop because the company's share price fell. This altruistic argument is usually enough to pacify the speculators holding their shares. What the corporation is really doing is rewarding a lack of creativity and innovation.

Until 1982, under the Reagan administration, buying back shares had been illegal since the Great Depression where it had been recognized as a form of stock manipulation. The US Securities Exchange Commission stated the rule change would increase stock prices. Supposedly this would benefit all investors.

Who really benefited most were the investment dealers e.g. higher stock prices = higher trading commissions? It has made the wealthiest 1% in the US even wealthier. Thanks to stock options, Chief Executive Officers now have an income on average 144 times more than their average worker. In 1982 it was 40 times greater. Trillions of dollars in share buy backs are now being bought by public companies every year. Since 1982 the average worker's income has seen little improvement.

(CH 1/T8) **RECESSIONS AND PANDEMICS**

In my earlier book, *"Income and Wealth from Self-Directed Investing",* I warned speculative investors that the future is unpredictable and that constantly rising stock prices is unusual. It had been twelve years of increasing capital gains since the last recession. We were due for another. My advice to the speculators in 2019 was to invest in financially strong companies that paid good dividends

In 2020, North America's 25 million business were plunged into a recession by the COVID-10 respiratory pandemic. Millions of employees have been laid off with no certainty as to when they would be called back to work, if ever. Hundreds of thousands of small businesses closed their doors and quietly disappeared while many large corporations began formal bankruptcy proceedings.

The hard-hit airline and cruise industries, have hung on, teetering on the edge of insolvency, hoping that a miracle would soon bring back the customers who were now barely willing to risk going to the grocery store for necessities. Companies in threatened industries have taken on billions of dollars in new debt in a desperate bid to survive. There future is cloudy at best.

Some businesses have flourished. A few like Amazon and Netflix, who cater to those sheltering at home from the virus, have flourished. Makers of plexiglass shields for retailers expanded their operations. The demand for liquid sanitizers was initially so great that prices soared to outrageous levels. The shares of such companies have soared. Interestingly, the liquor companies should be doing well. Not only are those in isolation drinking more booze but the liquor companies are also suppliers of industrial alcohol to the sanitary supply industry.

Despite how much some ignore its seriousness, deaths from COVID-19 in North America are projected to approach 500,000. Those ignoring the pandemic's demand for isolation jeopardize not only their own lives but the lives of millions.

(CH 1/T9) **GENERATING INCOME**

With social activity restricted many of those in isolation turned to on-line activities to fill their time and create opportunities for generating income. This included investing in the stocks. Investors all over the world have read *"Income and Wealth from Self-Directed Investing"*. Many of its readers were in the United States. They asked if my dividend investment system applied to US stocks. I assured them that it did. They then asked why no American stocks were scored in the book. I had limited the book's examples to those Canadian stocks with which I was most familiar with. I had not expected the book to be of interest to international investors.

In *"Safer, Better Dividend Investing"* but you will now find 628 US scored stocks. They are all the US common stocks paying a dividend of 6% or better. 250 US preferred stocks were not included because preferred shares can not be referenced to financial statement data. Unlike common shares they do not have operating margins or book values that are used in calculating the composite stock scores. This lack of good financial data left all preferred shares with low scores. The scores were also impacted by the fact that many have average daily trading volumes below 2,000 shares which further impacts their score.

Preferred shares are of little interest to investors. Investment analysts ignore them which inhibits their being traded. Another inhibitor was that only about 1% of the preferred shares show a miniscule share price increase from when they were first issued to investors. The share price drops are not offset by their dividend payments which are often in the 5% to 6% range.

In 2019 I had set the dividend selector for the Canadian stocks at 3.5% so the major Canadian banks would be included This resulted in the selection of 654 stocks including366 preferred shares appearing in "*Income and Wealth from Self-Directed Investing*". In this book, Canadian stocks paying a 3.5% dividend or greater, again appear but the irrelevant preferred shares have been removed. This resulted in 199 Canadian common stocks being listed.

Canada is a much smaller country than the United States with fewer public companies to invest in. The charts in this book show that the chance of realizing a good dividend income of 6% or more, is much easier to realize with US stocks than it is with Canadian stocks. Why do not more Canadians invest in US stocks? Currency conversions, US withholding taxes and the income tax breaks given to Canadians who receive dividends from Canadian stocks discourage many, but not all, Canadians from investing in US dividend stocks.

Before we look closely in the next eleven short chapters that describe the elements that make up the stock scoring program, let us review what the other investment vehicles have to offer. You now know that there is a wealth of current, accurate, free information available to select a good stock. This is information that government departments insist must be made available to investors.

You have read what motivates the executives of these public companies to pay dividends in pace with rising inflation and do all they can to increase their share price.

The ability for you to instantly buy or sell a share in the stock market for a negligible processing fee greatly improves your chances to make a good profit. It greatly exceeds the benefits the following investments can offer.

(CH 1/T10) **SAVINGS ACCOUNTS**

A savings account is a form of investment. How does it compare to a dividend stock? First you must accept that you are paying a fee to a bank to keep your money “safe”. The bank pays a minimal interest rate of less than one half of one percent at a time when inflation is close to 2%. Your money is then loaned by the bank at 8% for over drafts and at 22% for those who do not pay their credit card balances in full. That meagre interest paid to bank depositors is taxed at the full income tax rate. Is it any wonder the banks can afford to pay generous dividends to their shareholders? Carefully chosen bank shares can anchor a stock portfolio.

(CH 1/T11) **BONDS**

Until recently investment advisors would recommend that all investment portfolios contain at least 40% in bonds. What are bonds? Bonds are an inexpensive way for governments and corporations to borrow money. They are a loan, paying a fixed interest rate at specific intervals for a fixed number of years. At the end of the term you get back the original amount you loaned. Unfortunately, since bonds are not stocks, there is no chance for capital gain nor is there any lower income tax benefit.

In a bankruptcy bonds rank ahead of unsecured creditors and share holders in realizing any funds from a liquidated company. This is promoted as a major benefit. Unfortunately, there is rarely anything left for bond holders or anyone else in a corporate bankruptcy. The banks with their floating debentures on all assets rarely leave anything for the bond holders and other creditors.

Unlike the negligible cost to acquire $50,000 worth of stocks, bonds are expensive to acquire. They are bought and sold through a broker. If you were buying $50,000 worth of bonds, expect to pay thousands of dollars in commission. Due to a lack of investment information on bonds, you are never quite sure if the price you paid for a bond was a fair price or not. It is difficult to determine how safe the purchase is since the company issuing the bond pays the bond rating company to rate them. The positive ratings of mortgage backed securities by bond rating companies in 2008 was an example of their unreliability.

(CH 1/T12) **DEBENTURES**

Some investment advisors may propose investing in debentures. They are almost identical to bonds. They are unsecured loans in which the borrower pays a specific interest rate for a fixed period. Unlike bonds they do not have special rights in an insolvency.

(CH 1/T13) **MUTUAL FUNDS**

What most investment advisors are keen to sell investors are mutual funds. They will realize between 2% and 4% in management fees and commissions, every year that your fund is in their possession. Any gain on your mutual fund will most likely be eaten up by those fees and inflation which is running at close to 2%.

The investment advisor will always assure you that the mutual fund portfolio is going to increase in value. In the year 2000, I lost $300,000 in a mutual fund in which my advisor put my life savings. Studies have shown if a mutual fund gains one year it lessens the chances a gain will occur in subsequent years. A significant number of mutual funds do not last five years.

One big concern when you give up control of your money and entrust it to an unknown mutual fund is that the manager will buy and sell investments in your fund without consulting you. You are just along for the ride. You are never sure in what you are invested. If you do go to the trouble of looking at the shares in a mutual fund, what will you find. You will usually find the fund invested in hundreds of companies. The benefits of diversification diminish once you get beyond 20 companies. This means you are not going to get much better results than index funds whose management fees are much lower. The larger the mutual fund the poorer the results.

If you sell some mutual funds within a year or two of buying them, expect to incur thousands of dollars in penalties. This is done so the mutual fund can recover the 2% to 4% they have paid in commission to the institution that sold you the mutual fund.

When you own a portfolio of dividend stocks, you live off the regular dividend income being paid monthly or quarterly. That portfolio will continue to get larger, year-after-year. For my portfolio of mutual funds, I was told that I would just sell off a piece of it every year to pay my living expenses. Is it any wonder retirees fear outliving their life savings when they see their mutual fund portfolio shrinking every year as they sell off enough of it each year to live on?

(CH 1/T14) **ETFs - EXCHANGE TRADED FUNDS**

An ETF is a cheaper kind of mutual fund. You can buy them on the stock exchange the same way you can buy stocks The management fees are lower than mutual fund, perhaps 0.25% of the fund because the ETF fund managers invest in a fixed group of stocks that requires virtually no management analysis. You pay this charge every year just like mutual funds.

If it is a fixed investment that does not change from one year to the next why are you paying for it every year? One reply I got back was a shrug and the comment that it was not much, only 0.25 of one percent. So, if I had $1,000,000 in an ETF that 0.25% would be working out to $2,500 for doing nothing. In 10 years, that becomes $25,000. If you had invested $1,000,000 in 20 carefully chosen good dividend stocks, which would cost you nothing for 10 years, you could expect a $1,000,000 return from the reinvestment of your dividends and capital gain.

An ETF may buy every stock in a specific group. This includes financially strong companies and financially weak companies. This leads to mediocre results. If the whole group falls, one strategy to protect the fund is to sell everything in it. They then speculate on when to buy back in. Timing it right can be dangerous. To diminish such gyrations some ETFs have wandered away from investing in just one group which further waters down the results.

(CH 1/T15) **HOME OWNERSHIP**

One of the biggest tax breaks for Canadian is that no tax is paid on the capital gain of your primary residence when it is sold. With the average house in Toronto now above a million dollars, and prices still climbing, this gain can be a significant motivator to purchase the most expensive house you can afford.

With mortgage rates hovering below 2% for good risks, it can be significantly less expensive to live inside one of your largest investments as it appreciates 5% to 10% a year, than to rent. The equity in a house becomes a reliable emergency source of funding. A mortgage can be added or increased. A house can provide the equity security for loans. When you eventually retire, your house is paid for and most of life's major expenses are behind you, you can live in it, inexpensively and in comfort.

(CH 1/T16) **RENTAL PROPERTIES**

Owning rental property is not an easy investment. Finding tenants who will pay their rent on time and become long term renters can be a challenge. The constant costs of maintenance, taxes, heating, cooling, landscaping, security, replacement of appliances, cleaning and complying with landlord-tenant laws can make this marginal investment demanding and stressful. Having to police parking, storage lockers, laundry rooms, noise and squabbles between tenants can be a constant irritant .

The complications of finding, buying, and disposing of rental properties can be time consuming and expensive. Your capital gain after taxes and real estate sales costs hardly make up for the time and effort. Since this would not be your primary residence, the capital gain is taxed the same as earned income. Hiring a property manager to avoid these challenges can eat up your operating profits.

(CH 1/T17) **REITs**

Real estate investment trusts typically pay more than a 7% dividend. It is one way to own property without the complications and demands of actual physical ownership. REITS are shares sold on the stock market.

To receive tax benefits most of the profits must be paid out to the unit holders. The real estate they invest in depends on what they choose to specialize in and may range from apartment buildings, to malls, office buildings and even hospitals. Dividends may be derived from both rents and the return of capital gains on properties as they are remortgaged. Some of the payments come back tax free as the REIT returns the capital you invested.

(CH 1/T18) **HEDGE FUNDS**

Before Bernie Madoff was sentenced to a hundred years in prison, destroyed his family and one son hung himself, Madoff operated a hedge fund which was eventually found to be an elaborate multi-billion-dollar Ponzi fraud. He got away with it because hedge funds are largely unregulated and invest in anything where they "think" they can realize a gain. Wealthy investors blindly entrusted their monies with him.

They are designed as an investment for the high-income individuals. .To join, you must have a minimum annual income of $200,000 and be able to invest a minimum of

$1,000,000. A sales commission of 2% or $20,000 is immediately paid as an entry fee. Many famous wealthy investors invested with Madoff and lost millions.

There are no guarantees of a capital gain. If there is a gain, the fund gets 20% of it. A few big winners in a hedge fund draw in the speculators, the foolish and the greedy.

(CH 1/T19) **COLLECTIBLES**

Paintings, coins, rare books, postage stamps and antiques are just a few of the items that collectors buy. Many of them are speculators who believe they can buy a collectable at a fraction of its true value that they can resell it at a higher price for a profit. Unfortunately for them, something is only as valuable as what people will pay for it. Unlike stocks there is no established exchange that brings buyers and sellers of collectibles together for a quick, easy sale.

There are dealers that will sell collectibles on a consignment basis; however, they have limited wall space and do not come cheap. You could find yourself paying them 50% of the sale price. Some unscrupulous art galleries are known to sell paintings on consignment and "forget" to inform the consignee when the painting is sold. If they are in another city, it can be an irritant to constantly check on the status of your consigned painting. If you sell the painting without the benefit of a gallery, the logistics of delivering a collectible to a buyer can be complicated and expensive.

To find a buyer can take years of effort. People's taste change and what was once a popular collectable can fall out of fashion and be difficult to sell. There are closets full of art that have shrunk in value and are not worth the effort to dispose of them.

(CH 1/T20) **PREFERRED SHARES**

A preferred share is a business loan. Corporations wanting to raise money for capital projects like them because the distribution costs are low and does not dilute the value of the common shares. Most preferred shares are sold at $25 each. They pay a fixed dividend percentage which is usually a percent or so higher than the dividends that the same company pays on its common shares. Like common shares they can be bought and sold on a stock exchange.

Unlike common shares, preferreds have no voting rights. Since they do not dilute the value of common shares this protects the stock options provided as an incentive to a company's executives.

They are not a good investment for individuals. The chance for a capital gain in a preferred share is about 1%. While the chances are that 50% of them will lose 20% of the initial $25 price. That they can be recalled and reissued at a lower dividend rate also makes them unappealing. They rank above common shares if the company is liquidated. However, in most bankruptcies, the only creditor that is likely to be have their risk covered is the company's bank. A bank usually has a floating debenture on all assets of the company. The only security a preferred share offers an investor is the reputation of the company selling the preferred share.

Stock analysts ignore them because, so few preferred shares are traded daily, they are of no interest to speculators. Since preferreds are not common shares in an operating company you can not use a company's financial accounting reports to judge the investment risk.

CHAPTER 2

PRICE

(The ideal (1) "A stock price greater than $100.")

The current price of a stock is just one of eleven factors taken into consideration by the stock scoring software. Supply and demand determine the value investors put on a stock. The stock market is an auction vehicle that manages the bids from millions of stock buyers and sellers. A high price for a stock reflects the desire of thousands of investors to own a specific stock.

Of the 14,982 stocks traded in the USA and Canada, only 3 Canadian stocks paying a dividend over 3.5% are valued at more than $100 dollars a share and 55 stocks at valued at under $5.00 a share. 4 US stocks paying a dividend over 6% are priced over $100 dollars and 33 are under priced under $5.

Stocks under $5.00 a share are referred to as being penny stock and are often denigrated by investment analysts You will find 3 Canadian "penny stocks" that are financially strong and have scores over 50. No US penny stocks score over 50. Stocks falling below a score of 50 are in an area of higher risk

The scoring matrix applies the following numerical values to a stock based on the price the stock was trading at on the day the total composite score of the stock was calculated:

#1

1. 0 to 99 cents scores = 1
2. $1 t0 $1.99 scores = 2
3. $2 to $4.99 scores = 3
4. 5 to $9,99 scores = 4
5. $10 to $14.99 scores = 5
6. $15 to $19.99 scores = 6
7. $20 to $29.99 scores = 7
8. $30 to $49.99 scores = 8
9. $50 to $99.99 scores = 9

10 Over $100 scores = 10

The sub score derived from the stock's current value is added to the other sub scores in arriving at the stock's composite score.

CHAPTER 3

HISTORICAL PRICE

(The ideal (2) "A stock price that was greater than $100 four years ago.")

A stock that increases over time is an indication that the stock will continue to grow. Looking at where a stock was trading at four years ago on, gives insight into historical stock price stability and indicates in which direction it is now heading.

If the stock were much higher four years ago then it is now, it gives you an insight into what the stock could possibly achieve again or suggests you seek more information to determine whether the stock is unlikely to recover.

If the stock is now higher than it was four years ago, it could indicate that the stock has potential for continued growth.

Why chose the price four years ago instead of six years ago or ten years ago? Most stock information sources seem to easily display 5 years of data. Choosing 4 years fit within the 5 years of data and gives more of a historical perspective than 2 or 3 years.

Traditionally when looking at corporate financial statements you will see only the last three years of trend information. Going to a price four years ago is within the normal five years of information that is re. It is current enough to pick up upward trends.

New businesses have great difficulty in surviving to five years. The fourth year is a make or break year.

#2

1. $0 to 99 cents scores = 1
2. $1 to $1.99 scores... = 2
3. $2 to $4.99 scores... = 3
4. $5 to $9.99 scores ...= 4
5. $10 to $14.99 scores = 5
6. $15 to $19.99 scores = 6
7. $20 to $29.99 scores = 7
8. $30 to $49.99 scores = 8
9. $50 to $99.99 *scores = 9*
10. over $100 *scores ...= 10*

To obtain the price fours years ago from most stock information systems requires you to pull up a historical 5-year chart that records historical share prices and dividend payment amounts. As you run your cursor across the historical chart, the desired information is displayed by date. You choose the same date four years ago or the closest date to it.

CHAPTER 4
PRICE TREND

(The ideal, (3) A stock price now that is 99.50% greater than it was 4 years ago.")

A stock that is now much higher than it was four years ago gives you confidence that the share price will continue to grow. If it is less than what the stock was four years ago you would have concerns about its potential for growth. The following gradations between the two extremes give insight into the stock's overall strength and price trend. . *(The program that is available to all buyers of this book automatically calculates this score)*

#3
1. The Stock has been sold for less than 4 years = 0
2. The Current Price is less than the price 4 years ago, by more than 50.50% = 1
3. The Current Price is less than the price 4 years ago, by 11.50% to 50.49% = 2
4. The Current Price is less than the price 4 years by .50% to 10.49% = 5
5. Current Price is within .51% to 1.49% of the price it was at 4 years ago = 6

6. Current Price is 1.50% to 10.49% more than the price 4 years ago ... = 7
7. Current Price is 10.50% to 99.4% more than the price 4 years ago = 9
8. Current Price is more than 99.50% greater than the price of 4 years ago = 10

CHAPTER 5
BOOK VALUE

(The ideal, (4) A stock with a book value greater than $100.

The book value of a stock is arrived at by accountants. They look at all the assets of the company minus such things as depreciation and liabilities. The calculated figure is then divided by the number of shares outstanding. If the "book value" is higher than the current share price, then this is often viewed as a bargain priced stock. You might be able to buy a stock with a book value of $20 for only $15 on the open market.

It is a rather vague valuation. If the company had to be liquidated or sold, the assets are only worth what someone will pay for them. This is dictated by the laws of supply and demand. The value could be more or less than the book value or the stock market value. It surprised me when scoring the 628 US stocks how so many had book values of zero. This would of course lower their overall stock score. Many also had operating margins of zero.

#4

1. $0 to 99 cents scores = 1
2. $1 to $1.99 scores = 2
3. *$2* to $4.99 scores = 3
4. $5 to $9.99 scores = 4
5. $10 to $14.99 scores = 5
6. $15 to $19.99 scores = 6
7. $20 to $29.99 scores = 7

8. $30 to $49.99 scores = 8
9. $50 to $99.99 scores = 9
10. over $100 scores = 10

CHAPTER 6
VALUE to PRICE

(The ideal, (5) A current stock price greater than 49.5% of the book value)

This calculation compares the stocks value on the stock market with the book value the accountants have arrived at. The software provided to this book's buyers automatically calculates the score, to save you having to work it out manually. A book value close to or higher than the stock price is an indication that the stock has good potential to rise in price. In designing this scoring system, I was not only seeking a steady dividend income, but I was also looking for an annual increase in the total value of the portfolio from capital gains.

#5

1. Current Price is less than the Book Value by more than 49.49% = 10

2. Current Price is less than the Book Value by 10.50% to 49.50% = 8

3. Current Price is less than the Book Value by 0.50% to 10.49% = 6

4. Current Price is between 0.51% and 1.49% of the Book Value = 4

5. Current Price is 1.50% to 9.49% greater than the Book Value = 2

6. Current Price is 9.50% to 49.49% greater than the Book Value = 1

7. Current Price is 49.50% greater than the Book Value = 0

CHAPTER 7
BUY RATINGS

(The ideal, (6) Five or more analysts rating the stock a "buy".)

Some stocks attract the attention of many analysts from the major banks and brokerage companies. They provide a projection of where they anticipate the share price will go along with a recommendation that the stock is a buy, a strong buy, a hold or one that should be sold. One information source has started to rate how accurate these projections are. Since it is difficult to consistently predict the future, their projections are just guessing. The reason I put " buy recommendations" into this scoring system is that buy recommendations do encourage some investors to buy a stock. We want to consider all influences on the price of a stock.

#6
1. 0 analyst = 0
2. 1 analyst = 2
3. 2 to 3 analysts =.3
4. 4 to 5 analysts . =.4
5. 5 or more analysts =.5

CHAPTER 8
STRONG BUYS

(The ideal, (7) "Five or more analysts rating the stock a "strong buy")

In my 2019 book, "Income and Wealth from Self-Directed Investing" it was easy to identify "strong buy" recommendations because the TD software specifically identified stocks as a "strong buy". Unfortunately, they stopped doing this doing the last year. This required me to come up with a definition that would identify an analysts' recommendation as a "strong buy". What I settled on was that any analyst that projected a future share price 50% higher than the current share price was giving a "Strong Buy" recommendation. It required more work on my part but gave me something to work with.

Last year I had accepted on blind faith analysts strong buy recommendations. Now I have what I think is a better measuring stick.

Strong buy recommendations do encourage some investors to buy a stock. Recognizing this influence helps to identify dividend stocks with growth potential.

Since, readers have access to a multitude of analytical stock research data bases, definition of a “strong buy” may make it easier for everyone.

#7

1. 0 analysts = 0

2. 1 analyst = 3

3. 2 to 4 analysts = 4

4. 5 or more analysts =5

CHAPTER 9
DIVIDEND PERCENT

The ideal, (8) "A dividend yield percent between 7.50% and 10.49%.")

What investors like about good dividend paying stocks is that you get two opportunities to make a profit on your investment: the dividend paid and the stock's capital gain. However, as you will see when you review the charts for the hundreds of dividend stocks in this book, that those companies paying a dividend greater than 11% rarely have high stock scores. This could possibly be because some of them are paying too high a dividend from their profits. Perhaps the company's executives see little benefit in reinvesting their profits in the company. This attitude may be reflected in low operating margins, low book values and other weaknesses. Be wary of company with a low operating margin that is borrowing money to maintain their dividend payouts.

The total score for a business is the deciding factor not the dividend payout. On the positive side, when a company pays a dividend it is an indication that it has the surplus funds to weather any downturn in the economy.

The following Canadian companies were paying 6% dividends in September 2020. Most are traded on both the TSX and the NYSE. Their generous dividend payouts have not been cut in 20 years. Their share prices are down significantly from where they were a year ago. When share prices climb back to pre-recession levels, even though the dollar dividend payout will remain the same or be higher, the dividend yield percent will probably decline to the 3.50% to 4.50% range.

COMPANY	TSX SMBOL	DIVIDEND YIELD
Royal Bank of Canada	RY	6.0%
Bank of Nova Scotia	BNS	7.7%
TC Energy Corp	TRP	6.7%
Bank of Montreal	BMO	7.5%
Canadian Imperial Bank of Com	CM	8.6%
National Bank of Canada	NA	7.3%
Canadian Tire Corporation Limited	CTC-A	6.2%
Atco Ltd.	ACO-X	6.2%

Algoma Central Corporation ALC
6.6%

These are stocks that can anchor a portfolio. The consistently pay their dividends year-after-year. They are not "flashy". They have little appeal to speculators hoping to quickly double their money. They are widely held, and their share prices increase and decrease slowly from one day to the next. Some have been operating for more than 200 years.

#8

1. No Dividend Paid = 0
2. 0.001% to 1.49% Dividend = 1
3. 1.50% to 2.49% Dividend = 4
4. 2.50% to 4.49% Dividend = 6
5. 4.50% to 7.49% Dividend = 8
6. 7.50% to 10.49% Dividend = 10
7. Over 10.50% Dividend =2

CHAPTER 10
OPERATING MARGIN

(The ideal (9) "An operating margin greater than 79.50%")

When all expenses are subtracted from a corporation's revenues, whatever is left is the operating margin. The chief executive then decides what do with these profits. They could be invested in new equipment and acquisitions to make the corporation even more profitable. They could be kept in reserve for downturns in the economy or a portion could be paid out in dividends to the company's shareholders. Many companies consistently payout about 40% of their operating margins in dividends.

Companies who have consistently paid ever increasing dividends each year will most likely continue with this practice, as we have reviewed in Chapter One. I was surprised when scoring the 629 US public companies paying dividends greater than 6% how many were showing operating margins of zero. This is why the total composite score is so important.

#9

1. A margin less than 1.49% = 0
2. 1.50% to 4.49% = 1
3. 4.50% to 9.49% = 2
4. 9.50% to 14.49% = 3
5. 14.50% to 19.49% = 4
6. 19.50% to 29.49% = 5
7. 29.50% to 49.49% =6

8. 49.50% to 69.49% = 8
9. 69.50% to 79.49% = 9
10. Over 79.50% = *10*

CHAPTER 11
TRADING VOLUMES

(The ideal, (10) "An average daily volume of shares traded greater than 2,000,000")

It can be difficult to both buy and sell a stock that trades only a few thousand shares a day. Such stocks are generally ignored by analysts because few investors are interested in them. The reason they are lightly traded is that investors see little potential in the share price increasing. Low trading stocks can have dramatic increases and drops in the share prices because there is so little demand for them. Some stocks can have no trades in a day or at most a few hundred. Many preferred shares trade at these low levels.

Stocks that trade on average millions of shares in a day rarely show dramatic price fluctuations. These are usually established companies with potential who may not have high operating margins because they are investing all their money in new product development. An example would be a company like Tesla that does not pay a dividend.

Several of the major banks that do pay good dividends also trade millions of shares each day. Since one of the scores objectives is to identify companies with the potential to show a capital gain of 9% or better, the trading volumes are important.

#10

1. Fewer than 10,000 shares….. = 0
2. 10,001 to 30,000 shares……. = 1
3. 30,001 to 50,000 shares……. = 2
4. 50,001 to 100,000 shares…... = 3
5. 100,001 to 250,000 shares…. = 4
6. 250,001 to 500,000 shares.... = 5
7. 500,001 to 750,000 shares….. =6
8. 750,001 to 1,000,000 shares. = 8
9. 1,000,001 to 2,000,000 shares. =9
10. Over 2,000,001 shares …… = *10*

CHAPTER 12

PRICE-TO-EARNING'S

(The ideal (11) "A stock's price-to-earnings ratio between 0.1x to 5.49x.")

The way I like to interpret the price-to-earnings figure is that it indicates how many years it would take to recover what I have paid for a stock from earnings. The lower the number the less time it would take to recover your investment.

Of course, an earnings figure must appear to do the calculation and many companies have zero price-to-earnings ratios. Usually a price-to-earnings ratio below 20x is considered "good". It is not unusual to see a "hot" stock with a price-to-earnings rations in the hundreds, even over a thousand.

Speculative investors are bidding the share price up to stratospheric levels. Far beyond their earnings. The expectation is that these prices can not be maintained and the frenzy that drove the price up will bring it crashing down at the first time their potential looks questionable.

#11

1. 0 or a minus figure = 0
2. 01x to 5.49x = 10
3. 5.50x to 15.49x = 9
4. 15.50x to 20.49x = 8

5. 20.50x to 25.49x = 7
6. 25.50x to 30.49x = 6
7. 30.50x to 35.49x = 5
8. 35.50x to 40.49x = 4
9. 40.50x to 99.99x = 2
10. 100x or more =1

CHAPTER 13
INVESTMENT ADVISORS?

The purpose of this book is to explain the benefits of self-directed investing where no one touches your money but you. However, most investors still blindly entrust their investment dollars to the management of investment advisors. . There are more investment advisors per capita then there are medical doctors. This indicates that the investment industry is generates enough revenue to support this gigantic army of people.

(CH 13/T1) **POLICING INVESTMENT ADVISORS**

When money is the focus of an industry is it surprising that it attracts the greedy whose purpose is to separate you from as much of your money as they can. Almost every day I receive news releases from IIROC (Investment Industry Regulator Organization of Canada) reporting how some sticky-fingered investment advisor has used a client's portfolio like his private piggy bank. Tens of thousands to millions of dollars are being easily stolen from naïve, trusting investors.

These thieves do not go to jail. They receive light punishments and are allowed, after a cooling off period, to return to an industry which has a reputation for problems with greed and trust. An example of this would be the ruling for John X in October 2020. He was accused of altering client documents after the client had signed off on them. Fee schedules, the client's stated investment objective and their degree of risk tolerance levels were altered. This allowed John X to take mutual fund fees from the client's account to which his client had not agreed to.

His punishment was typical he was banned by his industry's monitors from employment as an investment advisor for 12 months, paid a fine of $50,000 plus costs of $50,000.You would wonder if his peers who were sitting in judgment of him were saying to themselves, "There but by the grace of God go I". Having an industry police its own members lacks the stiff penalties and true objectivity of a court trial for criminal theft.

(CH 13/T2) **SELF-DIRECTED INVESTING**

The desperation level of investment industry is under attack. Their future looks troubled. The internet is eroding their customer base. Using free internet information and an on-line stock trading services it is possible for an investor, with a little effort, create a portfolio that will give them better income and portfolio growth than an investment advisor.

Why are intelligent investors still paying 2% of their portfolio's value to an investment advisor year-after-year for decades. The advisor gives them no guarantees on results. They take their 2% and other fees whether that portfolio gains or loses.

(CH 13/T3) **ADVISOR INSIGHTS**

You rarely get insight into how investment advisor's see their job. An interesting book put out by John J. De Goey, entitled "*The Professional Financial Advisor IV*" gave me the insight I had been seeking for several years. For example, did you think that an investment advisor saw his job as one of making you rich or at least acting in your best interest? Quite the contrary, according to De Goey, "*When things to wrong....people are often shocked to learn that all an advisor had to do was recommend products and strategies that they deemed "suitable"* for their client's circumstances." De Gooey is a recognized authority in the financial service industry with decades of investment advisory experience.

What is the primary concern of the financial institution that handles your portfolio? It is to enhance their wealth not yours. They will profit from your portfolio whether it increases or deceases in value. Like any sales organization they expect to get the maximum dollar return from the efforts of the investment advisor who is "servicing" your account

I am told each investment advisor manages about 150 clients. Typically, a sales representative loses about 20% of their clients each year. This would be about 30, every year (losses are through death, changes in financial conditions, switches to competitors, etc.). To replace these 30, would probably require approaching 300 prospective customers. This leaves little time to service existing clients. Even clients with million-dollar portfolios report never seeing an investment advisor from one year to the next. One,-million-dollar portfolio investor, I know was unknowingly paying $20,000 each year for the services of a phantom advisor. Over ten years they had paid out over $200,000 while watching their portfolio shrink.

To encourage prospective clients to see their "salesmen", financial institution's will often give the best closers a vice president's title. Be on your guard whenever the advisor wishing to see you about your investments is a "Vice President".

If you thought your investment advisor is the one who decides where to invest your money, you are mistaken. Another employee, a portfolio manager is tasked with investing your money in a pool with perhaps thousands of investors who have a similar tolerance for investment risk.

Whenever a stock is added or subtracted from that pool, the thousands of investors in the pool are all charged a small transaction fee. Most of the investors will not pay attention to a $7 charge. An investment service can make tens of thousands of dollars for a two second computer transaction. You have no control over this "active management" of "your" portfolio.

The portfolio managers have monthly revenue quotas to meet. They are judged by their employer on how much income they can generate.

Many investors hold banks and financial advisors in awe. Financial institutions are not churches. Financial advisors are not priests. They are salesmen who work hard at convincing you that they are wealthy knowledgeable investment professionals. The reality is that they are sales representatives. How they are paid depends on their employer. It can range from straight commission, to salary plus bonuses. Selling is never easy. If you were an investment expert why would you not be living off your investments instead of having to tolerate the stresses of a sales job?

Every sales representative knows they are only as good as their last month's sales results. Every month is a challenge to reach their dollar objectives. Does it not raise question of an advisor's hidden objective in their recommendations and behavior?

(CH 13/T4) **FULL-SERVICE WARNING**

An investment adviser will never recommend that you become a self-directed investor. Their sole objective is to acquire full-service clients. You will be strongly advised that becoming a self-directed investor would be a terrible mistake that will result in you losing all your money. *(Please note, I have been a self-directed investor for 20 years and lived very well off my 100% stock portfolio made up of financially strong, dividend paying companies. That portfolio is much, much larger than what I started with)* They will tell you that your only chance of making money it to open a full service investment account and leave its management to the "professionals". They will gloss over the reality of fees for those who use their services. You will pay these fees whether your portfolio makes you money or not. Since they have your undivided attention, they will also try to up sell you on their attorney and estate services.

If you go to a bank branch to open a self-directed investment account, expect to be pressured to open a full-service investment account. If you already have a chequing account with that bank, you do not need to go into the branch. It is possible to open a Cash Stock Trading Account over the internet. It allows you to buy stocks only up to the amount you have deposited in the trading account.

Another option is buying on margin. This is paying for stocks with money that the financial service lends you. Like any loan you are paying interest. In this case the stock you buy secures the loan. If that security should fall in value, the bank will sell the stock if they lose money on the loan. If the sale is insufficient to cover the money they leant you, you will be liable for what is still owing. You are in effect losing control over your investment which is never a good idea. Buying on margin can be dangerous.

(CH 13-T5) **OPENING YOUR TRADING ACCOUNT**

Your online bank account should provide directions on how to open a self-directed trading account. There are self-directed investment services available from companies independent of banks, they should still be able to allow you to transfer money between the investment account you have with them and your bank account.

If you are transferring an investment portfolio from an old bank to a new bank, let the new bank handle the whole transaction otherwise it could cost you thousands of dollars in dollars. The new bank should waive the fee for such a transfer.

Sign nothing before you go over it line by line. They may try to slip a full-service contract by you. If they succeed, it could take months before you regain control of your money in a self-directed portfolio.

If you are opening a self-directed investment account, you should never be requested to complete a Risk Tolerance Form. If this is presented to you then you have been unknowingly signed a full-service contract. However, without your signature on a completed Risk Tolerance Form, an investment adviser can not legally complete the set up of a full-service portfolio. While forging your signature is possible, it would be improbable. Since self-directed investors are totally responsible for their own investment decisions, a risk tolerance form is irrelevant.

In Canada, every major bank (and a few other sources) offer self-directed investment accounts. E*TRADE, Charles Schwab, and TD Ameritrade are a few of the US companies providing self-directed investing accounts.

Once your self-directed account has been opened the objective is to realize a dividend income of 6% plus show an annual capital gain in your portfolio of 9%. Supposedly a stock exchange measuring all stocks being traded in it grows at about 6%, thus 6% is reasonable.

Capital gains are not as predictable as dividends. Over several years a portfolio of financially strong companies grows. The task is to carefully buy common shares in 20 financially strong stocks, from diversified industries, paying good dividends. The charts in this book and the free stock scoring software makes this easy. Your objective is to only buy shares that you intend to own for 20 years or more. Such companies have most likely been operating for 20 years and consistently paying ever increasing dividends either monthly or quarterly.

The only one-time, total-fee you may ever incur, as a self-directed investor, when acquiring 20 stocks should be less than $200. The fee for acquiring a company's shares should be less than $10 no matter how many of that company's shares you acquire.

Those who provide trading services for "free" make their money through volume processing. While you may have put in a bid of $10 for a stock and be happy that you got it for that price, the stock trading service may have got the stock for a few cents less than $10 and pocketed the difference. . Occasionally, I have got a stock for less than my bid price from my bank. I pay a transaction fee of $9.90. There is no free lunch in this life

CHAPTER 14

TRADING

There is a choice of 8,961 stocks that can be purchased on US stock exchanges and 6,021 on Canadian stock exchanges. Out of thousands, how do you find those 20 that are best for your portfolio? Your investment dealer should have free software for self-directed investors that allows you to use selectors to reduce the number of stocks to be considered for purchase down to a workable number. Such software was used to identify the stocks that appears in the charts in this book. The US possibilities were reduced to 629 possible and the Canadian possibilities to 199 stocks.

(CH 14/T1) **FINDING STOCKS TO INVEST IN**

The journey to select safe, strong stocks for your portfolio begins by accessing an easy-to-use free database which provides standard information on stocks. While your investment dealer's system may be the easiest to access you can also consider other stock screening services. . Some I have considered are: **Questrade Market Intelligence, Google Finance, Globe Investor, stockcharts.com, Yahoo Finance, Finviz, and Atom Finance.** Several of these sites, once you get into them, are not as free or as easy to access as they advertise.

Not all of them were able to supply data on all Canadian stocks. In several of them I found while they had much information, the information I needed for my scoring matrix was either not there or difficult to find. I kept on going back to the TD direct online service, which was simpler, easier to use, and had all the information I needed. TD provides good free data once you register as an investor with them. I understand that TD's US affiliate, TD Ameritrade, contains the same information and allows US clients the additional benefit of not charging them for the buying and selling of shares.

The important thing is, for consistency you should stick to one source of information, so that you are always comparing each stock with data derived in the same way. One would think they would all show the same data for each stock, but they do not.

The TD self-directed system is what I will use to describe how easy it is to analyze and find the 20 stocks for your portfolio. It is the system I used to score each of the 828 stocks that appear in the charts in this book. Much of the work for finding good stocks has already been done for you, but you should understand how to search for other stocks beyond the selectors that I used.

(CH 14/T2) **DATA SEARCHES**

(1) sign into your WebBroker Account
(2) select **RESEARCH**
(3) select **SCREENERS**
(4) choose the *selectors* you wish to use to find the kind of stocks you want to appear in your portfolio.
(5) choose the *high and low range* within each selector

If your selector choice had been *Operating Margin*, you could set the *minimum* operating margin at 17% and the high setting at the *maximum*. If you had chosen that range, you would receive back a list of 1,120 stocks in the US and Canada with an operating margin of 17% or higher. Since this is too many to work with, use the numerous other selectors to bring the number of stocks for consideration down to a reasonable number.

Average daily stock trading volumes would be a good selector to use to quickly reduce the number for consideration

. Once you have a reasonable number of prospective stocks to consider, you can get great volumes of detailed facts on each stock by clicking on the *Overview* button on the *RESEARCH* page.

This will open a window that will take you to an ***Overview Page*** for a stock. In the window that opens, you type in the stock symbol or the name of the company. A list of possible stocks will appear. Click on the stock that you wish information on. Far more information than you require for scoring a stock will appear.

To see actual TD *screener* views and *overviews* of sample stocks, review my four free ten-minute videos on YouTube.com. *Video #3* walks you through this process of searching for a good stock. *Video #4* shows what your on-line portfolio screens will look like after you have acquired the stock.

Enter the following titles into the **YouTube.com** search screen to bring up the videos. A narrative description accompanies the videos contents:

"First Lesson in Income and Wealth"
"Income and Wealth from Self-Directed Investing - Lesson 2"
"Income and Wealth from Self-Directed Investing - Lesson 3"
"Income and Wealth from Self-Directed Investing - Lesson four of 4"

While these videos were created for my first investment book, "Income and Wealth from Self-Directed Investing", they are also relevant to this book.

(CH 14/T3) THE OVERVIEW PAGE

In Video #3, the OVERVIEW page for a stock is where you will find the 9 information items required for calculating a stock score. The stock scoring software is supplied FREE to those who have purchased the book. To obtain the stock scoring software send a request for to imacd@informus.ca. Unfortunately, sometimes messages fail to get delivered. If you do not receive a reply within 24 hours send an email to ianduncanmacdonald@hotmail.com or phone 929-800-2397 (this is a New York number) or send a mail request to Informus Inc, Vista Humber Drive, Toronto, Ontario, Canada, M9P 3R7.

To calculate a stock's score the following data is extracted from the Overview Page.

(1) the last price the stock traded at

(2) the average volume of stocks traded daily

(3) (3) the number of analysts that rated this stock a buy

(4) (4) the number of analysts that rated the stock a strong buy (some databases do not separate "buys" from "strong buys" and you may have to calculate this number by looking at the price the analyst is projecting for this stock. If it were 50% higher than the current price then the analysts recommendation would be a "strong buy".

(5) the dividend yield percent

(6) the book value of the stock

(7) the Price to Earnings ratio of the stock

(8) the Operating Margin of the stock

(9) the price the stock was trading at 4 years ago. This historical figure is a bit trickier to obtain. There is a **CHARTS**. Selector. You click on it and a chart displaying the price of the stock and dividend information for more than five years will appear. Run your cursor over the graph. The price of the stock on historical dates will appear. Choose the price for the date that is closest to the current day's month and day 4 years ago.

(CH 14/T4) **ALWAYS CHECK FOR CHANGES**

No one likes unpleasant surprises. There are 8 chapters of scored dividend stocks in this book. It took many months, starting in May of 2020, to score all the 828 stocks. Occasionally the data would change as I was calculating scores, not much but enough to be noticed. While dividend paying stocks are stable, it is always recommended that before you purchase the stock that you rescore it .

It is also recommended that you do a final **google.com** search just before completing your purchase of the stock. Enter the company name in the google search pane, do your search, then do a second search in which you add the following to the company's name, **"problems complaints legal actions".** You are looking for any negative information that could dissuade you from purchasing the stock. Since these are public companies, Google will have immense volumes of data. Scan through it quickly. The most important, current items will normally be at the beginning.

(CH 14/T5) **THE PROCESS OF ELIMINATION**

You may have narrowed the stocks you are interested in buying to many more than is needed or wanted for your portfolio. Diversification is important but 20 stocks in a portfolio is more than enough diversification. It becomes a real chore to try to work with more than 20 stocks.

Initially, invest 5% of your portfolio money in each stock. The stocks you have chosen are financially strong. It would be very unusual if there are significant problems in the future with more then 2 of the 20 carefully chosen stocks. You have spread your risk.

To get your portfolio down to 20 stocks is a process of elimination. You may want to eliminate mining and oil companies. Their share prices fluctuate with world commodity prices over which these resource companies have little control. Over the last fifty years I have lived through the depression oil company executives when Saudi Arabia cut prices and North American oil companies became unprofitable. I remember how the International Nickle Company would stockpile nickel in anticipation that the price of nickel would soon drop. When it did drop, they would then force 23,000 employees to go out on strike. This allowed INCO to cut overheads by shutting down their operations until nickel prices recovered and reserve inventory needed to be replenished. In 1957 after being out on strike for six months, the desperate union employees came back to work for a one cent an hour raise.

As the world heads towards eliminating gas powered vehicles, the laws of supply and demand indicate a lessening use of petroleum products. When electric cars dominate the automotive scene, the impact upon the existing industries established to build, sell, repair and service internal combustion automobiles will be immense.

If you are considering stocks that score under 50, you may want to eliminate commodity impacted companies from consideration for your portfolio.

Since lower priced stocks have a better chance of doubling in value than higher priced stocks, lower priced stocks in your list of possible purchases may be ranked ahead of higher priced stocks.

Since stocks that trade less than a few hundred thousand shares a day are more difficult to acquire and are subject to greater price fluctuations than stocks trading in larger daily volumes.

It is absorbing work. Before you realize it, you will have reduced your possibilities down to 20 stocks. Accept that the perfect stock does not exist and that you have done your best to carefully choose financially strong stocks paying good reliable dividends.

(CH 14/T6) **BUYING YOUR STOCK**

To buy a stock, sign into your trading account in the investment dealer's website. There you will find a \ button normally called TRADING. Click on it. Another menu will come up giving you a choice to BUY or SELL. Since you are buying, click on BUY. The computer system will now ask what you want to buy. You are buying a stock. Click on STOCKS. A stock ordering screen comes up.

Type in either the stock's symbol or company's name. A matching confirmation name appears in a window. You click on it and are asked to enter how many shares you are buying and the price you wish to pay for a stock.

While there is no minimum order limit to purchase the shares, depending on the service, there would most likely be a charge of under $10 for the order.

It would not usually be cost efficient to buy a single stock that was costing you $5 a share if your investment service charged $9.00 for handling the order. You would pay the same $9.00 for 1,000 shares of the same company.

Under "price" you are given the option of accepting the current market price or choosing to LIMIT the price to a lower priced bid. As soon as LIMIT is selected .a window appears to enter in your offered lower price. You then hit the button to place the order. If a seller accepts your price, the ordered is immediate filled. I usually put in a buy price a little lower than the offered share price, just to see if someone will pay less than the offered price. All you need is one person to accept your buy order for the sale to be made.

After placing your order, return to the TRADING screen and click on ORDER STATUS. You will see if your bid for the stock was filled. If it has not been taken up by a seller, you can go back, increase your price, and bid again.

If you want to, you can leave your original bid open for a few days to see if someone will sell the shares to you at your price. You can set how many days you want to leave the bid open.

Once a bid is accepted by a seller, it will take a day or two to appear in your account's RECORD OF STOCKS OWNED.

Millions of stocks are being bought and sold every day. The system of ordering stocks is quick, easy, and virtually fool proof. If there is not have enough cash in your account to pay for the stock you are bidding on, the bid will not be processed.

This order process will be repeated 20 times while buying the stocks for your portfolio. The 20 stocks you purchase will require you to make twenty compromises. If you can not make stock buying decisions, you will never receive a dividend income nor see your portfolio increase in value. The result will be that you will never be in control of your investments and never be able to protect yourself from running out of money in your old age.

(CH 14/T7) **MANAGING YOUR PORTFOLIO**

Unfortunately, you, not someone else, must go through this process because no one cares as much about your future financial well being as you do. You must understand why you chose these stocks for your portfolio and why you have faith in their long-term performance. Over the years the price of the stocks will rise and fall on the normal fluctuations of the stock market. If you are going to sell a stock every time a stock declines in value, you are going to create a lot of work for yourself and most likely lose money. A stock market downturn is not a signal to sell stocks, you will continue to receive most of your regular dividend payments as you sit back and wait for share prices to recover as they have after every downturn for the last 100 years.

Once the 20 stocks are bought, the amount of time you need to spend on them becomes negligible, maybe a few minutes a week, just to keep an eye on the total value of your portfolio and to see what cash the dividends are spinning off.

Most dividends will arrive as expected on the 15th and the 1st of each month. The money can be transferred into your bank account or re-invested in buying more shares of your 20 stocks. Until you have faith in your stock choices and understand that your money is not going to disappear, it is natural to feel you must constantly be checking the status of your portfolio. Eventually you will relax.

Every quarter you might want to score all 20 stocks or at least those where the price has fallen below their original purchase price. Since the objective is to hold the stocks forever, very rarely will you impulsively sell a stock until there is significant negative change in the score and the financial strength of the company.

If an unexpected amount of cash is deposited in your trading account, it is important that you investigate why it is appearing. Do this by going to the ACCOUNTS option in your main entry scree. . You click on it and are presented… with a list of options. One of these is

ACTIVITY. When you click on it, a screen appears that details every input and extraction of money in the account.

Above the ACTIVITY option is the HOLDINGS option. Clicking on it displays the gains or losses in every stock as measured against its initial purchase. The gains are displayed in green and show both the dollar gain and the percentage of gain. Losses are in displayed in red.

Also displayed is what percentage of the total portfolio each stock represents. If you are adding more money to the portfolio, you may want to put more money into those of the 20 stocks whose share of the portfolio has fallen below 5%. This 5% distribution can be a difficult objective to maintain since over several years some of your stocks will likely double or triple in value over their original purchase price.

Your concentration should be on the total value of the portfolio not on the value of the individual stocks in the portfolio. Having a few of your stocks slip below the price you paid for them is tolerable. The remaining stocks in your portfolio will usually have capital gains that offset any capital losses in the portfolio. Stocks down this week can be up next week.

In a recession 90% of your stocks will continue to pay dividends even if most of the share prices are down. If the financial information confirms the stocks are strong and paying a good dividend, you can wait for their share price to recover.

There is not much point in reviewing individual stocks in your portfolio every day. Perhaps, every 3 or 4 months, you might want to rescore the stocks in your portfolio.

Where are you going to keep these 20 stocks? If you are years away from retirement and want to grow your portfolio without having the government take a bit out of your dividend revenue or hit you for a capital gain every time you sell a stock then you will want to own a tax sheltered registered account where your dividend income can grow without being taxed. There are annual limits as to how much money (value of your stocks) you can put in these special accounts. The bank you open these sheltered accounts with will tell you what are the limitations and rules you must follow.

(CH 14/T8) **CANADA TAX FREE INVESTING**

In Canada these are Registered Retirement Saving Plans (RRSP) or Tax-Free Savings Accounts (TFSA). Your bank will be more than pleased to open a RRSP account or TFSA for you and provide the literature that explain them in detail.

One big benefit for Canadians is that all the allowed deposits in your RRSP are deducted from your employment income tax. As the stocks in the RRSP and TFSA accounts spin off dividends, this money can be used to buy more shares of your 20 stocks. It is surprising how quickly an RRSP portfolio can grow with deposit from both dividends and normal capital gain.

In the US and Canada at 72 years of age you are forced to begin withdrawing money from these registered plans. Initially it starts at 5% and the percentage grows a little every year. Since you are earning 6% or more in dividends in the RRSP, you can draw enough dividend cash from your RRSP to pay the taxes on this forced withdrawal and have money left over to invest in your regular trading account.

Using the dividend money that has been accumulating negates the need to sell any stocks in your portfolio (unless there us an urgent need beyond paying taxes on the withdrawn money. Withdrawing the accumulated dividend cash keeps the capital gain in your RRSP stocks growing even in retirement).

If you should live to be ninety, the increase in the volume of money you are taking out each year will reach a point that you will eventually have to sell your stocks in these tax free accounts. If asked, your bank will tell you each January how much you must withdraw from your RRSP that year.

If you are a Canadian older than 71, your possibilities for sheltering large amounts of income from taxes in a shrink. If most of your money is in a non-registered tracing account and that account is the source of income that you live on, any surplus funds, exceeding your needs can not be transferred into an RRSP. They can be reinvested in the regular trading account from which the money is coming, or it can be tax sheltered in a TFSA (Tax Free Savings Account). (If Canadians earn dividend income from US stocks in a TFSA, unfortunately unlike the dividends received from Canadian companies, they are fully taxable). A big benefit of TFSAs is not only that dividends and capital gain are being protected from taxes, but you can withdraw money from the TFSA at any time tax free.

You must be 18 years of age to open a TFSA. They were created in 2009. That year and for four subsequent years investors could contribute $5,000. It increased to $5,500 in 2013 and then to $6,000 in 2019. If you have never contributed to a TSFA savings account since 2009, then you can play catch up and open it with $63,500.

(CH 14/T9) **USA TAX FREE INVESTING**

In the United States you have IRAs (Individual Retirement Accounts). They are savings accounts held by a financial institution to provide income when you retire, their distributions are not subject to income tax. Payments are made into them by individuals, or in some types of IRAs employers can match and contribute directly from the employee's paychecks

Individuals can manage their own self-directed IRA or Roth IRA. They usually invest in stocks or mutual funds It has been about two decades since they were established. Since the custodian (the investment service) need not be involved in selecting the investments in a self-directed IRA the financial institution's charge can be minimized.

The Internal Revenue Service has established rules as to when and what can and can not be taken out of IRAs. For example, account holders can not use the IRA funds as security on personal loans. They do allow for the IRA to be invested in a specific list of other investments like real estate if the account holder is not living in the property.

As with Canadian retirement accounts, you must start withdrawing money from in your early seventies. The service where you establish your IRA and your accountant have detailed information on how to best to invest your retirement account.

CHAPTER 15
QUESTIONS
&
ANSWERS

Since I published *"Income and Wealth from Self-Directed Investing*" in 2019. I have spent hours every day fielding questions from investors. Following is a selection of questions that they have asked and my answers. Many of the questions are particularly relevant to financial and pandemic conditions in 2020. Answering the questions gave me great confidence in my belief that the secret to successful investing is investing in the shares of financially, diversified strong companies that pay good dividends.

(CH 15/Q1) **How does the Great Depression 1929 compare to the 2020 recession?**

The NYSE reached a peak valuation in September of 1929. It never exceeded that peak again until 1954 The crash had ended the "Roaring Twenties". It had been 10 years of exceptional growth and social change following the First World War. The Great Depression began with the market crash in October of 1929.

Thousand of banks failed, a quarter of those employed lost their jobs, thousands of speculative stocks listed on the exchange went bankrupt, and millions of investors lost their life savings. What caused the crash? Buy low, sell high speculators were buying shares on margin in anticipation of getting rich from stock prices that were always rising. Value investing in low risk of profitable companies had no interest.

Buying stocks on margin allowed an investor to only pay a third of the stock's price up front. The balance was paid for with loans from their broker or a bank. The acquired stocks became the lenders security for their margin loans. It seemed a reasonable lending arrangement in booming markets.

When the stock market value dropped to a tenth of its worth prior to the crash, the banks and stockbrokers called in their loans to cover their risk. They were left holding worthless securities. The stocks could not be sold to cover their loss because there were no buyers.
Thousands of banks went bankrupt wiping out the deposits of millions of their customers.

The market did not bottom out until the summer of 1932. The crash impacted the economies of all countries in the world.

Prior to the crash, many companies were optimistically producing more goods than the market could absorb. Their optimism was fueled by being able to arrange easy cheap financing from selling their shares in a hot ever-growing stock market. The inability to sell what they produced in either domestic or in foreign markets (because of barriers to export trade), these companies became unprofitable and failed. This triggered losses on the stock market.

As a result of the Great Depression, those who reached adulthood in the nineteen thirties forever looked upon the stock market negatively. They not only shunned investing but borrowing as well.

Many other changes came about because of the Great Depression. Unions were formed to protect workers. Buying stocks on margin was tightly controlled. Banks were closely monitored by the government. Bank savings accounts were protected by the government. Companies selling shares on the stock market were tightly regulated by the Securities Exchange Commission.

These safeguards are still in place and have tempered the impact of subsequent market crashes. The 2000 failure was caused by investors irrationally investing heavily in unprofitable dot com companies. The 2008 market crash was caused by mortgage backed securities which allowed those without sufficient income to buy houses they could not afford. Houses were being built then to meet a demand that could not be financially supported. The 2020 crash unlike the other recent crashes has not been triggered by financial errors, but by the fear of a deadly virus. It caused businesses to curtail their activities, millions of employees to be laid off. all travel to almost cease, schools to close and most leisure activities to shrink.

Not all companies have suffered. Marketers and entertainment services that utilize the internet have boomed. The world's economy was going through a period of adjustment before the pandemic and the pandemic has only been accelerated by it/

(CH 15/Q2) **What are the benefits of a 100% stocks-only portfolio?**

Over the last 20 years I have dabbled in almost every possible investment from rare coins to mutual funds. The safest and easiest investment is a portfolio made up of the shares of 20 carefully chosen financially strong corporations that pay dividends averaging over 6%.

For the last 15 years I have lived very well off those dividends and watched my portfolio more than triple in value. Even in a recession and a pandemic the dividends get paid by 90% of the stocks. Yes, shares and the portfolios values go up and down, but share prices almost become irrelevant if you have no intention of ever selling your stocks. If you own the same number of shares, you regular dividend income flows in. Strong companies tend to increase their dividend payouts on a regular basis. This keeps your income and portfolio value ahead of inflation.

The objective is to choose of course the right 20 stocks. There are almost 700 stocks in Canada and the United States paying dividends of 6% or more. A stock scoring matrix I created makes it easy to apply a numerical value to all stocks so the "best" can be recognized.

I have yet to find anything with less downside risk than having 100% of your investments in such a self-directed stock portfolio. Involving investment advisors in your portfolio eats up most of your portfolio's income.

(CH 15/Q3) **Is there a difference between and ETF and an Index Fund?**

Index funds and ETFs have many things in common. Both represent a "slice" of the market. That slice can be narrow (such as sector like Energy), or broad (like the S&P 500).

The difference is how they are purchased. Index funds can only be bought for a set price which is determined at the end of each trading day. ETFs can be bought and sold throughout the trading day like a stock. This makes ETF's prices volatile. It also negatively impacts investor behavior by frequent buying and selling easy. When an ETF does get treated like a long-term investment it then closely resembles those index funds that are bought and held for the long term.

(CH 15/Q4) **Why do many investors not trust investment advisors?**

While there are efforts to bring professionalism to the investment industry, the industry is certainly not helping itself. Today I received the usual IIROC *(Investment Industry Regulatory Organization of Canada)* daily epistle. It reported Peak Securities, *"almost 500 clients who held fee-based accounts were erroneously charged trailing fees."* Peak had similar complaints in British Columbia and Quebec in 2018. This negative registered against Peak is contrary to how they see themselves. The company's advertising sees itself as offering the same level of professionalism as medical doctors:

Promoting independent financial advice

For almost a quarter-century, PEAK Financial Group has been promoting independent advice for clients throughout Canada. Since its inception, the Montreal based company has served 150,000 Canadians.... the company has approached $8 billion in assets under administration and grown to support a passionate team of 1,500 advisors, employees, and registered professionals....

"I think in general, Canadians are either not aware, not that interested, or in some cases not that familiar with what's out there, so they rely on financial professionals. Getting independent advice is very important because there is no conflict of interest. A lot of people are looking for that: for advice first, before considering which products to choose. It's kind of like going to a doctor and having a full physical assessment before getting any prescriptions," explains President and CEO Robert Frances.

Frances states that when it comes to PEAK's selection of independent advisors, "integrity is number one." This is because PEAK values transparency with the end investor in all dealings. Moreover, their fully independent status is what sets them apart from many other financial companies that may only offer their house products...Their ability to offer completely unbiased advice in the customer's best interest, coupled with an ability to offer a variety of products under one roof is what enables PEAK to meet the needs of so many Canadians, each with different financial needs."

How could a company with 1,500 advisors not have had controls in place that would catch "erroneous" billings to 500 clients? The question of whether management condoned what was going on is sure to raised by some investors. Every day I seem to be getting infraction notices from IIROC.

These incidents only reinforce my belief that investors are better off managing their own investments. It is the least expensive way to invest and the cost of the investment is the most important factor to consider.

An honest investment advisor told me that retaining the current value of your portfolio is about all you can expect after about 5% in costs and inflation are deducted from a mutual fund's typical gains. For the last 15 years I have been getting a much better return on my investments than 5 or 6 percent - with zero costs.

Doing your own investing forces, you to know exactly what and why you have invested in a particular stock. When you invest in an ETF or Mutual Fund you have only a vague idea of what you are invested in. A typical mutual fund holds shares in hundreds of companies, if I scored those companies, half of those hundreds of shares would be rejected as being below my cut off point of 50.

Another problem with mutual funds is when they lose value, the whole mutual fund suffers. In a dividend portfolio of 20 carefully stocks not all stocks shrink, some always continue to grow in value even in a recession. 90% of them will always continue paying dividends. This reality reassures investors that the "sky is not falling" and a recession is just another passing phase in your investment experience.

Recognizing that investors are a minority in a population makes you question why there are far more investment advisors than doctors. Most investors invest through financial advisors. Only the opportunity to make an exceptionally good income would attract so many to a career in the investment industry. If advisors were made to adhere as rigidly to professional standards as doctors, there would be a significant reduction in their numbers. However, investment advisors are not greatly interested in appearing to be professionals and millions of investors do not really consider their advisors' level of professionalism when choosing them. They often choose their advisors just like they choose real estate agent to sell their house (everyone has a friend in the industry). Most think that one advisor is just as good as another.

+It is not until the ability to make an exceptionally high income disappears that you are going to see a shrinkage in advisors. At some point in the future, Canada and the United States will adopt the controls similar toq those now in place in the UK and Australia.

(CH 15/Q5) **Why don't you invest in growth stocks and what are the best dividend stocks to invest in?**

No, I have no interest in recognized "growth stocks" like Tesla, Amazon, Apple, etc. I have more than enough income to live very well on and do not need the stress and uncertainty of buying stocks that shooting up like rockets. I spend two minutes a day monitoring my portfolios. Speculative stocks require constant monitoring to determine when to buy and when it is best to sell the stock to realize your profit. There is a limit to how high a stock will go. Pursuing speculative riches is an endless run on a treadmill that is constantly increasing in speed with a greater and greater chance that you will fall off and injure myself.

After an investment advisor lost $300,000 of my money in a mutual fund, my objective for 20 years has been in realizing a steady, income that lets me do everything I want to do for the rest of my life. I own most of the shares I have always owned, yet my portfolio has grown by several multiples. Why? Because the companies who give me the exceptional, reliable dividends are and have always been financially strong companies. Such companies increase their dividend payments as their stock prices rise in tandem with their rising sales and profits. While their stock prices in 2020 are down, the companies in my portfolio are still financially strong.

As for the stocks I own that pay at least 6%, you can find some among the 5 major Canadian banks. These banks are recognized by the magazine Global Finance as some of the safest banks in the world. Several have been operating for 200 years. Most are traded on the NYSE.

I spent almost 40 years working with these banks on systems to predict commercial risk. They are conservative, careful businesses, almost to the point of being too conservative.

My portfolio also includes several REITS paying close to 10%. Only 10% of my stocks have cut dividends.

While about half my stocks may now have lower share prices, half have held steady or increased over the last 6 months. When I recently scored my stocks, I confirmed that they are all still financially strong.

I have had no pressing need to buy or sell any stocks in the last year. In January of 2020 I may start buying again. My cash reserves are up because my spending is inhibited by. COVID-19. Until January, I will keep this cash in a bonus savings account paying me an exceptional 2.5% interest.

(CH 15/Q6) **Do you see Tesla as an overpriced stock**?

Tesla is considered by many to be a hot, overpriced stock . It currently gets much more publicity than any other car company even though it has not yet joined the top 10 automotive countries in the world. It has only begun to realize profits in the last year. It pays no dividend.

By comparison, Honda is a member of the top 10, has had profits for decades, pays a good dividend and a share can be purchased for a small fraction of what it costs to buy a Tesla share. Honda has a long-established reputation as a reliable, affordable car.

This comparison of two auto companies would lead one to believe that a car company's stock price has little to do with a car company's perception by most car buyers. Tesla is viewed by many speculative investors as the next "hot thing". They are sure it has the potential to be another Microsoft or Apple. They missed getting rich from those two stocks and they are determined not to miss buying a Tesla stock no matter how much they must pay to join the herd.

The typical speculative investor chases performance especially when stock markets reaches new highs. Seeing an opportunity to get "rich" slipping past them, they jump on the latest hot new stock that is rising like a rocket. Taking all their free cash and even borrowing money they invest it all in that one stock. No thoughts of diversification or careful analysis is considered.

When inevitably stock crashes they bail out after the stock drops down below what they bought it at. This is the buy high, sell low formula that guarantees most speculators will never become rich. If you run with the herd, expect to suffer the same fate as the herd when it plunges over the cliff. Human beings are social creatures. They band together. They follow the herd.

To be a successful investor you must isolate yourself from the herd and look at investing objectively and unemotionally. It requires that you make hard logical decisions based on facts.

(CH 15/Q7) **Who are the US companies paying the highest dividends?**

I have just finished a study of 629 US companies paying a dividend of 6% or more. The highest dividend paid was 36.34% by PER (Sandridge Permian Trust). I am sure there are special circumstances for it paying that high a dividend. There were 6 other stocks paying more than 30%. There were about 200 paying more than 10%. (*Since you are reading this book you can view all 629 US stocks in the following four chapters).*

(CH 15/Q8) **How can I realize a 1% weekly return from my portfolio?**

1% weekly return equates to an annual 52% return. I know speculators who have seen portfolio growth greater than 52%. So, it is possible but is it probable? Winning the lottery is also probable. A stock market usually grows at about 6%. There are thousands of stocks being bought and sold. Some are shrinking while others are growing. It is not difficult to build a portfolio that will achieve 6% growth in a year.

(CH 15/Q9) **Can investing become addictive?**

I would not use the word "addictive" but it can sure hold your interest and make you spend endless hours acquiring information about investing, writing books about it, creating videos, answering questions and helping people who want to learn about it. I would describe it as a passion for the subject.

(CH 15/Q10) **We are in a recession. Is now the time to liquidate my portfolio?**

Why would you pull money out of the stock market? Have you found a better investment with more potential? If you are invested in financially strong stocks, they will come back. If you are not invested in financially strong stocks, why did you invest in them? I have not bought or sold any of my portfolio in over a year. I live off my dividends and wait for the market to return to new highs. It may take two or three years.

CH 15/Q11) **My shares have plunge 50%. What can I do to salvage this loss?**

In 2008 my portfolio dropped by 50% but by February 2020 it had more than doubled from where it had been before that drop.

It dropped by 50% in March 2020 and has regained about half of that loss. It took 3 years to fully recover in 2008. I expect it will recover to where it was in February within 2 or 3 years.

Why doesn't it bother me? Because I only invest in the common shares of financially strong, diversified companies that pay on average a dividend of 6% per annum - even in a recession or pandemic. I have lived very well off my dividends for 15 years and I am still living well off my portfolio. I have never been put in a position where I had to sell shares to generate cash for my living expenses. As long as I own the same number of shares, I expect my income to continue.

I did re-score some of the stocks that were down. I found that they still had good operating margins, etc. They were still fundamentally strong companies. I only buy shares in companies that I never intend to sell.

(CH 15/Q12) **If I can buy a stock and sell it within 5 days for a gain of 20%, why would I invest for the long term.**

Everything is fine until you lose your gain. You can not consistently predict what will happen next. You are on a treadmill requiring you to take a risk on every investment decision you make. It is a bit like having lucky hands in poker.

If you were a self-directed investor in 20 financially strong, diversified companies paying on average a dividend of 6% or better, you will not only get capital gain, but you will have a steady income that continues even in a recession. Such companies also increase their dividend payments regularly which keeps you ahead of inflation.

(CH 15/Q13) **What are the 3 best pieces of personal finance advice that almost nobody takes?**

(1) Stay far, far away from investment advisors.

(2) Stay away from mutual funds.

(3) Every month you keep money in a bank savings account it is being eaten by inflation. Become self-directed investor

and invest in 20 diverse, financially strong corporations that pay dividends averaging 6% or better, who have potential for an annual capital gain of at least 9%.

(CH 15/Q14) **When is a risk not a risk?**

A risk is not a risk when it is an obvious benefit that you can acquire with nothing to lose.

(CH 15/Q15) **Will Canadian banks cut their dividends in 2021 if we get a second wave of COVID-19?**

While it is not impossible, it is improbable that the Canadian banks will cut their dividends. Too many bank executives have their stock option bonuses tied into the share price which would be hurt if they cut the dividends.

Banks are infamous for nickel and diming customers to death with small charges. So far, they have not resorted to increasing fee charges. They are still flush with cash and are not paying any higher interest rates to attract more money to lend out. Almost all of them still have multiple options for generating more income and for cutting costs. Historically cutting dividends is just something they do not do (I subsequentially learned the government had prohibited increasing executive income, increasing dividend payments and allowing buybacks of bank shares).

(CH 15/Q16) **Which stocks pay a dividend yield as high as pipeline stocks?**

Which pipeline stocks? Just because a stock pays a high dividend does not make it a good investment. There are about 200 stocks paying dividends higher than the best pipeline stock I could find.

Of the 7 best dividend scored risks only one was a pipeline paying a dividend of 7.83%. I have just finished researching and scoring all 629 US stocks paying a dividend greater than 6% .

(CH 15/Q17) **What are risk management's goals?**

I have been involved in risk management for decades and have never been asked or seen anything that laid out the fundamentals of risk management. So, let me try.

The first thought that came to mind was the rather cynical saying of, "Trust but verify". While designing risk scoring systems, I found that 15% of any population is made of deviants. 85% of a population (no matter what kind of risk you are considering) follows the rules and does as they are expected to do. Within the deviant 15% are various levels of deviance from mild to extreme. The extreme would be a small percentage of that 15%.

As a risk manager you job is gather data that allows you to sort your "population" into various levels of risk. You then establish different rules for dealing with those different levels of risk. Often you are working in a political environment where several parties will try to put pressure on you to ignore the rules.

Ideally what you are trying to achieve is a flexibility that allows you establish limits as to how much deviant risk your organization can tolerate while maximizing potential sales.

I also have a theory that deviants are the ones who bring about both positive and negative changes in a population. They push the limits of the rules and can open new possibilities that the rigid 85% can not see.

(CH 15/Q18) **Is it too late to start investing at 35?**

Too late for what? I did not start investing until I was 56. My portfolio is many times larger than when I began, and I have lived very well off it for 15 years. Waiting so long certainly focused my attention on what needed to be done. My investments had to serve me for the rest of my life.

(CH 15/Q19) **Should I invest in in GICs and mutual funds?**

Investing in a Mutual Funds will make the investment advisor who sells them to you rich. It costs you money to buy them and to keep them. They will give a mediocre return.

Investing in financially strong companies that pay exceptional dividends are safer, more rewarding and cost almost nothing if you buy them as a self-directed investor. Most importantly you know exactly what you are invested in rather than having to put blind faith in the choice of investments going into a mutual fund.

GICs do not generate enough of a return to offset inflation. They are not an investment. They are a refuge for those who incorrectly think they could not possibly manage their own investment portfolio.

(CH 15/Q20) **How many stocks do I need to invest in before I see any money?**

One stock paying monthly dividends gives you money next month. Investing in 20 financially strong companies that pay exceptional dividends gives you much more money and the diversity helps protect you from recessions and pandemics. How much you reap from such a strategy depends on how much you invest.

(CH 15/Q21) **If a company's expenses are greater than their current income, how could they survive?**

What are the underlying assets owned by the company? Money can be borrowed to keep a company going.

What is the company's potential? Speculators will invest money now if they can be sold on expecting a high return on their investment in the future. The money they invest can keep an unprofitable company going.

(CH 15/Q22) **How can Oprah be a billionaire if her company is not publicly traded?**

There are many companies in the world that are billion-dollar companies that are not traded on stock exchanges.

Until the last few years the company that owns and operates oil production in Saudi Arabia was not a public company. It is now one of the largest public companies in the world.

There are about 25 million companies in North America. Fewer than 20,000 are public companies. Some individuals put great value on the privacy and flexibility they have as private companies. Many private corporations have profits that allows them to grow and expand without having to raise money in the stock market.

(CH 15/Q23) **If a "company" is unwilling to give up control but needs additional capital. Which would be better issuing new stock or issuing bonds?**

A bond is a loan. A stock is usually a share in a public company . Borrowing money from a bank or other sources is usually the quickest easiest option for a corporation to get necessary funding. The bank secures the loan with a debenture on all the business' assets.

If whoever is worried about losing control of the company can control the majority of shares, then they do not lose control. Both issuing new shares and bonds requires significant time and effort. The need for capital could be realized from a bank within days depending on their relationship with the bank and how much money was required.

(CH 15/Q24) **What is the primary purpose of a company's dividend policy?**

The primary purpose of a dividend should be to focus all the executives and all the employees on a realizable objective. Dividends are paid out of profits. Profits are made by increasing sales and by reducing or controlling expenses. These two factors should be constantly monitored.

As a shareholder I resent companies using profits to buy back shares in their own company. This distorts share prices, it I often done so executives can realize their bonuses and stock options which are often based on ever increasing share prices. I would want the operating margin to be split between corporate development and dividends paid to shareholders.

(CH 15/Q25) **How much should I budget for a potential loss when I buy my first stock?**

This is like asking, "How long is a string". The first thing is you never invest in one stock. You spread your risk equally among 20 financially strong stocks that have paid exceptionally strong dividends on a regular basis for years. If you do that you might find that 10% of the 20 pause paying dividends (even in pandemics and recessions). None will disappear and perhaps half might lose half their value temporarily in a severe recession. Since you only buy stocks you intend to hold forever, the constant fluctuations of the stock price becomes irrelevant as the shares you own remain the same and continue to provide you with a dividend income to weather the recession.

(CH 15/Q26) **What is buying and selling stocks with the idea of making a quick profit known as?**

Speculative wishful investing

(CH 15/Q27) **The highly volatile company I work for has gone public. I have been given S4,000,000 in shares. Can I get a high return without too much risk if I invest in real estate?**

If it were my 4 million, I would invest $2 million equally in 20 financially strong companies paying more than a 6% dividend. This would give you a safe, diversified dividend income probably between $150,000 and $200,000 a year plus show an additional 9% or more in capital gain annually. The dividends get steadily paid even in pandemics and recessions. These companies tend to increase their dividend payouts annually. This keeps you ahead of inflation. Your intention is to live off this capital and never sell these carefully chosen stocks.

The other $1,900,000 would go into my primary residence which, depending where you are, could increase at 10% a year. Owning property controls a big chunk of your living expenses. Another $100,000 go into a safe cash account earning the best interest I could find, but available almost instantly if needed.

You have now achieved financially independence for the rest of your life. I would continue working always with the thought at the back of my mind that I do not need to put up with the B.S. of the corporate world. This then allows you to put up with the B.S. or to look for something else that is going to be more interesting and challenging. You would continue to add the dividend payments and the surplus cash from your salary to those 20 shares.

The 4 million is now only hypothetical because you are probably going to have to pay capital gains tax if you liquidate the shares you are receiving. The company you are working for may not be crazy about you selling your shares, but diversification is important in giving you lifetime security, freedom, and self-confidence.

Find a good accountant and pay him to give you tax advice. Stay far, far away from investment advisors who will take 2% to 4% of your wealth every year in direct and indirect charges but give little of value in return. Anyone with a brain in their head can easily build and manage a portfolio as a self-directed investor. It takes several hours to set up a good portfolio but once it is set up, you spend 2 minutes, 5 times a week keeping an eye on it. The first task is finding the 20 good dividend stocks.

While 4 million dollars may seem like a lot of money, it can disappear in a year or two if you are not careful. The sharks will come looking to take a bite out of it. I take the attitude that it really is not my money, I am just its steward who is going to be passing it on to future generations

(CH 15/Q28) **What is the difference between a shares' book value per share and market value?**

The book value is calculated by accountants who calculate the value of the company's assets (based on standard accounting principles) which are then divided by the number of shares. It is a bit of mythical valuation. The only real value of a company is what a buyer would be willing to pay for it at the time the company were liquidated. The share value is the stock market value as established by what buyers are willing to now pay for the stock in the stock market.

Where the book value is useful, is in picking stocks. If you can find a stock that you can buy for $1 that has a book value of $2, then you have probably identified a bargain. The book value is just one factor out of 9 in my scoring system that helps you identify good stocks for your portfolio.

(CH 15/Q29) **Which would be better, to work for a successful established company or to start my own business?**

The question should have read or "to be a **successful** employee in a well run, profitable,established company". Your chances of achieving great success in your own business is not great, no matter how smart or hard working you may be. Very few new businesses survive their initial 5 years.

Establishing a new business is difficult. In a competitive environment, you must convince prospective customers to abandon their established source of supply and try whatever you are selling. Few people can cause this habit change. Once you gain a customer you must then learn how to consistently deliver your product to meet their expectations. You normally start off under financed and limited in what you can do. It could take decades of deferred gratification and long hours of work before you achieve even a moderate success.

If you join a large, established successful company, the hard work of establishing corporate credibility and reliability are already there. All you need do is follow the established patterns of successful behavior that would have brought that company to its elevated status.

You must be prepared to work longer, harder, and smarter than all the other employees that your results will be compared to. The executives of large companies are always looking for new employees who accept and flourish within their corporate culture. Step-by-step, consciously, or unconsciously, the outstanding "new" employee will be given more and more opportunity to show the company how they can make money for the corporation. Within 5 to 10 years the outstanding money makers can be in a very senior position in a large company.

Once you have proven yourself and risen to position of great knowledge and respect, you are in the drivers' seat. You can stay with that company or move to any other large company that would appreciate your proven experience and abilities. The rewards are not just in a high income but in the size of the challenges, the opportunities, the fringe benefits, the easy access to the financial resources that allows you to grow the business in new directions and the respect you enjoy in being a recognized success in a large company that may have existed for a hundred years or more.

Whatever path you choose, achieving "success" (however you define it) is never easy or without sacrifices.

(CH 15/Q30) **Isn't Benjamin Graham's book, "The Intelligent Investor" difficult for beginners to understand? What alternative books would you suggest?**

I have read many books about investing, including the "Intelligent Investor". Most seem to be written by financial advisors who are trying to impress other financial advisors.

This usually makes them as relevant and difficult to read for me as a textbook about quantum physics. They take the relatively straight forward function of a stock market, which is an auction, and do their best to turn it into a complicated incomprehensible machine that somehow predicts the future. The reality is that no one can accurately predict the future e.g. COVID-19 sure was not a well-known prediction.

Companies have little control over their share prices. What companies can control, is what they do with their profits. Dividends are paid out of profits. Future research and development are also paid out of profits. Companies that pay good dividends know that if they stop paying good dividends that those who bought the shares to receive good dividends will be inclined to sell those shares at a lower price.

A simple, easy way to invest is to find and buy shares in the best 20 financially strong companies that pay the best dividends. Through pandemics and recessions financially strong companies continue to pay dividends despite their share price going up or down. Over time, such companies' shares will increase in price. The stock market is not a casino. Be happy with steady growth and a reliable, ever increasing dividend income (such companies regularly increase their dividend payouts. This keeps you ahead of inflation).

The initial challenge is finding the 20 best dividend stocks. This book comes with software that allows you to sort out potential stock purchases. Since things are neither big nor small except by comparison, a scoring system allows you to give a mathematical value to each stock you consider in your quest for the best stocks to add to your portfolio. Such a tool becomes extremely useful in finding your 20 best stocks to buy within the 628 US stocks paying a dividend greater than 6%.

(CH 15/Q31) **Is it a good idea to invest in the stock market when my life is busy 24/7?**

It is a cost/benefit decision. What is it costing you to ignore the benefits of investing? I spend 2 minutes, 5 days a week monitoring my portfolios. I have lived very well off my portfolio's dividend income for 15 years while watching the total value of the portfolios more than triple in value. Yes, it will require several hours to choose the 20 best stocks to add to your portfolio, but free tools provided by self-directed investment services make it easy.

(CH 15/Q32) **If the value of a stock is 100% greater than what I bought it for, should I sell it?**

A question like this is only one that a speculator would ask, someone who believes that investing is all about buying low and selling high.

A value investor would want to evaluate the stock e.g. (1) share price now (2) share price 4 years ago (3) book value of the stock (4) operating margin of the company (5) dividend yield percent (6) number of analysts recommending the stock as a buy (7) the price to earnings ratio of the stock (8) the average number of shares traded daily.

If they could find a stock with better numbers than the jewel, they already own, they might consider selling. If they could not find a "better" stock they would continue to hold it and collect the dividends.

(CH 15/Q33) **Why are bank stocks in the toilet right now?**

I have owned several bank stocks for 20 years. I have watched them go up and go down, but I am still far ahead of what I originally paid for them. I bought them for their good steady dividends. Some have paid rising dividends consistently for over 100 years. The fluctuation of the stock price is almost irrelevant to a long-term investor. I pay for my groceries with the hard cash I get from a bank's reliable dividends not from the fuzzy value of a bank's shares I own

Banks are money machines. It is not very difficult to show a profit when you are paying interest of 0.02% on a savings account while charging a borrower 8% when they use their line of credit or 22% when they don't pay off their credit card balances every month.

The banks have limited control over their share prices, but they know how to make steady profits. The sophisticated credit scoring systems they now have helps them to minimize their bad debt losses - even in a recession. You will notice that despite the record low interest rates banks pay depositors that consumers are not charged lower interest rates on their unpaid credit card balances.

(CH 15/Q34) **Bank shares have dropped about 20% since June. Would you wait until they dropped even lower before buying them?**

I can not time the market. All I know is that the sky is not falling and within six months to two years the market will most likely be ahead of where it was in January of 2020. Meanwhile I will continue to live off my dividends from the bank stocks and other stocks I own which continue, for the most part, to be paid. The banks have significant control over their profits, but their widely held share prices are controlled by the "market". Not having to worry about timing is why I am not a speculator but a value investor. I buy good stocks knowing they will rise in time.

(CH 15/Q35) **Why does the expense ratio of different mutual funds vary?**

It is called whatever the market will bear. The high expense ratio allows the mutual fund company to pay the seller of the mutual fund a bigger commission than lower priced mutual funds are paying. It also allows them to pay for the advertising that portrays their mutual fund as a leader of all mutual funds. The interesting thing is the difference in content and results between a high-priced fund and a low-priced fund is often insignificant. The expense ratio is all about paying for marketing costs.

(CH 15/Q36) **Where is it easier to make profit, investing in real estate of in stocks?**

I own property and I own stocks. To realize a profit on my primary residence I would have to sell it. On the rental property, it generated revenue but much of it got eaten up by taxes, maintenance, and many other expenses. To realize the capital gain on that property, it had to be sold. Selling property is rarely quick or easy. Real estate agent commissions, taxes, lawyers, bureaucracy, and other complications eat into the profits.

I only invest in the shares of financially strong companies that pay good dividends e.g. more than 6%. I live off that dividend income. It requires 2 minutes of my time 5 days a week to keep an eye on it. The portfolio has more than tripled over the last 20 years despite my regularly withdrawing a good income from it. In an emergency part or all of it can be liquidated within minutes.

I do not miss owning rental property.

(CH 15/Q37) **How can I get investors to invest in my great screen play?**

What objective source has determined that it is a "great screen play"? How much time and money are you prepared to spend to find sponsors or investors?

Like any creative project you are competing with thousands of others seeking funding from a small number of investors who only want to invest in a "sure thing". It may require years of effort to find and approach investors who would consider it.

It is easier to get a book published. Can the screen play be turned into a book that can be the vehicle to reach screen play investors - especially if the book gets recognition?

(CH 15/Q38) **How can you earn more than a 6% return annually?**

I have just finished scoring hundreds of stocks traded on North American exchanges that pay a dividend of 6% or greater. Some pay dividends as high as 35%. Many high dividend companies did not score well but several were financially strong companies that scored very well. Pick your portfolio from these stocks which are identified in the following chapters.

(CH 15/Q39) **Should "Don't lose the money!" be the first rule of investing?**

What does "don't lose the money" mean in investing? If you have a portfolio of 20 financially strong stocks, at various time a small percentage of the stocks may show a loss but the total portfolio can still be well ahead of the price you paid for all 20 stocks. No matter how careful you are in choosing stocks, you can not predict future events accurately. Stocks go up and stocks go down, but a financially strong company whose shares are down is still a financially strong company. Paper losses only become real losses if you sell the financially strong company. The first rule should be buy value.

(CH 15/Q40) **I am 18 and have saved $30,000 at 18 from casual employment. What should I invest in for both the short term and the long term?**

I would invest equally in 6 financially strong companies in diversified industries paying dividends averaging among all 6 at 6%. Such companies pay dividends even during recessions and pandemics. In addition to the dividend income I would expect, in most years, to see the stocks show a capital gain of 9%. To get these gains it is important to stay away from financial advisers whose fees and the cost of the investments they recommend will eat up much of your gain. You set up a self-directed account which will allow you to buy the stocks for less than $10 per company.

As you acquire more spare cash you continue to add another 14 stocks to your portfolio. The objective is to own these 20 stocks forever. As the stocks spin off dividend income you keep investing it in your portfolio of 20 stocks. To get help in how to identify financially strong companies go to my website where you can gain access to 4 free investment videos. I have lived very well off such a portfolio for 15 years.

(CH 15/Q41) **Are investors internal stakeholders or external?**

It all depends upon how many shares of the company you own. If you were the largest shareholder in the company, the executives and directors of the company will give you their full attention. You would then be an internal stakeholder. You could cause real change in that company. Most likely you would be on the company's board of directors.

If you own a few thousand shares in a billion-dollar corporation, you are just along for the ride. If you do not like the way the company is being run, you would be expected to vote with your feet, sell your shares and move on. To the officers and directors of such a company, you are just another external irritant like a small, disgruntled customer complaining about a product.

(CH 15/Q42) **What are the benefits of being an investor?**

What is the opposite of an investor? I would say it is a borrower. Borrowers pay interest for the money they borrow. Investors are the beneficiary of interest and other benefits from those who "borrow". The borrower incurs an obligation to the investor. Investing is positive and borrowing is negative.

(CH 15/Q43) **What are the chances of showing a good profit by investing in several companies' IPOs (initial stock placement orders) and selling them in a day or two?**

What you are doing when you invest in IPOs for few days is speculating. Speculators generally lose money. A 6% return in a portfolio is a good return. The stock market is not a casino. If you carefully invest in established, financially strong companies that pay dividends averaging6%, you will receive income even in recessions.

(CH 15/Q44) **What are your greatest stock market investment trades of all time? What are you investing in now?**

I have no great stock market investment trades because I know that a good return on an investment is 5 to 6 percent. I bought shares in 20 financially strong, diverse, carefully chosen companies that pay dividend averaging 6% with no intention of every selling them. It costs me almost zero to buy shares as a self-directed investor. The cost of investments is important if your objective is to make money.

Even in recessions and pandemics 90% of my shares continue to pay dividends. As their share prices increase, these companies tend to increase their dividends. While the share prices will go up and down, over the years you will find your portfolio showing a steady capital gain. In time it will triple, etc. You continue to invest your dividends until you retire and then you live off your dividend income, just as I have done for 15 years. Your portfolio continues to grow despite your dividend withdrawals.

I gave up chasing "great stock buys" 20 years ago once I proved to myself that I could not predict the future. I set out to find a better safer way to invest.

(CH 15/Q45) **If you worked for a company in which you owned a significant number of shares, would its managers have to listen to you?**

Why are they not listening to you now? Why would you work for a company and own its shares if they do not listen to employees? Unless you owned a significant percentage of all the issued shares of the company, they can continue to ignore you.

(CH 15/Q46) **What are some lies stockbrokers tell themselves?**

That they can consistently pick stocks that will increase in value.

That the costs to acquire the investment are unimportant.

That self-directed investors need the discipline that investment advisors provide to hold on to their stocks during a recession.

The higher the cost of acquiring a mutual fund, the greater will be its return.

That an investment that increases in value over the last 3 years guarantees that the investment will keep increasing.

That they are expert investors.

(CH 15/Q47) **Can you overdiversify? Would 50 different types of stocks be bad for your portfolio?**

There are not 50 good stocks out there that I would want in a portfolio. I like to invest equally in 20 carefully chosen stocks, so that I never have more than 5% of my wealth at risk. Keeping track of 20 diversified stocks is reasonable. Trying to periodically score 50 stocks would require more effort than I would want to spend.

(CH 15/Q48) **How reliable is 'capital protection' in mutual funds?**

What kills your capital in a mutual fund is cost. The company managing the fund expects to be paid, maybe 1.5%, the salesman (investment advisor) who puts the fund in your portfolio expects to be paid, maybe 2.5%, inflation will eat up maybe 2%. A fund tied into stock market performance might generate 5 to 6 percent. According to my math, investing in mutual funds is a losing proposition. That is why I am a self-directed investor who invests in 20 financially strong diversified companies that pay dividends averaging about 6%.

The cost of buying such shares can be close to zero depending what investment service you use. Even in a recession or pandemic, 90% of my dividend income is not affected. What turned me into a self-directed investing was losing $300,000 in mutual fund that an investment advisor had put my money into. I have lived off the dividends of my self-directed portfolio for 15 years as I watched it grow by several multiples.

(CH 15/Q49) **What happens if everyone invests in index funds?**

If everyone invested in Index Funds, this would mean mutual funds would disappear as an investment. Thousands of investment advisers who depend upon the high mutual fund fees embedded within them, would have to find other employment. It would make investment advisers who charge fees for their advice incredibly happy as they would be quite willing to promote index funds because their fees would not change. Self-Directed investors who buy their stocks individually for their portfolios would not be happy to be forced to buy index funds. The cost to buy their investments is now almost zero and they would not appreciate even the relatively low index fund charges.

(CH 15/Q50) **What is an example of one stock with a minimum 6 % dividend that you personally like to own?**

Are you a self-directed investor? If you go to the research section of your provider and put in a selector for Canadian stocks paying a dividend of 8% or more, with trading volumes on average exceeding 414,000 and a stock price greater than $1.82.

The first 4 stocks that come up should include 3 of the companies I have owned for probably 15 years. They are currently paying dividends between 8.40% and $10.08%. The dividend percentages are high because the share prices are down because of the pandemic. I did not sell them in the 2008 recession, and I have no intention of selling them in this recession.

Why don't I just tell you who they are? Because I want you to see how easy it is to find good stocks. You do not need to be asking what stocks other people have. You just need to understand how to pick good stocks that you will have confidence in because you understood why they are good.

(CH 15/Q51) **How can I know which investments will be profitable in the long term?**

Do you want stocks who will still be here in 20 years?

Have the companies already existed for 20 years? Has their share price steadily increased over 20 years? Have they been paying ever increasing dividends for 20 years? Is their operating margin over 20%? Are analysts recommending them as a buy? Is their current share price over $20 a share? Is their book value higher or close to their share price? Are they trading more than 100,000 shares on average each day? Is their price to earnings ratio below 20.0x?

All this information is free and available.

The perfect stock that meets all these criteria does not exist but those that come close are most likely to be around for 20 years or longer with a share price worth more than it is now. Although they are inanimate, companies do form a "character" which persist for decades. Those executives exposed to the company culture will find creative ways to survive against competitive and technological changes.

(CH 15/Q52) **If a business had 1 million in its operating margin, should it pay a dividend or investment in more equipment?**

It all comes down to who has the power in the corporation. If the dominant shareholder needs cash for other ventures the money may get paid out in dividends, if the profits are a result of a new technology the money may get poured into maximizing the technology for even greater profits in the future, etc. There is no hard and fast rule. You are dealing with several directors with all their hidden objectives. They will have to debate the options and vote on it.

(CH 15/Q53) **Is real estate a riskier investment than stocks if you are relying on property appreciation?**

The problem with real estate is the expenses and bureaucracy associated with owning rental property which can be a drain on cash flows. Selling and buying property is never quick and easy. While the property will most likely appreciate over time, until it does it is an expense. If you carefully invest in financially strong dividend paying companies, you can immediately gain income and realize an increase in your capital investment. The stock market requires far less work, it is easier with fewer headaches.

(CH 15/Q54) **What stocks can I invest in that will make me a millionaire?**

The stock market is not a casino, it is an auction? To win big you would have to bet big on long shots. Companies that are small and marginally profitable. Are you prepared to lose? The odds are about 2 in 100 that you will make money betting that you can time when to buy a stock at a low price and when to sell it at a high price. Would you keep investing your money until it had all been lost?

The stock market does not move in a logical way because it is reacting to actions of millions of people with competing ideas. When you buy a stock that you think is going to increase in value, someone who thinks it has reached its highest price point is selling it to you.

The only way I have found to make consistent revenue is to buy shares in financially strong companies that will give me a dividend income of 6% or greater. They have a long history of paying such dividends even during recessions. Over time it is possible for the stocks of carefully chosen, financially strong, dividend companies to exceed one million dollars, if you had started with a few hundred thousand dollars.

(CH 15/Q55) **I am new to investing. Should I buy equity advisory services for stock tips?**

There are many free sources offering "stock tips", however it is better to create your own "stock tips". What kind of stock are you looking for? Do you know how to recognize a "good" stock? You might get some benefit out of reviewing the 4 free 10-minute investment lessons in my website, informus.ca. I would never buy a stock just because I was told it was "good". I want to research and confirm it is good.

(CH 15/Q56) **How unjustified do you think the exclusion of Tesla from the S&P 500 was, given the recent volatility of that index?**

The following is a reply I wrote July 21, 2020 which I think probably explains why Tesla was excluded from the S&P 500 in September, despite finally achieving profits for 4 quarters. *(Subsequently, it has been announce in November of 2020 that will be included in the S&P 500.)*

"There is no strong reason for Tesla's stock to be at the price it is now at. The price seems to indicate that many investors do not research "glamour" stocks. They want to believe that there is no price limit in a hot stock.

(1) Tesla has a book value of $36.50. This is the current reported value accountants say a share is worth. No one would really know its liquidation value until it was marketed.

(2) 8 analysts are recommending it be sold. One of them expects it to drop to $300. It is unusual for analysts to recommend a stock be sold. 6 analysts did recommend it as a buy with one projecting it going to $2,322.

(3) It has a price to earnings ratio of zero which reflects a lack of profit at the time it was calculated. (since I wrote this, they reported a profit).

(4) It was trading at $222 four years ago.

(5) It has an operating margin of 2.83%.

Things are neither good nor bad, except by comparison. Compare Tesla to Honda which has a share price of $26.36 and 4 years ago was trading at $26.82.

(1) Honda has a book value of $43.28. (what a bargain you can buy a $43 stock for $27)

(2) The 3 analysts reporting on it, all rate Honda as a buy

(3) Honda's price to earnings ratio is 10.7. Anything below 12.1 is good.

(4) Honda's operating margin is 4.1% compared to Tesla's 2.3%

(5) Honda is paying a 3.93% dividend.

If you had $100,000 in lifetime savings to invest and you could only invest it in one stock which of these two stocks would you choose?

At some point in the future, reality will rear its ugly head and bring Tesla's party to an end. In a capitalist society great commercial success leads to great competition. It is all about supply and demand and Tesla does not have a monopoly on electric cars."

(CH 15/Q57) **Is it a good idea to keep holding stocks forever or should you sell them occasionally, make a profit and reinvest?**

Most dividends get paid in recessions and pandemics. If you are living very well off your dividend flow, why would you sell the stock?

The ups and downs of the stock prices of carefully chosen dividend stocks (in financially strong companies) are only of passing interest to shareholders who have no intention of buying low and selling high. Their objective is retention of the wealth they have accumulated. They know If you sell and take a profit you now must pay a tax on it plus the uncertainty of trying to find another stock as financially strong that pays as good a dividend.

If the company got into financial difficulty, looked like it was going to become insolvent, and had stopped paying dividends then you would go to the trouble of finding a replacement. However, with 20 good stocks, the chances of this happening are small and for added insurance, most of the other stocks would have capital gains that would more than offset the loss of one piece of your portfolio.

Companies are not inanimate blocks of wood. Those employed by the company would be doing everything they could to return a company to its usual operating margins e.g. adjusting prices, creating new products, improving old products, selling off assets that were redundant, cutting salaries, reducing all expenses, etc. etc.

(CH 15/Q58) **Why do financial advisors push annuities?**

Financial advisors love to recommend annuities. Annuities give them a high immediate commission. I am told the commission can be as high as 10% of the amount you pay the. When they sell a mutual fund, they might only receive 2%. Financial advisors are salesmen being paid to sell you what will most benefits their employer.

If your investment objective is capital gain, there is no capital gain in annuity. If your objective is income, you can do much better with a carefully chosen diversified portfolio of 20 financially strong stocks paying dividends of 6% or more (there are over 600 US stocks paying 6% or more).

When you own stocks, it is an asset that you can use as security on a loan or to establish your net worth for credit rating purposes. In an emergency you can always sell off a few shares from your portfolio.

Once you buy an annuity, that asset is no longer yours. That money now belongs to the insurance company that you signed the annuity contract with. They will invest that money and even after paying you as agreed for the next few years, they will make a profit from that money. When you die, then they will get it all.

They are no smarter than you. You can learn the basics self directed investing in a few days.

(CH 15/Q59) **How do capitalists avoid paying taxes?**

A capitalist can directly own a billion dollars in shares but if he does not sell those shares, he has no income and thus pays no income tax. If he or she has a corporation, many of their expenses can be paid by their corporation as a "legitimate" business expense e.g. cars, entertaining clients, computers, travel, health insurance, parking, etc.

As well, the more influence you have, the more free meals and perks you get from corporation trying to gain your favor. The banks want your company deposits. Hotels want your employees to use their facilities. What these businesses spend to gain your favor is their legitimate business expense.

A need to show a big taxable income vanishes if many of your expenses are being covered by the company. Warren Buffet once said his secretary was paying more income taxes than he was.

It is not that they are trying to "get away without paying taxes", they are in the peculiar situation where the position they hold does away with the need to show a large taxable income. Their stock options could be worth hundreds of thousands of dollars but are not taxable if they do not sell those stocks. They are in the position of choosing how much income they wish to be taxed on. Accountants paid by their companies will make sure it is legally as little as possible.

While those trying to scrape up enough money to feed their children are required to pay more in taxes than some of these capitalists. The capitalists will have their corporations pay millions of dollars to lobbyists to ensure that no new tax laws are passed to disrupt the status quo.

(CH 15/Q60) **Can I borrow money from a bank in which I own stocks and get paid dividends?**

Of course, you can. If the bank is also the one holding your portfolio you should be able to get a better interest rate on any loan because they can see exactly what your assets are. Banks like to lend to their shareholders especially ones whose assets are far greater than the loan they want.

(CH 15/Q61) **Would you make a great investment scammer?**

I would not make a great investment scammer. I am not greedy enough.

Being in the corporate risk business for decades, I have seen just about every type of scam that exists. When I was young, the hole-in-the-wall investment dealers were pushing "pump and dump" penny mining stock to naive investors who would be sold on the potential of a hole in the ground. They would bid up the price. The scammers would sell out at the top and the naïve investors would be left holding worthless stock . Later these scammers were into emeralds, then it was copier toner. Now, it seems to be bit coins.

Then there were those who would set up corporations to rip off suppliers. They would send in big orders and after delivery disappear with the goods without paying for them. Some would rip off the banks by showing the bank a warehouse full of appliances that was securing their inventory loans. The boxes were empty, and no one at the bank had checked. They too would skip, and the bank would have an inventory of empty boxes to cover their loan.

These crooks were clever and hard working. Was it the sheer joy in pulling the con that motivated them? They had no empathy. They appealed to people's greed and felt their victims deserved to be taken.

(CH 15/Q62) **Is stock investing more a game of mass psychology musical chairs than intrinsic economic factors, given that most companies do not pay dividends proportional to their profits?**

Most companies do not pay dividends. Dividends are paid out of their operating margins along with money that they put into their reserve account to finance the purchase of equipment and other expenses that will keep the business healthy and growing. A dividend is an incentive to encourage new investors and to keep existing shareholders. The dividend only needs to appear to be as generous or more generous than their competitors.

Running a profitable public company is never easy. The more profitable you are the more competitors you attract. Competitors will undercut your prices to take sales away from you.

Operating a business is like being on a treadmill that is constantly accelerating. Yet, there are companies who are constantly able to increase their annual dividend payments through good times and bad times. Such companies are not playing "financial shenanigans". They are just well run. It is extremely hard for a public company to fake having the profits from which their dividends are paid.

(CH 15/Q63) **If the stock market crashes by the end of 2020, how can investors protect their capital, and where can they safely invest their money ahead of a possible crash?**

Even in a recession most financially strong companies, who pay dividends, continue to pay dividends. You live off your dividends, sell no shares, and wait it out. The sky is not falling, the market and your capital will recover. Speculators who must sell their shares to generate income to pay bills are screwed because they are forced to sell their shares at the worse possible time, when share prices are down. It is not always about buying low and selling high.

(CH 15/Q64) **Is frugal living and investing early in life better than having a pile of cash and investing later?**

Life is to be enjoyed. Do not waste your youth. Concentrate on building a lucrative career so that you will not only have the funds in your forties to invest but in your forties your living expenses will also start to decline. Building a portfolio in your forties should be easier. I always find it interesting how investment advisors want you to set up a retirement portfolio long before you hit your prime earning years. Could it be that they want to take their bite out of your investments every year for the next forty years?

(CH 15/Q65) **What is the primary reason to avoid risk?**

It is not a question of avoiding risk, it is a question of accepting that risk exists and that you must hedge your bets. Thus, you carefully researching your investments. You spread your money among several stocks but not too many, etc. No one can accurately forecast the future e.g. the 2020 pandemic's impact was certainly not anticipated.

(CH 15/Q66) **Is there such a thing as investing in too many mutual funds?**

One mutual fund is one too many. You are paying, every year, 2.5% to 4% of your portfolio's value to a financial institution who has no better idea what the future holds than you do. They will take that 2.5% each year whether your mutual fund has made or lost money.

You typically have no idea what the mutual fund is invested in. You have naively accepted what the financial institution has sold to you. They love clients who never want proof that they are getting something of value.

As a self-directed investor with minimal effort you could manage a million-dollar portfolio that would never cost you more than an initial $200 in fees. . I lost $300,000 in a mutual fund a financial advisor put my life savings into. This motivated me to find a better, safer way to invest that allowed no one but me to touch my money.

(CH 15/Q67) **If I bought one share of every stock traded on the New York Stock Exchange, would I have more or less money in my portfolio in 1 year?**

For each share you purchase you would incur a fee over the cost of the stock. You would have to buy thousands of stocks. One share could cost more than $1,000. Hypothetically you would show an average gain of about 6% in your portfolio but the time, effort, and cost of acquiring each share would probably make it a money losing proposition.

There is probably an ETF that you could buy into that would contain every share in the New York Stock Exchange. You would incur some charge, but you should show a gain on the fund, of about 6%.

(CH 15/Q68) **What percentage of the population invests in the stock market?**

A small percentage of the population invests in the stock market. To most the stock market is alien, frightening, complicated, confusing, only for rich people, dangerous, gambling, immoral, foreign, and verging on evil. The idea of achieving total financial independence by investing in the stock market is seen as a ridiculous pipe dream.

They will buy lottery tickets, fly to Las Vegas, and go to the horse races but to invest the same amount of money in the stock market is something that they will never do. Yet, they will eat, drink, and buy the products of the thousands of companies that are traded on the stock exchanges.

They do not seem to grasp the simple concept that you are buying a piece of a company when you buy a stock, and that that company will share their financial success and profits with you. This simple concept gets hidden behind the financial industry's jargon and froth e.g. puts, calls, ETFs, preferred shares, bonds, shorts, going long, mutual funds, annuities, buy backs, candle stick charts, etc. Does the industry do this deliberately to make investing seem beyond the comprehension of the common man?

(CH 15/Q69) **Does real estate have 'corrections' similar to the stock market?**

Yes, real estate does not always go up. Remember Florida a few years ago. You are probably going to see another "correction" in Florida when all those foreigners who are afraid to return to the USA because of COVID-19 start to dump their Florida properties over the winter. Real Estate prices are sensitive to population changes which are caused by economic and technical changes. Want to see some great property values in Detroit?

(CH 15/Q70) **Does it make sense to own an ETF that contains individual stocks that are already in my portfolio?**

The interesting question is why do you have ETFs? They incur a management fee and will contain some stocks which are mediocre. You have no control over this investment which the fund manager can change at will. With a little effort you can have a self-directed portfolio of diversified dividend stocks giving you a steady income of 6% while growing most years at 9%.

Why would some stocks in an ETF be mediocre? Fund managers aim at never doing worse than the stock exchange measuring sticks. Since they can not predict the future, they spread their prediction risk over as many stock's as possible.

If you score hundreds of stocks as I have done, you soon realize that unless you objectively score each stock in an ETF yourself you really do not know what your money is invested in.

(CH 15/Q71) **Should gold be a part of a retirement portfolio?**

You pay brokerage fees to buy gold. You pay to store it safely. You pay brokerage fees to sell it. It is a commodity that is subject to fluctuations in world pricing that can go up and down depending on stressful situations are playing out thousands of miles away. You must sell it to get income to live on.

Investing in 20 stocks of financially strong companies that pay dividends greater than 6 % as a self-directed investor is safer and more cost effective to own. Even in a pandemic or recession your dividends get paid. As a self-directed investor it costs less than $10 to buy as many shares of a stock as you want. There are no storage fees. You can buy them instantly and easily. Such stocks increase in value over the years while paying you dividend to hold on to them. They raise their dividend payouts as their share prices increase.

(CH 15/Q72) **Would you take a million dollars in pennies?**

How much would 100.000,000 pennies weigh? What is the price of copper? A penny is both a commodity and legal tender. I would take the pennies.

Since pennies are only thinly clad with copper over zinc. You can get more for the zinc content than the copper content. That surprised me. They probably add the zinc to make the coin more durable. Copper is soft. The following advertisement shows the commodity value of the pennies:

"Scrap Metal Prices Per Pound

All the prices that are listed on this website are a direct representation of a variety of local scrap metal yard's prices for a range of metal types. Please get into contact with us if you are searching for prices in a specific state or region in Canada, or elsewhere around the world: Aluminum,$0.76 - $0.88/ Brass$1.25 - $1.92/ ***Copper*** *$2.34 - $3.65/ Iron$1.22 - $1.57/ Lead$2.56 - $3.74/ Magnesium*

$4.87 - $6.62/ Steel$1.34 - $2.99/ Tin$1.66 - $2.89/ ***Zinc****$3.23 - $4.59."*

(CH 15/Q73) **What happens if I max out my credit card and disappear?**

Hundreds of thousands of people every year max out their credit cards and move, leaving no forwarding address. It is assumed most do it deliberately. After about 90 days from last receiving a payment, the bank being able to find you, will forward their claim to a collection agency.

The collection agency has skilled skip tracers working for them. The agency will receive a substantial commission if they find you and get you to pay.

It is difficult to disappear in this internet world. You would have to keep changing residences about every two months to stay ahead of the skip tracer.

If you are able to remain hidden for several years (the length depends on the jurisdiction) without the bank being able to serve you with a writ (which would allow them to commence legal action,) the debt would most likely be written off to bad debt. If you ever, after it is written off, paid one dollar towards that debt, the whole amount would be reinstated and again be owing.

You will have to assume a new identity which is difficult but not impossible. Employment, bank accounts, apartment rentals, library cards, and doctors, almost all of them require being able to confirm who you are. Some want to check legitimate references and you will not be able to give any and remain hidden. You will not be able to use any other credit cards you may have and getting new credit cards would be almost impossible. You enter a cash only world.

It is not worth the stress and inconvenience. If you are unable to pay your debt, first approach the bank. Tell them the only option you see is to go bankrupt. They would rather take prolonged payments or a reduction in the amount owed than to completely write off the debt.

If they do not wish to work out a settlement, let them sue you. They will likely get their judgment and then try to execute the judgments against your assets. I will assume you have nothing worth seizing. However, for the next twenty years they will be able to seize any assets you might acquire. Fortunately, we no longer have debtor prisons.

The other option is to go bankrupt. A bankruptcy trustee charges a fee, but it will wipe out the debt. You get to start over again. For seven years creditors will be aware of your prior bankruptcy.

It may be difficult to get credit but not impossible. Some creditors see you as a good risk - a debtor with zero debt. Other creditors are not so tolerant. They are aware that many who go bankrupt once will do it again.

(CH 15/Q74) **College isn't for me. Is it possible to work for Amazon, live frugally, and invest in dividend paying stocks until I can live off of them within 10 years?**

If you have an interest in stocks, why not find an entry level job with an investment company. You will learn a lot and if you can make money for them, you can probably make much more than you would make at Amazon. You may enjoy it so much that you will want to show up for work for the next 40 years.

(CH 15/Q75) **The "efficient market" hypothesis says that all public information is instantly factored into stock prices. If everyone believed this, investors would not analyze stocks. Thus, the hypothesis does not make sense because investors do analyze stocks. Do you agree?**

It is doubtful that if there are more than 2 people in a room that they can all ever agree on anything. While the public information may be read by thousands of people, they interpret and react to the information in hundreds of ways based upon their unique experiences, knowledge, and investment strategies. Thus, to say "all public information is instantly factored in" is meaningless because it suggests that the need for specific information can be determined in advance and it can only result in one reaction. This would make the stock market totally predictable and logical. It does not take long before you learn the stock market is not predictable and you can quickly lose your money if you think it is.

Diversity of investment is important. The investor with a million dollars who invests in 20 "good" stocks is more likely to survive for decades than the investor who puts the million dollars in one stock.

The stock exchange is an auction. For every buyer there must be a seller. Both believe they are making a wise transaction. Only time will tell which one is right.

Not all corporate information is made public. Much of the information that impacts stocks is derived not from the company but from the environment the company is operating in.

(CH 15/Q76) **Why is it important to save money early?**

It is not necessarily important to save money "early", and by early I think you mean when you are young. When you are just starting off your expenses are high, and your income is low. When you enter your forties, your expenses start to shrink, and you are reaching you peak earning years.

Just meeting your day-to-day expenses is difficult when you are young without being made to feel guilty if you are not investing for your "retirement". I believe that the only ones who benefit from early investing are investment advisors who get to take a percentage of your savings every year for decades as they "actively manage" your "portfolio".

I think it is more important for you to concentrate on making a success of your career when you are young. The money follows with success.

(CH 15/Q77) **In which ETFs should I invest in if I want to retire in 30 years with $600,000 to $1,000,0000?**

I wrote the following to respond to a question about index funds. It also applies to EFTs, just substitute ETF where you see "index fund."

Index funds means you wish to settle for the mediocre results of an entire index which includes both good and bad investments.

It also means if the index crashes that you crash with it or you sell out and wait for when you think it is safe to reinvest back into the index fund (which turns you into a speculator which removes the safety net).

It also means you are paying someone every year to manage the index fund which is a bit illogical since no analysis is required to gather all the stocks going into an index fund. Admittedly the fee is much less than a mutual fund, but it is still a fee for doing basically nothing which is one reason investment companies push them.

A self-directed investor who carefully chooses to invest in 20 financially strong diversified companies that pay good dividends can do much better than investing in index funds. Yes, it might take you a few hours to put together a portfolio that will cost you less than $200 to buy all the stocks required, but it is a one time fee as your intention is to hold these stocks forever and live off the dividend income. Even in pandemics and recessions these companies continue to pay dividends.

(CH 15/Q78) **If everyone knows that the stock market will perform better in the long term, why do people sell in panic and not hold their investments?**

People are not necessarily logical. They are emotional beings.

If you see your life savings drop by 50%, as it did *in March of 2020*, most people who have never been through a market crash would become anxious This is especially true if the income from their portfolio is all that stands between being able to pay your rent and being homeless. Rather than confirming that you have financially strong investments that can weather any storm, people panic and conclude that it is better to cut their losses and liquidate their investments to save what little is left. In their illogical minds they think their portfolio's value can go to zero.

They do not look at the history of recessions nor carefully evaluate their situation. Most do not have cash reserves, as insurance, to draw upon in a stock market crash. They feel they must quickly liquidate to survive. They then wait too long to buy back into the market because they have been shaken by the crash and think the recovery is only temporary. Their loss becomes permanent.

Recessions occur about every 4 years. You anticipate them. They are one reason I invest in the stocks of 20 financially strong companies that pay good dividends. Even in a recession or pandemic these companies continue to pay their steady dividends, if you maintain the same number of shares. I have watched the value of my portfolio steadily increase after each recession over the last 20 years.

(CH 15/Q79) **Is short selling morally defensible? It seems pretty much like "hoping for the worst"?**

Is there a moral difference between buying a stock you think is going to go up in value and short selling a stock you think is going to go down in value? The person selling you the stock you think is going to go up thinks you are a fool because he thinks he is selling it at the best possible price. He believes he is taking advantage of your stupidity.

The person short sellers thinks the stock is over valued and believes anyone owning such a stock is a fool.

Morality is not a factor in the buying and selling of stocks. It is just a bunch of game players thinking they can predict the future. Sometimes they win. Sometimes they lose.

(CH 15/Q80) **How much capital would I need to invest in the stock market to earn 20 dollars daily?**

There are many good safe dividend stocks that pay out 6% of their value in dividends. $20 a day is $6,300 a year. To get a return like that you would need to invest $105,000 dollars.

(CH 15/Q81) **Can you really invest $5,000 in the stock market and make 5 million?**

There are about 14,000 stocks listed in North American stock Markets. One of them that you can now buy for $1 in 20 years is going to worth $1,000 a share. All you must do is figure our which of the 14,000 it is. Of course, in 20 years with inflation a car might cost $5,000,000.

(CH 15/Q82) **When were all the stock market crashes?**

RECESSIONS	GDP DOWN	LENGTH	NEXT
08/1929 to 03/1933	-26.7%	43 mths	50 mths
05/1937 to 06/1938	-18.2%	13 mths	80 mths
02/1945 to 10/1945	-12.7%	8 mths	37 mths
11/1948 to 10/1949	-1.7%	11 mths	45 mths
07/1953 to 05/1954	-2.6%	10 mths	39 mths
08/1957 to 04/1958	-3.7%	8 mths	24 mths
04/1960 to 02/1961	-1.6%	10 mths	106 mths
12/1969 to 11/1970	-0.6%	11 mths	36 mths
11/1973 to 03/1975	-3.2%	15 mths	58 mths
01/1980 to 06/1980	-2.2%	6 mths	12 mths
07.1981 to 11/1982	-2.7%	16 mths	92 mths
07/1990 to 03/1991	-1.4%	8 mths	120 mths
03/2001 to 11/2001	-0.3%	8 mths	73 mths
12/2007 to 06/2009	-4.3%	18 mths	116 mths
02/2020 to ?	%	?	?
AVERAGE	**-2.7%**	**9 MTHS**	**50 MTHS**

Source: National Bureau of Economic Research

(CH 15/Q83) **Is playing the stock market gambling? If it is gambling, why is it legal where gambling is illegal?**

Some investors treat the stock market like a casino. They are called speculators. They win and lose fortunes. No matter how much they might acquire it is never enough to satisfy their lust. I assume they get a rush from the risk,

A few investors treat the stock market like bankers. They carefully invest their money in the shares of many financially strong, long established companies. They expect to get regular dividends, the same as they would also expect to get regular interest in a savings account. However, their dividend return can be 20 times greater than they would get in a savings account which is why their money is in stocks and not in savings accounts.

They have no intention of ever selling a stock and taking a profit. They get no rush when the dividend payments come in or when their share prices double or even triple in value. It is a "ho-hum" occurrence when a share price drops down below the price, they purchased it at. Since they are living off their dividend income, they do not need to sell shares to pay living expenses. They anticipate that share prices will recover at some point. If prices did not recover, the increases in the majority of their shares would offsets any loss. The gyrations of the stock market are only of passing interest.

A stock is just like their real estate investments. They expect both to increase in value over the decades. These people are not trying to become "rich" or even appear to be "rich". They see their purpose as one of preserving their "wealth" for future generations just like it was probably saved for them. They have things that turn their crank other than “making money”. Thus, to refer to this as “illegal gambling” would hardly be accurate.

(CH 15/Q84) **How can I solve my financial problems?**

A debtor who takes on more debt than they can afford can get caught up in a sophisticated relentless collection machine. They have a legal responsibility to live up to the agreement they reached with creditors to repay their debt.

Coping with debt problems depends on which country you are in, how deeply you are in debt, how great your income is, what assets you own and your attitude.

If your creditors are banks or large companies, as much as 5% of their consumer debt gets written off to bad debt. You are just one of millions of debtors who are not paying creditors as you legally agreed to pay them. If their efforts to get you to pay fail, they will place you with a third-party collection agency in 3 to 4 months after you stopped paying them. Since the creditor could end up paying the collection agency a third of what ever is collected, they would always prefer to negotiate a settlement of the debt than to involve a third party in their efforts to get paid.

Creditors are also reluctant to spend the money to go through the court system to get a judgment that would allow them to seize the debtor’s assets to sell and recoup their loss. To get to trial can take years. Court costs are often not recovered. Before the legal action gets to court the debtor’s, assets may evaporate and there will be nothing to seize or the debtor may become formally bankrupt.

If a legal judgment is won in court it allows a creditor to legally seize a debtor's assets fort the next 20 years. If they can not find any assets to seize, there are some speculative entrepreneurs who buy such judgments for pennies on the dollar and follow the debtor's finances for those 20 years, waiting to seize any assets the debtor might acquire.

Your options may be bankruptcy or doing your best to disappear. If they can not find you, Skip tracers can be hired to find debtors if the amount owed is large enough to make their expense worthwhile. Bankruptcy no longer has the negative stigma it used to have. We no longer have debtor's prisons. Society accepts that a mistake was made and allows the bankrupt debtor to start over with a clean slate. Credit reporting agencies will report a debtor's bankruptcy for up to 7 years before it is removed from their credit report. While you may have some trouble getting credit from some creditors, other creditors will see that you now have no debt and are less of a credit risk. However, it costs money to go bankrupt. Trustees in bankruptcy do not work for free. Shop around for the best price.

If you skip, be prepared to move each time it appears that a skip tracer has tracked you down. If they do reach you, tell them you do not owe the moneys and that they should sue you, then disappear again. If they can not find you, then they can not serve the writ. If they do serve the writ, you are obligated to appear at the set trial date. If you do not appear the judge will grant a default judgment to the creditor.

If your debt is small the creditor will usually t write it off as" uncollectable" or if they are efficient, they will sell that debt to a third party who will now pursue it. Your avoidance of creditors does not go on forever. There is a statute of limitations which varies on where you are located. It might be 2 to 7 years. If they have not started legal action within that period, they legally can not do so. However, during this phase never offer to pay one penny towards the debt or the total debt will again be legally due for another seven years.

There are some people, commonly referred to as "deadbeats," who deliberately never pay debts. They know all the tricks to avoid paying bills and think they are cleverer than the creditors. They are the exception. Usually about 85% of the population pays their creditors according to terms. It is the remaining 15% who provide various degrees of difficulty in getting paid.

Creditors have become very sophisticated. There is a credit report available on every adult in North America. Through scoring systems, large creditors make decisions on how much risk they want to take on. If they need to increase revenues, they will loosen credit and sell more marginal accounts. They can predict how much bad debt they will be taking on and what it is going to cost them. So, if you have financial problems the first thing is to face the reality, meet with your creditors and work out a solution. They may be more co-operative than you think.

(CH 15/Q85) **I scored very highly on a wealth management risk questionnaire, does that mean I should invest?**

Who sponsored the questionnaire? Was it a financial institution? Could it have been a marketing tool to rope in new investment accounts. If you have never invested and want to get some insight into the good and the bad that you would be getting into, go to my website and review the 4 ten-minute free video lessons. The website is, informus.ca.

(CH 15/Q86) **How do people make big money trading stocks if the average S&P 500 annual return is only 9.8%?**

Is the purpose of the stock market to make "BIG" money? What exactly is "BIG Money"? What is the point of investing in the stock market?

I invest in the stock market because I have found it to be the safest way to steadily grow my wealth. This is after losing $300,000 in 2000, in a mutual fund an investment advisor put my life savings into. I took what was left of my life savings and learned how to self invest.

By carefully investing in 20 financially strong companies that pay good dividends, for 15 years, in my retirement, I have realized a dividend income of about 6% a year while my portfolio also grew by about 9% a year. This sure beats the typical advice from professional investment advisors that recommend you should expect to liquidate your portfolio by about 4% a year so you do not outlive your savings when you retire. My portfolio is now many times greater than when I first started direct investing after losing all that money 20 years ago.

I never set out to make "Big" money, but I am now, by any measurement well off. I suspect that the vast majority of those who see the only way to realize wealth is by betting on the long shots in the stock market) are destined to fail to achieve wealth. If you treat the stock market like a casino, you get the same results as you get in a casino.

(CH 15/Q87) **When is someone ready to invest in stocks?**

You invest when you have unallocated funds not earning you money. You do your research and find a low risk investment with the highest return. You then invest with the intent that you will never sell this stock because you know all markets rise in time. Thus, any time is investment time.

(CH 15/Q88) **How can I convert $100 to $1,000 in a week online?**

You open a bank account online with a $100 charge to your credit card. You also sign up for a line-of-credit with the bank at the same time. After your line of credit is quickly established because you have a good credit rating, you go in the bank and extract $1000 from your bank account. You get the money because you have the preapproved line-of-credit. You now owe the bank $900 and are paying probably 8% interest per annum on the $900 loan.

You did not ask how you could make a profit of $1,000. You got what you asked for. The only positive thing is that if you had borrowed $1,000 on your credit card, you would be paying close to 22% interest.

If you are a hustler, you now take the $1,000 and buy something wholesale that you can retail for at least a 100% markup.

(CH 15/Q89) **Is it better to buy a few popular stocks that cost hundreds of dollars or several cheaper ones?**

It is unusual for a hundred-dollar stock to increase to $150 in a few months, but it is not unusual to see a $1 stock increase to $1.50 in a few months. If you had $100,000 to invest, although it would be riskier, you would have a much better chance of getting a $50,000 return on investing that money to buy 100,000 one dollar shares than 100 one hundred dollar shares. The percentage increase potential is what is important, not the price of the stock. To minimize your risk, you would want to spread the risk over the stocks of as many good companies as possible.

(CH 15/Q90) **What is a good amount to invest if I have never done it before?**

Why are you investing? What do you hope to achieve? When do you want to achieve this objective? When do you plan to retire? It is only after answering these questions that you can come up with a reasonable answer as to how much you should invest? If you just want to invest enough to say you are an investor, a hundred dollars would be fine. If you want to draw upon this portfolio for retirement then you should be investing as much as you can afford but only after you have learned how to identify what are a good stocks.

(CH 15/Q91) **Do companies pay dividend stocks for life?**

No. I know of some major banks that have paid ever rising dividends for more than a hundred years. However, at monthly or quarterly meetings the directors of the company always vote on the dividend recommendations. They are not automatic, and companies concerned about a possible problem that may require them to call upon their cash reserves can always suspend dividend payments. They also know the repercussions cancelling the dividend would have on their stock price, so it is one of the last things they would do.

(CH 15/Q92) **Why is the stock market detached from economic conditions?**

Nothing is completely detached from economic conditions. The fact that the "economy" seems to be heading in one direction and the stock market heading in another is only one's perception of events. The reality may well be that the reason the stock market is going up when the economy is going down, is because the economy is going down. Speculators are greedy and they are opportunistic. What may be driving them is the fear if they do not buy now, when the stock is cheap, they will lose out in the next bull market. Only a small percentage of the population buy stocks. The stock market is just one factor impacting economic conditions.

(CH 15/Q93) **Why does the stock market so often give surprises?**

The stock market does not give surprises. People interpret activity in the stock market as a "surprise". The stock market is just an inanimate transfer vehicle reflecting the decisions by millions of people and thousands of companies being influenced by changes and adjustments taking place in many marketplaces. The only way it could not be a surprise is if the stock market were simple and easy to predict.

(CH 15/Q94) **When companies pay out quarterly dividends, have they passed their prime?**

What does "past their prime" mean"? Does it suggest that companies who pay dividends are about to cease to operate? Does it suggest their sales and profits will never reach new highs? I only invest in financially strong companies that pay good dividends. I average an annual dividend return of about 6% and usually an additional capital gain of 9%. The dividends get paid even in a recession. Dividends focus the company and executives on a target that they must achieve. If the annual dividend is not achieved the executives know their stock options will be worthless and they will lose thousand of dollars in bonus money.

(CH 15/Q95) **Isn't it a scam for Apple to reach an additional trillion-dollar valuation in just a few weeks when it took 45 long years to reach the first trillion- dollar mark?**

No, that is just the way speculators have always emotionally jumped on "hot" stocks. The reality of the situation is ignored.

(CH 15/Q96) **Which is better in the long term, finding additional income or spending money carefully?**

No matter how careful you might be about spending your life savings, inflation will slowly diminish their purchasing power and leave you destitute in your old age. It is critical that you find additional income to offset what you are losing because of inflation. Therefore I developed software to help me choose stocks that not only paid dividends for consistent steady income but were most likely to show capital gains year-after-year.

(CH 15/Q97) **Why is it critical to incorporate alternative strategies into your investment portfolios?**

I think when most people have searched high and low to find a strategy that consistently makes money for them that they are not going to continue to search for the perfect strategy (if such a strategy exists). The problem for most new investors is finding a workable strategy - period. Most people have no “strategy”. They buy because they have heard rumours, read analyst reviews, or rely on an investment advisor to tell them what to buy. They do not know the difference between a “good” stock to buy and a “bad” stock to ignore. They have no idea of how to find a good stock or how to analyze it to confirm that it is good.

I was like that until I lost $300,000 in a mutual fund a “trusted” investment advisor put my money into. After this loss, I took back what was left of my savings and set out to find an investment strategy that could give me a steady income and increase the value of my portfolio, year-after-year. I have now lived very well off my portfolio for 15 years. For my friends who asked what my strategy was, I put together 4 ten-minute free video lessons that show them how to find the stocks to build a solid money generating portfolio. The lessons are available in my website informus.ca.

(CH 15/Q98) **Besides emotional control, what skills or concepts should I learn that a stock market simulator can't teach me?**

To understand the market, it helps to first understand how large corporations work and what motivates them. This is learned by working as an executive in a large public corporation. The stock market is not a video game with programmed rules.

There are thousands of public companies, employing millions of people, fighting for survival, beating off their competition, growing, shrinking, dying. Nothing is certain. No one can accurately predict the future. Executives must make decisions every day based on data that is suspect. Often, they make mistakes. Sometimes they are just lucky to be at the right place at the right time.

The stock market is just a place where the leading companies come together to facilitate their corporate growth. The speculators and the financial institutions feed off them. While the opportunity for financial gain motivates all the players, any success they realize is only temporary as the game never stops evolving.

(CH 15/Q99) **Has the stock market become such an essential part of the retirement system, that it is "too big too fail"?**

Failure of the stock market implies that it has some goal that it is aiming for. There is no goal.

The stock market is a simple tool or process like a sewage plant or an elevator that moves something from one place to another. In this case it is transferring the ownership of shares between one capitalist entity and another. If the current physical machinery were to be destroyed, the transfer of shares would continue to take place, even if the transfer were done manually. If there is a collective will to raise capital or speculate, it will exist. The retirement system is just one of the volume motivators, it is not the machine.

(CH 15/Q100) **How will business intelligence play a part in helping corporate entities regain market share after this current pandemic?**

A large company can be drowning in business intelligence data, but it means nothing unless someone can interpret it correctly and has the power to implement the strategy that they see being revealed. It is not something that automatically happens. It requires creativity and the ability to sell the vision to the executives who will have to implement it. Some will regain market share, and some will not. It will be an opportunity for smaller, nimbler companies to gain market share.

(CH 15/Q101) **How does Tesla have a P/E ratio of 800? Is this sustainable?**

The P/E ratio of 800 is sustainable if there are investors who see the price, they are paying for a share of Tesla as reasonable. However reasonable investors would say that the share price is unsustainable. Share prices often have little to do with reason or logic.

(CH 15/Q102) **Is missing out on Tesla Stock be the biggest financial mistake you will ever make?**

There will always be another Tesla. I am very picky about the stocks I buy. My scoring system gave Tesla a 48. I avoid stocks scoring less than 50. It just did not measure up. It's book value was a tenth of its share price, too many analysts saw it as over priced and would not recommend it, its operating margin was too low, its price to earnings was too high, it wasn't paying a dividend, etc. It is now a pure speculative play and I do not speculate. I buy quality stock that have had profits for years. There are hundreds of stocks I would buy with better fundamentals than Tesla. I do not look at the stock market as get rich quick slot machine. Perhaps in a few years Tesla will have the numbers that indicate it is a solid company but not now and I can wait.

(CH 15/Q103) **Why did Tesla's stock suddenly skyrocket? Is it totally overvalued?**

How do you judge "value"? According to the accountants who prepare Tesla's financial statements, the "book value" of a Tesla share is only about one tenth of a share's current market value. The liquidation price, if the company were to be sold, is worth whatever another company is willing to pay for it.

50 years ago General Electric, IBM and General Motors were the Tesla companies of their day. They are now just shadows of what they once were. Value is not only subjective but fleeting.

All businesses eventually fail. It is extremely hard for a successful large company to adapt to the inevitable changes that slowly take market share away from them. They are the target. The successful company continues to appeal to what it thinks are what its market has always wanted while its competitors goes after those open to new designs, new technologies and new ideas. The joys of capitalism.

(CH 15/Q104) **Is the stock market based on luck?**

The stock market is based on a communication device that allows businesses to connect those with sufficient wealth to buy a share of their "new" business. They buy with the expectation that through the shares they will share in future profits of the business.

After the shares are bought, those buyers who then want to sell the shares use the same communication device to connect to others with wealth who would be interested in buying their shares. Since these shares were now proven money makers, they could sell their shares for more than what they had paid for them. Thus, in addition to making money on dividends (a share of the profits), they could also make money on selling their shares at a higher price (capital gain).

Of course, sometimes the companies did not make profits, and the shareholders had to sell their shares for less than what they paid for them. Speculators then bought these discounted shares on the "hope" that the share price would again increase. Since profits are never 100% certain, buying on the potential profits is a "guess" which could be interpreted as "luck" if the share price again increases.

(CH 15/Q105) **Can anyone really say they understand the stock market?**

Can you understand how the executives who run businesses work? Yes.

Can you understand how speculators look at investing? Yes.

Can you understand how people want to make money in the stock market? Yes.

Can you understand the greed and manipulation of the financial institutions? Yes.

Can anyone fully understand the market? No because the market is made up of millions of investors and thousands of companies all making independent decisions. However, you can understand it enough to avoid the traps and make a steady reliable income if you are careful, diversified and do your independent research.

(CH 15/Q106) **How do I avoid losing money already invested during the covid-19 pandemic?**

The only way you lose money is if you sell the stocks you have purchased. Why do you want to sell these stocks? Are they teetering on the edge of bankruptcy? Are their operating margins lower than their competitors? Is their book value a small fraction of their share price?

If the shares have dropped because of the pandemic but the companies are fundamentally strong then the prices should come back. The typical recession lasts about 9 months. We are only about 6 months into it. If you had chosen stocks that paid dividends, you would most likely still be receiving monthly dividend payments. Are you are planning on selling at a loss because you need money?

(CH 15.Q107) **What is greed? Is there a difference between WANT, GREED and NEED?**

Greed is never being satisfied. A constant compulsion to acquire more. A compulsion that sees “need” as a mediocre desire or an objective that satisfies the average person. “Want” is just a vague idea that may or may not grow to become a “need”.

(CH 15/Q108) **Why do people with little investment knowledge take high risks in intraday trading?**

People who take high risks in intraday trading without knowledge are no different than thousands of people who buy a stock because someone "told" them it was a good one to buy. No one has taught them how to tell the difference between a good stock to buy and bad stock to buy. They are convinced it all depends on luck, just like putting quarters in the slot machines in a casino. They do not understand that carefully choosing a diverse selection of several "good" stocks increases their chances of showing more gains than losses.

(CH 15/Q109) **I have just lost 30% of my principal investing in stocks. How do I recover from this?**

What do you mean by "lost"? Have you now sold those stocks at a price lower than what you paid for them? If you sold them, why did you sell them? Are these companies financially strong? Do you know how to determine their strength?

Suppose they are financially strong companies who have taken a temporary hit but will recover and be profitable. It is not unusual in a recession for a portfolio of "good" stocks to lose 30% of the value they were in January. I would not sell them unless I saw an indication of financial difficulties that would take years before they would recover. In those companies there may be thousands of people working towards recovery.

In 2000 I lost $300,000 in a mutual fund that an investment advisor put my money into. I took what money that was left and set out to find a better safer way to invest that did not involve investment advisors.

I recognized then that I knew little about investing. In a few years I found a system that works and have recovered many times more than what I lost in 2000. What I came to realize was that with that mutual fund, I had no way to easily and accurately assess the components that made up the fund's total strength and value. I was flying blind and I sold that mutual fund because I could not established faith in its management. However, with a subsequent portfolio of 20 carefully chosen stocks it was now easy to quickly see the strength of each individual stock. This gave me confidence to hold on to those stocks in a recession. I could see even in a recession some of them were stronger not weaker.

My portfolio declined in the 2008 recession. I sold nothing and within 3 years it was gaining and kept gaining until February of 2020. It has declined this year, but I have sold nothing because I scored my stocks and confirmed that they are still financially strong and will come back. Meanwhile I live on the dividends that still get paid, even in a recession.

(CH 15/Q110) **Considering their decreasing share prices, are airline stocks a good investment for the long term?**

No airline is making a profit. Some weaker airlines will go bankrupt. Those who are financially strong and can weather the recession will eventually be stronger as they absorb the customers left by their departed competitors. The problem is no one can accurately predict the future. Who are now the strongest airlines? They are most likely the ones who will survive but investing in an airline right now is a speculative gamble. Why invest in airlines when there are many financially strong companies in other industries to invest in?

CH 15/Q111) **At 16 what should I do to become rich in the future? Learn programming, investing, or trading, develop skills like sales, advertising or learn finances and how money works?**

Most successful Chief Executives were first successful salesmen. If you learn how to sell, it is a skill that every business in the world requires in one form or another. You can write an impressive computer program but if you cannot sell it, you will be a failure. You can learn how money works but if you can not sell investors in buying your shares or in borrowing money from you, then you too will fail. Selling requires perseverance, diplomacy, intelligence, competitiveness, and creativity. You learn how to achieve success by influencing other people. With that ability almost anything is possible.

(CH 15/Q112) **What is the difference between a shareholder and an owner of a company?**

I think what you are really asking is what is the difference between a limited corporation and proprietorship. A limited company is an "artificial person" that is legally created and recognized by a government. It allows its owners, who are called shareholders to operate businesses. Legally the shareholders benefit from this "limited liability". They are only responsible for the amount that they have invested in the business. If the company were to fail and leave behind unpaid bills, creditors can not seek payment from the shareholder "owners" of that business. A mountain of laws exist that define the rights of shareholders and the responsibilities of a company's management to their shareholders.

A proprietorship is owned by a single person who is totally responsible for all the debts and obligations of the business. There is a third possibility and that is a business operated by partners. The partners can be held responsible for all the businesses' debts.

(CH 15/Q113) **When a stock drops to a low price, how does it affect the company's borrowing?**

The loan managers at their bank and a business' suppliers would generally not even be aware of the stock price of their corporate customers. What they are looking for is current trade payment experiences from other suppliers, especially their client's competitors; whether any legal suits or judgments have been registered against the business; whether they have been placed for collection by other suppliers. Interestingly they would rarely pay much attention to a financial statement on corporate customer, even though such data is public record. Their attitude would be that the public financial data was months old, they want to see current data when judging the risk.

I once tested a theory that credit worthiness of a corporation some how or other impacted the share price. I had free access to current credit risk data on 2 million corporations. I could never find a useful connection between credit risk and share price. Even short selling the stocks I knew were on the edge of bankruptcy failed to be a profitable investment experience.,

(CH 15/Q114) **Which investment turned out to be your greatest?**

The house I live in. I bought it for $125,000. I am told that it is now worth about 15 times what I paid for it. I only had to wait 42 years. None of the carefully chosen stocks I have held for 15 to 20 years have grown to 10 times what I paid for them, however they have provided me with a steady dividend annual income worth about 6% of the portfolio's value. The portfolio in February 2020 was worth about 5 times what I started with. When a portfolio's value shrinks, I live off my dividends the same as when it is p, as I wait for it to recover.

(CH 15/Q115) **Can Tesla stock still crash after record highs?**

Any stock can fail after reaching record highs. Success breeds competition. Every business eventually fails. The question is how long before its crash. It is not going to be anytime soon.

(CH 15/Q116) **How do professional investors psychologically cope with long periods of underperformance?**

Is a professional investor who lives off their investment income? If so during a recession I continue to live off my dividends, knowing that eventually my portfolio will once again begin to rise because I only invest in carefully chosen, financially strong companies that I never intend to sell. You learn to recognize that the gyrations of the stock market are just background noise. You go off and do other things that interest you, like write books on investing.

(CH 15/117) **Why does the stock market and gold have an inverse relationship?**

Gold is a commodity whose price is impacted by the rules of supply and demand around the world. It is also a refuge in times of disaster.

When the stock market collapses, those who are sure the sky is falling and the price of their stocks will never recover, rush to sell their stocks and park their money in a safe refuge like physical gold. A few speculators who see this rush to gold buy shares in gold mining companies because suddenly a mine's inventory and deposits buried in the ground have increased in value. Their sudden profits will reward investors.

Once the panic is over, investors see gold as the lump of metal it is and as its value starts to shrink back to a "norm", they cash in their gold and jump on the next hot stock that they think is going to make them rich.

(CH 15/Q118) **As a first-time investor, how are you supposed to understand "Interactive Broker Fees"?**

You are not supposed to understand investment fees. You are just supposed to pay them without question. Confusing fees is just one reason to become a self-directed investor where there are no broker fees.

(CH 15/Q119) **How can the stock market in America doing so well despite a crippled economy?**

Speculators must speculate. They hate sitting on cash. They are "active investors". The economy may be "crippled" but millions of investors see opportunities to make money in a volatile, fluctuating market. Some find it exciting. Fortunes are being made and lost.

The state of the economy to them has little to do with their speculating on a "hot" stock. To a degree they are right because the state of the economy is a backward assessment. The speculators are focused on the future. Today's economy is almost irrelevant.

The average recession last about 9 months. The worse recession lasted 43 months. Even what we are now in will come to an end and some of those who have gambled by investing now will reap a reward.

(CH 15/Q120) **Would you bet against the current stock market?**

The stock market is not a casino. It is possible to realize a steady reliable income from your stock market shares if you carefully select a diversified mix of financially strong companies that pay good reliable dividends - even in a recession. You do not have to be a speculator to do well. I have lived very comfortably off my dividend income for the last 15 years. There is no reason to "bet". You choose financially strong companies that pay dividends in the good times and bad.

(CH 15/Q121) **How did investors in 2008 that bought "Asset Backed Securities" from commercial banks expect to make a profit?**

Those who bought the Asset Backed Securities as an investment saw them as being similar to a mutual fund, that would give them a good "safe" return on their money. A salesman got a commission for selling this investment. These funds were made up of mortgages, instead of stocks like in a mutual fund. Because they were backed by mortgages, they were in turn secured by real estate,

They were sold as being safer than if they were backed by stocks. Doesn't real estate always go up in value? Isn't the stock market risky?

There was such a demand for these "safe investments, offering a good return" and the greed of the advisors and lenders were so great, that sellers of mortgages could ignore a house buyer's financial strength. Mortgages were granted without the buyer having to put any down payment on the property being "bought". No credit checks were done on these new homeowners.

The banks selling the mortgages knew their risk in the mortgage was going to be immediately passed on to the investment industry. The bank recognized that there were hundreds of thousands of people who had never previously been able to get a mortgage (because they were lousy credit risks). All they needed was to find such people and get them to agree to "buy" the property. Why bother with a credit check if you were going to immediately pass on the risk to naïve investors.

The construction industry jumped in to meet the demand for new houses. It was a feeding frenzy

The demand for houses with no checks on credit created a fierce demand. Mortgage rates increased. (mortgage rates mean nothing if you do not intend to pay them). House prices soared (the price of a house means nothing if you do not expect to pay for it).

Reality soon caught up to the bubble. The market crashed when hundreds of thousands of new home buyers without money defaulted on their mortgages. Investors tried to sell their mortgage backed securities. No one wanted them. They were now junk for the vultures who bought such junk for pennies on the dollar.

The banks who had sold the original mortgages had made their profit when they sold the mortgages to the investment dealers. The investment dealers had made their profit when they sold their risk, the mortgage backed securities to investors.

All house prices plunged in value when the cheap houses from defaulted mortgages flooded the market. It took years for house prices to recover.

Was it a fraud? It all depends upon your definition of fraud. No one went to jail. Billions of dollars were made by banks and investment dealers. Billions were lost by investors.

A credit risk score on any adult in North America can be obtained in seconds for a modest charge. Those selling the mortgage back securities did not check the value of the asset in the security. They did not care, nor want to know. All they cared about was getting their sales commission. Those buying the investment would not be aware of who owned the mortgages that backed their "investment".

Lesson Learned: never invest in anything in which you can not easily determine and control the risk - no matter how wonderful and safe an investment advisor may say it is. Buyer beware! This is why I am a self-directed investor.

(CH 15/Q122) **I'm a senior citizen with some health issues. If COVID-19 destroys our economy and stock market, I probably wouldn't live long enough for it to recover. Should I pull my money from the market?**

I too am a senior with health issues. I learned a long time ago that I could not time the market well enough to make enough money to survive on. I found speculating to be a stressful way to invest. Why am I not about to sell my stocks?

Twenty years ago, after experiencing an investment loss of $300,000, I set out to find a better, safer, easier way to invest. After much trial and error, I found the answer by investing in 20 diversified financially strong companies that pay good dividends. For the last 15 years I have lived off the dividends and watched the portfolio grow as much as 500% from where I started.

In a recession the portfolio total value shrinks but I still have the same number of dividend sources and they keep paying my living expenses. The gyrations of the stock market have almost become irrelevant. A year can go by without me buying or selling a stock.

Interestingly, the bad times weed out the weak companies which allows the strong companies to then scoop up their clients and get stronger. Do you have your money invested in financially strong companies paying good dividends? If you do, you can weather the storm.

The average recession lasts about 9 months. The worse recession in the last 100 years lasted 43 months. No one can foretell the future, but history shows that after every crash the market comes back and reaches new heights.

Part of your problem may be that you really do not know how to judge if you have strong or weak stocks. If this is the case, I would suggest you go to my website and go through 4 ten minute free video lessons I put together for friends. This may help you determine what your options are.

(CH 15/Q123) **Should you not invest in a company if they are filing for chapter 11 bankruptcy even though they have solid fundamentals for value investors?**

There are about 14,000 companies out there you can invest in and probably fewer than 50 are filing for chapter 11 bankruptcy. Why invest in this company? To buy shares in this company is a speculative play not a value play. To invest in a company filing for Chapter 11 bankruptcy is a bit like a bride marrying the town drunk and then complaining after the marriage that he is a drunk and not a good husband.

There is a reason they are in Chapter 11. It may take many years before this company could once again be a solvent, well run company. It could take years to resolve settlements with secured and unsecured creditors. Shareholders are at the end of the line with claims on the assets and usually they end up with nothing.

If they were solid, they would be able to meet their obligations as they come due and would not need to go bankrupt. What is there operating margin? What is their book value? What is their Price to Earnings? If these figures are strong, then this is a very unusual bankruptcy.

(CH 15/Q124) **How do the analysts and market watchers know exactly why the stock market is reacting the way it is?**

They don't know exactly why the stock market is reacting the way it is but they are expected to come up with a response when asked and will come up with some kind of logical reason. It is called creativity.

(CH 15/Q125) **How can you expect returns in trading stocks as a private investor, (with no experience) while competing with professionals and funds?**

Whether you are a professional or a first time self-directed investor, if you carefully select 20 financially strong stocks with dividends you can expect to receive a dividend income each year worth about 6% of your portfolio plus in addition expect to see your portfolio grow by about 9% each year (maybe not this year). Even in a recession the dividends of most financially strong companies get paid as you wait for prices to recover.

The investment industry with its argon, arrogance and B.S. does a good job of discouraging people from becoming self directed investors. It is not difficult to get these results. All the information you need to select stocks is available free of charge.

I have lived very well off my self-directed investments for 15 years and watched my portfolio grow by about 500%. I set out to find a better, safer way to invest after an investment advisor with 40 years of experience lost $300,000 of my money that he had put into a mutual fund.

Do not be intimidated by professionals and funds. They are no smarter than you are and have no magic crystal ball that allows them to predict the future, even though they will do their best to convince you that they do.

CH 15/Q126) **How accurate are financial statements of publicly traded companies?**

First, financial statements are historical records. It can be many months after a company's year end before you will typically see their annual financial statement. Think of how glowing some 2019 annual financial statements were for some companies now hit hard by COVID-19. Companies who are now insolvent or moving towards insolvency.

It has always concerned me that the accounting firms who prepare the financial statements are paid to make a public company's annual financial statement appear as glowing as possible. They want to get next year's audit. If they did not, the accounting firm could lose hundreds of thousands of dollars in income if that public company starts shopping around for another accounting firm. An annual financial statement potentially puts millions of dollars at risk not only with the company's investors but with their lenders. The jobs of high paid executives in the company can also threatened.

Large accounting firms know how to gild the lily. What they do is not "illegal", but it certainly is not objective. You must learn how to read "between the lines" and determine what is really in that annual financial statement that they hope no one looks at too closely.

I used to design commercial risk scoring system for banks, insurance companies, manufacturers and wholesalers that totally ignored financial statement information as a factor in determining risk. I only used current, factual, verifiable, trended information e.g. trade payment experiences of a company's suppliers, legal suits, judgments, NSF checks, company starting dates, etc. When 3,000 bad accounts were test scored by a major bank, they found the scores to be "amazingly predictive" of forecasting commercial bad debt write offs. For everyone of these commercial loan customers the bank had bee receiving annual financial statements. It did not stop them from having to write off hundreds of millions of dollars to bad debt.

(CH 15/Q127) **Is investing in cruise lines currently a good move?**

Did you ever try to defend investing in the stock market when the risk adverse shouted that no one can foretell the future and investing is just luck?

The Canadian Pension Fund's purchase of several million more shares of Royal Caribbean Cruises Ltd in the fourth quarter of 2019 is an example of our inability to foretell the future. Due to COVID-19, Royal's shares dropped a billion dollars in the first quarter of 2020. With assets of $420 billion, our pensions are not in jeopardy, but it may well be years (perhaps decades) before Royal Caribbean share price recovers to its former glory.

"Capital value is going to fluctuate over time", was the pension funds response to the hit. They are right. As long at the pension fund does not sell these depreciated shares, they will technically never take the billion-dollar hit. Not having to sell is the joy of investing with the public's money. The next time you lose a few thousand on your stock pick you can tell your spouse, who is questioning your investment skills, "It's a long-term play. At least it wasn't a billion dollars like those professionals at the Canadian Pension Fund."

Until COVID-19, investing in cruise lines looked like the safest of investments. Every year their boats were full of more and more baby boomers with the time and money to splurge on the non-essentials of life.

The $46 billion-dollar cruise industry is dominated by Miami based Carnival Corporation (CCL), Royal Caribbean Cruises Ltd (RCL) and Norwegian Cruise Line Holdings (NCLH). In 2019, these three gave boat rides to 80% of the 26 million cruise passengers in the world. Between them they employed 272,000 in 200 ships. These now under-utilized assets are tied up at docks with only a hope that some of them might tentatively begin cruising again August 1, 2020.

Would cruise shares make a good edition to now add to your portfolio? The following chart gives you an idea of how speculative an investment they might be:

CRUISE LINE DATA May 14, 2020

	ROYAL	CARNIVAL	NORWEGIAN
Current Share Price	$40.70	$14.15	$12.78
Share Price 4 yrs ago	$77.77	$48.60	$45.73
Daily Volume	21,281,530	64,777,331	36,306,463
Dividend Percent	7.40%	0.00%	0.00%

Book Value of Share	$58.26	$35.46	$30.58
Price to Earnings Ratio	4.58	7.62	6.89
Operating Margin	19.16%	14.97%	18.33%
# Analysts Rating Stock a "Buy"	10	9	10
# Analysts Rating "Strong Buy"	7	6	4
IDM SCORE	**78**	**60**	**64**

Do you find it interesting that despite the pandemic, analysts are rating all these stocks as buys and strong buys? Based on this limited data, did the pension fund choose the best one to add to their portfolio? Interestingly Royal paid a dividend in April, this appears to be the last dividend they will be paying for the foreseeable future. The other two have not paid dividends this year.

The book values of these three companies are well ahead of their current share price which indicates a bargain. Admittedly, “book values” are calculated by accountants and are not the same as the “market values” that might be realized if the company’s assets were liquidated. Currently, the supply for cruise ships is probably 20 times greater than the demand.

The price-to-earnings ratio is low confirms that the shares are not overpriced. The operating margins for the three reflects their historical sales minus the expense to realize those sales. With little new revenue now coming in, their operating margins will probably be a minus figures when more current financial information is released.

The IDM score at the bottom of the chart is a measuring stick and summary to quickly evaluate stocks. It is based on the data currently available to the public. It does not reflect the dire straights that these businesses are now in. The scores reflect those of the profitable well-run companies that these three once were just a few months ago. Normally any score over 70 indicates a very desirable stock to own. Anything over 50 is normally a safe stock purchase. (You can learn more about the IDM score at informus.ca).

No matter how good a score it may be, an internet searches always needs to be done to determine whether recent negative information might disqualify a stock from being purchased. For example, the cash burn for Royal Caribbean Cruises is reported to be $250 million a month. They have pledged as security several of their ships to secure a 3.3 billion bond issue. Those buying the bonds are gambling that Royal's revenues will have recovered within the next 12 months. They may be basing this optimism on the fact that 55% of the Royal Caribbean clients, who had booked cruises in 2020, are accepting vouchers for a future cruise instead of a cash refund. This willingness to forego cash may reflect the "high end" market that Royal Caribbean caters to in its brands like Silver Sea Cruises, Azamara Cruises and Celebrity Cruises.

Carnival Corporation caters to a different market. Their focus is on "first-time" cruisers This strategy has captured 47.4% of the world's cruise passengers in their 105 ships sailing under their brands: Carnival Cruise Line, Princess Cruise Line, Costa Cruises, AIDA Cruises, Holland America Line, P&O Cruises, Cunard Line and Seabourn Cruise Line. Their annual sales were 21 Billion and from this they netted out 2 Billion in Net Income. This revenue represents 39.4% of the industries' revenues. It is a high-volume operation that needs to fill 254,000 beds and requires 150,000 employees to cater to their clientele.

Royal Caribbean's emphasis on quality captured 23% of the passengers and 20.2% of the industries revenue.

Norwegian Cruise Lines is considerably smaller but very cost efficient. With only 9.5% of the passengers they have captured 12.6% of the industries revenue.

On January 10, 2020 Royal Caribbean shares opened at $134.17 (probably helped by the massive purchase by the Canadian Pension Fund). On March 23, 2020, the shares hit their most recent low of $24.03.

On January 21st Norwegian Cruise lines shares opened at a high of $59.00 by March 19 they hit a low of $8.03.

On December 30, 2019 Carnival Corporation hit its high of $51.64 but by April 2, 2020 their price as down to $8.01.

The good news is that they have all recovered substantially from their recent lows. The bad news is that they are a long way from their highs of just a few months ago.

For every pessimistic seller, there must be an optimistic buyer. Those who bought at the recent lowest share prices have already made nice gains. Will the shares continue to climb? The optimists will say yes and buy. The pessimists will take their money and invest in companies that are not contingent on the desire of those able to spend on luxuries like cruise vacations. With unemployment expected to climb into the plus 20% range, companies providing necessities will probably seem like a safer investment than cruises. Uncertain times bring both great opportunities and great risk.

CHAPTER 16

US STOCK MARKETS

The New York Stock Exchange (NYSE) and the NASDAQ are the primary stock markets where equities are bought and sold by Americans. These two exchanges trade shares of companies from all over the world. The major difference between them is that the NYSE maintains a physical trading floor in New York and the NASDAQ trades electronically though a data center in New Jersey. Since shares in both locations are done electronically the self-directed investor will not notice any difference in how their buy and sell orders are processed.

Established in 1792, the NYSE sees itself as serving the more stable and well-established corporations. This is reflected in the higher fees they charge companies wanting to get listed on either exchange. The NASDAQ's listing fees are lower. It sees itself as the home for the more volatile, cutting edge technology and innovation growth stocks.

It is only in the last 20 years that both the NASDAQ and the NYSE moved from being private companies to being public companies. Anyone can buy shares in them.

The Federal Government's Securities and Exchange Commission (SEC) oversees both entities. They administer laws that protects investors from unfair or illegal stock trading practices.

In the following 4 chapters you will find all stocks traded on the NASDAQ and the NYSE that pay a dividend of 6% or greater. The stocks are sorted in descending order by:

(1) Dividend yield percent
(2) Stock score
(3) Alphabetical by company name
(4) By the stock's share price.

The data was extracted in the summer of 2020.

=

US STOCKS

With A Dividend Yield of 6% or Greater

BY DIVIDEND %

In the summer of 2020, when the following 628 stocks were selected from all stocks listed on United States stock exchanges they were all reported to be paying shareholders dividends annually equivalent to 6% or more of their share price reported on that day. That dividend percentage will change as share prices change. The directors of the listed companies can also decide to cease paying dividends or raise or lower the dividend payments.

The directors can periodically declare what the dividend dollar payout will be and when it will be paid. While the amount of the dividend paid remains fixed a rising share price lowers the dividend yield percentage, and a shrinking share price causes the dividend percentage to increase.

I have seen several banks who were paying dividends in the 3.5% to 4.5% range last year now paying dividends in the 5.5% to 6.5% range. Their share prices have dropped about 17% because of the COVID-19 recession in 2020. Their scores are now in the sixties. Previously they were in the seventies. At some point their share prices will regain their previous highs. In the meantime, they will continue to pay good dividends. Several of these banks have not cut dividends in over 100 years.

It took me many weeks to calculate the scores. This involved locating and extracting the necessary 9 facts used in the scoring software. What you see below are the dividend percentages that were reported on the days I calculated that stocks score. This delay in processing is why, some stocks were no longer paying dividends by the time I calculated their score.

I have previously explained why a dividend percentage is an important consideration in choosing a stock to add to your portfolio. However, as you can see below those stock reporting the highest dividend payout do not usually have scores over 50. I avoid adding stocks to my portfolio that score below 50. I have highlighted all those stocks scoring over 50 so you can easily find the better stocks to consider.

It was interesting to see a stock paying a dividend over 30% that had a score over 50. This unusual occurrence would require research to find out if the stock were available for purchase. I might even contact the company for an explanation for its high dividend payout.

Stocks paying over 6% are generally stable. There should not be much change in the data used for scoring. However, <u>it is always important that before you buy a share that you always rescore that stock with the most current information</u>

available. Even while I was calculating a few scores for this book, sometimes the information would change as I was recording it.

In October 2020 I came across a stock that was paying a 6.43% dividend and did not show up in the following chart. This puzzled me until I investigated further and found that years could go by without that stock paying a dividend. The first dividend they paid in 2020 was in September, after I had extracted the list of stocks for this book.

This following list of high dividend payers is a snapshot at a specific time. It is unusual for dividend payers to not pay dividends on a steady basis either monthly or quarterly, but not impossible. Since I require a steady, dependable flow of dividends, I would choose stocks of comparable value before I would purchase one that paid stocks sporadically.

You will notice how I have truncated the names of most companies. This was necessary so that I could fit the share information on one line.

All stocks scoring over 50 have been high lighted. The list is sorted in descending order by dividend yield percentage.

Score /Stock Symbol/ Company Name/. Stock price/ Dividend%

48.PER..Sandridge Perm$0.45..**36.34%**

49.FRO..Frontline Ltd..$8.37**..32%**

20.CEN..Center Coast B..$8.45..**31.95%**

58.DHT..DHT Holdings Ltd...$6.12**..31%**

35.MVO..MV Oil Trust..$2.95**..30%**

20

38.NNA..Navios Maritime .$5.22...**23%**

31.NRT..North European O..$3.29..**20.76%**

14.EGI..Eagle Growth and .$5.03..**20.28%**

35.BSBR..Banco Santander ..$7.00..**20.24%**

22.OCCI..OFS Credit Co Inc..$10.74..**20%**

32.PTMN..Portman Ridge Fin..$1.17..**20%**

21.CLM..Cornerstone Strateg..$11.02..**20%**

20.CRF..Cornerstone Total Re..$10.81..**20%**

19

36.NGL..NGL Energy Partn.$4.16..**19%**

34.VEON..VEON Ltd.......$1.53..**19%**

29.OXLC..Oxford Lane Capit..$4.24..**19%**

53.ET..Energy Transfer LP..$6.64..**19%**

17

34.KRP..Kimbell Roy..$8.31..**17.91%**

36.USAC..USA Compr..$11.78..**17.83%**

43.GEO..The GEO Gr…$10.81..**17.76%**

30.SRLP..Sprague Reso..$15.08..**17.71%**

45.CEQP..Crestwood E..$14.20..**17.61%**

39.SHLX...Shell Mi.$10.61.**17.34%**

32.ICMB..Investcorp Cr.$3.46..**17.34%**

35.NRP...Natural Res...$10.55..**17.06%**

22.AM..Antero Midstre..$7.22..**17.04%**

7.YGYIP..Youngevity .$14.34..**17%**

16

52.HMLP..Hoegh ..$10.50..**16.76%**

35.IEP..Icahn Enterpri…$49.68..**16.10%**

55.WF..Woori Franklin..$21.37..**16.09%**

41.RVI..Retail Value ..$12.77..**16.05%**

12.MDRRP..Medalist D..$12.50..**16%**

12.CUBA..Herzfeld Cari.$3.83..**16%**

52.EURN..Euronav NV...$9.64..**16%**

17.JOC..Nuveen Credit..$6.07..**16%**

34.BBVA..Banco Bil...$2.97..**16%**

48.KNOP..KNOT Of...$12.81...**16%**

32.OXSQ..Oxford Sq..$2.62..**16%**

15

44.MBT..Mobile Tel..$9.55..**15.84%**

38.ARI..Apollo Comm..$9.01.. **15.55%**

30.ORC..Orchid Island..$5.10. **15.28%**

52. MPLX..MPLX LP..$18.22...**15.09%**

18.OPP..RiverNorth/D..$14.23..**15%**

48. FSK..FS KKR Capital..$15.80.. **15%**

24. FSKR..FS KKR Capital..$49.19..**15%**

10.HGLB..Highland..$6.56..**15%**

14

29.MARPS.. Marine Petro..$2.03.. **14.95%**

35.BKCC.. BlackRock ..$2.71.. **14.76%**

36.PFLZ..Pennant Park ..8.37..**14.74%**

38.DMLP..Dorchester $10.63..**14.72%**

34.CRT..Cross Timber..$6.11..**14.71%**

33.PNNT..Pennant Park..$3.27..**14.70%**

39.CGBD..TCG BDC..$8.76.. **14.61%**

42.RIV..Rivernorth Opport..$15.06..**14%**

36. PSEC..Prospect Capit..$5.11.. **14%**

20.RA.. Brookfield Real ..$16.96..**14%**

33.OFS..OFS Capital Corp..4.79.. **14%**

39.GLP.. Global Partne.. $12.75.. **14%**

37.MRCC.. Monroe Capi.. $6.96.. **14%**

26.NHTC..Natural Health ..$5.78..**14%**

13

45.WES..Western Midstre..$9.03..**13.85%**

45.SACH..Sachern Capita..$3.48..**13.78%**

31. RTLR.. Rattler Midst.. $8.50.. **13.68%**

42. CNXM.. CNX Midst..$10.26..**13.62%**

34.CINR..Ciner Resourc..$10.01..**13.59%**

36.EDF..Stone Harbor Emer..$7.09..**13.54%**

43.AINV..Apollo Investme.$9.18..**13.51%**

52.WHF..Whitehorse Fi..$10.52..**13.50%**

40.CIM..Chimera Invest..$8.96..**13.39%**

41.ACRE..Ares Comm…..$9.8…**13%**

32.CCAP..Crescent Capital..$12.24..**13%**

33.BCSF..Bain Capital S...$10.48..**13%**

49.OKE..ONEOK Inc……$28.07…..**13%**

34.CAPL…CrossAmerica Pa..$15.73..**13%**

52.PSXP..Phillips 66 Partn..$26.52...**13%**

12

13.FBIOP..Fortress Bio..$18.37...**12.76%**

45.IFN..The India Fund..$17.07..**12.54%**

20.MINDP..Mind Techn..$17.86..**12.53%**

38.DPG..Duff & Phelps..$11.19..**12.51%**

16.EOD..Wells Fargo ..$4.57..**12.49%**

38.SUN..Sunoco LP...$26.94…**12.49%**

50.NHF..Nexpoint Strat...$9.63..**12.46%**

16.USDP..USD Parnters..$3.57..**12.44%**

15.FGB..First Trust Spec..$2.66…**12.41%**

45.ENLC..EnLink Midst...$3.03…**12.38%**

15.FCO..Aberdeen Global..$6.82..**12.32%**

8.GDV..Gabelli Dividend..$9.76..**12.30%**

15.DDF..Delaware Invest..$8.37..**12.05%**

35.HCFT..Hunt companies ..$2.47..**12%**

35.GLOP..Gaslog Partners..$3.97...**12%**

20.ECC..Eagle Point Credit..$7.79..**12%**

37.ARR..Armour Resid…$9.86…**12%**

37.TCPC..BlackRock TCP..$9.90...**12%**

18.PCF..High Income Sec..$8.10…..**12%**

39.GOF..Guggenheim Str..$18.02..**12%**

20.GGT..Gabelli Multimed..$7.20..**12%**

31.BPMP..BP Midstream..$11.74..**12%**

8.BKEPP..Blueknight E..$5.93..**12%**

17.EDI...Stone Harbor E..$7.93..**12%**

44.SCM..Stellus Capital In.$8.20..**12%**

14.IRR..Voya Natural R..$2.61…..**12%**

53.STWD..Starwood Pr..$16.01..**12%**

19.GGM..Guggenheim ..$18.14..**12%**

15.GLV..Clough Global .$9.87..**12%**

47.NEWT..Newtek Bus..$19.00..**12%**

9.XFLT...XAI Octagon F..$6.02..**12%**

31.NLY..Annaly Capital ..$7.47..**12%**

50.MCN..Madison Covrd..$6.06..**12%**

41.NMFC..New Mountain F..$10.11..**12%**

17.NRO..Neuberger Berma..$3.90..**12%**

14.RSF..RiverNorth Mar ..$14.73..**12%**

15.HTY..John Hancock Ta..$11.04..**12%**

42.KYN..Kayne Anderson..$4.93..**12%**

54.TPVG..TriplePoint Vent..$11.78..**12%**

19.FEN..First Trust Energ..$10.02..**12%**

38.PBFX..PBF Logistics LP..$9.94..**12%**

30.AFIN..American Finance T.$6.97..**12%**

11

27.FCRD..First Eagle Alt ..$3.34..**11.98%**

44.DCP..DCP Midstream ..$13.13..**11.88%**

41.NS..NuStar Engergy ..$13.48….**11.87**

51.FDUS..Fidus Investme...$10.47..**11.46%**

48.HTGC..Hercules Cap..$11.20..**11.43%**

32.SFL..SFL Corp Ltd….$8.91..**11.23%**

53.ENBL..Enable Midstream ..$5.90..**11.21%**

21.CTR..Clearbridge Energ..$14.34..**11.16%**

38.SCD..Lmp Capital Inc..$10.98…**11%**

28.GMLPP..Golar LNG Part LP..$19.24..**11%**

43.GSBD..Goldman Sachs .$15.82..**11%**

19.FCT..First Trust Senior Floa…$11.22..**11%**

21.GLQ…Clough Global Eq…$11.86…..**11%**

19.GLO…Clough Global Oppo….$9.58..**11%**

19.KIO…KKR Income Oppo….$13.34..**11%**

44.CSWC..Capital Southwestr..$14.98..**11%**

37.CHMI..Cherry Hill Mortga….$9.77..**11%**

49.BPY..Brookfield Property…..$23.23..**11%**

29.BPYU.Brookfield Property..$11.95..**11%**

17..PGZ..Principal Real Estate ..$11.63..**11%**

22..PHK..PIMCO High Income..$5.43..**11%**

26.ANH..Anworth Mortga……. $1.76..**11%**

57.PCI..PIMCO Dynamic Cre..$18.88..**11%**

44.DSL..DoubleLIne Income S..$16.14..**11%**

21.GAB..Gabelli Equity Trust…..$5.48..**11%**

12.WTFCP..Wintrust Financial..$26.59..**11%**

16.FEO..First Trust/Aberdeen..$13.28..**11%**

21.PFL..PIMCO Floating R..$10.04….**11%**

34.FEI..First Trust MLP…..$5.34……**11%**

29.FPL..First Trust New Op..$4.05…..**11%**

59.PDI..PIMCO Dynamic ….$26.64…**11%**

20.FMO..Fiduciary/Claymore ….$8.61..**11%**

29.MTBCP…MTBC Inc…….$25.66….**11%**

13.IAE..Voya Asia Pacific …..$9.63..**11%**

51.PFN..PIMCO Income St…..$11.28..**11%**

17.CSSEP..Chicken Soup for ..$0.00..**11%**

43.DKL..Delek Logistics Part..$32.36..**11%**

16.IHD..Voya Emerging …...$6.77…..**11%**

10

15.DEX..Delaware..$8.96..**10.98%**

24.ERC..Wells Fargo..$11.26..**10.94%**

35.GEL...Genesis Ene..$5.51..**10.93%**

38.FTF..Franklin Lim.$12.06..**10.92%**

27.CYCCP..Cyclacel ...$5.50..**10.91**

54.ARCC..Ares Capit...$14.19..**10.82%**

23.MBNKP..Medalli ..$18.50..**10.81%**

11.NREE..NexPoint ..$14.99..**10.67%**

49.ABR..Arbor Realty ..$11.62..**10.67%**

52.MMP..Magellan Mid..$38.61..**10.67%**

13.BKEP...Blueknight E..$1.50..**10.65%**

35.APTS..Preferred Apar..$6.61..**10.61**

49.HFRO..Highland Inc..$8.90..**10.38%**

54.NCZ..AllianzGI Conv..$4.35..**10.34%**

40.MNDO..MIND C.T.I..$2.32..**10.34%**

20.AHC...A H Belo Corp..$1.55..**10.32%**

25..VGI..Virtus Global ..$11.64..**10.31%**

58.LADR....Ladder Capi..$7.77..**10.30%**

59.BXMT..Blackstone M..$24.08..**10.30%**

48..BHLB..Berkshire Hill..$9.35..**10.27%**

49.TWO..Two Harbors In.$5.47....**10.24%**

29.DMO..Western Asset M..$12.96..**10.24%**

63.EPD..Enterprise Produc.$17.60..**10.12%**

54.PAA..Plains All Americ..$7.12..**10.12%**

27.DNI..Dividend and I..$11.40..**10.09%**

20.CIF..Mfs Intermedi..$2.31..**10.08%**

38.PHT..Pioneer High In.$8.05..**10.06%**

24.MFV..MFS Special Val.$5.35..**10.05%**

44.MFD..Macquarie/First...$7.93..**10.04%**

50.RC..Ready Capital C..$10.49.....**10%**

47.EVV..Eaton Vance Ltd ..$11.7..**%10**

49.EARN..Ellington Resi.$11.62..**10%**

33.USA...Liberty All Star .$6.21..**10%**

58.NCV..AllianzGI Convert..$4.88..**10%**

43.AGNC..AGNC Invest..$14.14..**10%**

34.CDMOP..Avid Bioservic.$27.88..**10%**

25.HEQ..John Hancock Hed..$11.33..**10%**

43.GLAD..Gladstone Capital..$7.64..**10%**

58.ORCC..Owl Rock Capital .$13.31..**10%**

46.EMO..ClearBridge Ener..$2.90...**10%**

16.TECTP..Tectonic Financia..$9.00..**10%**

9

45.E..Eni SpA...$18.98….**9.97%**

29.RMT..Royce Micro-Cap ..$7.93...**9.96%**

32.CHW..Calamos Global ..$8.45..**9.94%**

47.NAT..Nordic American...$4.34..**9.92%**

19.SPKEP...Spark Energy ..$22.05…..**9.92**%

21.IAF..Abereen Australia ….$4.82**..9.9%**

26.VTA…Invesco Dynamic...$9.10..**9.9%**

23.PGP..PIMCO Global Sto..$8.49..**9.9%**

45.HRZN..Horizon Technol.$12.09..**9.9%**

22.JDD..Nuveen Diversified ..$7.99..**9.9%**

25.GGN..GAMCO Global ..$3.65..**9.89%**

37.HESM..Hesse Midstre..$17.66..**9.88%**

52.RVT..Royce Value Tru..$13.36..**9.88%**

40.PAGP..Plains GP Hold..$7.31..**9.85%**

24.AWP..Aberdeen Global..$4.87..**9.85%**

64.PKO..PIMCO Income O..$23.20..**9.83%**

48.HEP..Holly Energy Pa..$12.59..**11.18%**

51.SLRC..Solar Capital Ltd..$16.97..**9.8%**

64.DX…….Dynex Capital I...$15.85..**9.8%**

49.ITCB……Itau Corpban...$4.43…**9.74%**

22.AIRTP..Air T Inc……….$20.54….**9.74**

40.THW..Tekla World Healt..$14.39..**9.73%**

29.AVK..Advent Claymore C..$14.43..**9.73%**

34.SIM..Grupo Simec SAB de ..$6.13..**9.19%**

23.IDE...Voya Infrastructure I..$9.49..**9.7%**

26.IGR..CBRE Clarion Globa..$6.18…..**9.69%**

39.HQL ..Tekla Life Sciences I.$16.93..**9.69**

55.PCM..Pcm Fund Inc………$9.94…..**9.66%**

32.PTY...PIMCO Corporate .$16.18…..**9.64%**

67.BTI..British American T..$34.48..**9.62%**

57.NHS..Neuberger Berma..$11.30..**9.61%**

26.ETW..Eaton Vance Tax..$9.0..**9.6%**

63.SNP..China Petroleum ..$45.77..**9.59%**

51.RCS..PIMCO Strategic ..$6.39..**9.58%**

25.BGX…Blackstone / G..$12.55...**9.56%**

20.NYMTM..New York Mo..$20.60..**9.56%**

40.CMO..Capstead Mortga..$6.29..**9.55%**

25.BGH..Barings Global Sh..$13.31..**9.52%**

36.IGD..Voya Global Equity...$5.04..**9.52%**

43.LOAN..Manhattan Bridge.$4.20..**9.52%**

44.KREF..KKR Real Estate ..$18.11..**9.50%**

23.FAM..First Trust..Aberd..$10.10**..9.5%**

27.BTO..John Hancock Finan..$23.27..**9.5%**

26.JRS..Nuveen Real Estate ..$8.02..**9.48%**

23.NYMTN....New York M..$21.12..**9.47%**

51.CIK..Credit Suisse Asset..$2.85..**9.47%**

47.DHY..Credit Suisse High..$2.09..**9.47%**

56.BGB..Blackstone / GSO...$11.95..**9.44%**

64.AB..AllianceBernstein..$28.91..**9.44%**

28.CGO..Calamos Global..$12.73...**9.43%**

26.EXG..Eaton Vance Tax...$7.85..**9.42%**

35.JRI..Nuveen Real Asset…$12.34..**9.41%**

47.SPH..Suburban Propane..$12.75..**9.41%**

49.OLP..One Liberty Prop..$19.14..**9.40%**

26.MIE…Cohen & Steers ..$1.92..**9.38%**

25.FSD..First Trust High..$14.09...**9.37%**

47.WLKP..Westlake Che..$20.17**..9.35%**

43.EAD..Wells Fargo Inc..$7.52..**9.35%**

58.PMT..PennyMac Mor..$17.15...**9.33**

62.TSLX..Sixth Street S.$17.60..**9.32%**

66.SAR..Saratoga Inve..$17.19….**9.31%**

39.ARDC..Ares Dynamic..$12.58..**9.30%**

31.NYMTO..New York M..$21.18..**9.30%**

46.CVI..CVR Energy Inc.$17.21..**9.30**

57.GHY..PGIM Global Hi..$13.45..**9.3%**

25.DHF..BNY Mellon Hi..$2.75..**9.3%**

22.IGA...Voya Global Advan..$8.39..**9.3%**

62.OPI..Office Properties..$23.84..**9.23%**

36.NRGX..PIMCO Energy..$7.37..**9.23%**

53.BIT..BlackRock M…$16.O2..**9.22%**

55.GFNCP...General Fin..$100.00..**9.20%**

30.SLMBP...SLM Corp...$33.05..**9.20%**

26.PPT..Putnam Premier..$4.58..**9.18%**

59.CTL..CenturyLink Inc.$10.91..**9.17%**

52.GNL..Global Net Le..$17.52…**9.13%**

44.ETB..Eaton Vance Ta..$14.20..**9.13%**

24.VLT..Invesco Hi..$12.67...**9.13%**

58.TGP..Teekay LNG Part..$10.96..**9.12%**

47.IVH..Ivy High Incom ..$11.99...**9.07%**

39.TRTXTPG RE Finan...$8.82..**9.07%**

47.ETV…Eaton Vance Tax.$15.07..**9.04%**

26.MXF..Mexico Fund I..$10.29...**9.04%**

40.HNW..Pioneer Diversif..$13.65..**9.01%**

55.SUNS..Solar Senior Capit ..$13.34..**9.00%**

9

44.FUND..Sprott Focus….$6.24..**8.98%**

27.ISD..PGIM High Yield…$14.06..**8.96%**

39.NCMI..National CineMed..$3.13..**8.95%**

51.GAIN…Gladstone Invest..$9.39..**8.95**

24.JTA…Nuveen Tax Adva..$8.59..**8.94%**

40.AROC….Archrock Inc…$6.51..**8.91%**

24.EXD..Eaton Vance Tax..$9.54..**8.91%**

28.HIX…Western Asset Hi..$6.61..**8.90%**

50.ETJ..Eaton Vance Risk-..$10.26...**8.89%**

52.BSM…Black Stone Min…$6.75..**8.89%**

63.XOM……Exxon Mobil..$39.18...**8.88%**

24.MIN..MFS Intermediate I.$3.84…**8.88%**

44.HQH..Tekla Healthcare .$20.06..**8.87%**

59.SMFG..Sumitomo Mistu ..$5.95..**8.86%**

28.PDT..John Hancock Pre..$13.21..**8.86%**

49.GBDC..Golub Capita..13.13..**8.83%**

24.SPE..Special Opport.$12.82…..**8.81%**

29.FOF..Cohen & Steers ..11.86…..**8.80%**

33.ETY..Eaton Vance Tax-.$11.49..**8.8%**

43.GMZ..Goldman Sachs ...$9.33...**8.79%**

58.EMD..Western Asset ..$12.98..**8.78%**

59.TCP..TC Pipelines L...$29.65.....**8.77%**

70.RIO..Rio Tinto PLc.....$61.50....**8.73%**

44.GER..Goldman Sachs ..$7.12.....**8.71%**

27.DDT..Dillard's Capital ...$21.44...**8.7%**

47.NBLX..Noble Midstream..$8.67..**8.65%**

25.JTD..Nuveen Tax-advant...$13.63...**8.64%**

24.TLI..Western Asset Co....9.20......**8.61%**

53.EFC..Ellington Financia...$12.47....**8.6%**

28.GCV..Gabelli Convertible..$5.63..**8.53%**

59.PCN..PIMCO Corporate ..$15.79...**8.5%**

34.EVT..Eaton Vance Tax A..$20.42..**8.5%**

30.PIM..Putnam Master Inter..4.24....**8.5%**

46.BRG..Bluerock Resident..$7.57..**8.5%**

47.MVC..MVC Capital.....$8.04..**8.46%**

51.SHI..Sinopec Shanghai ..$20.00...**8.45%**

44.EDD..Morgan Stanley E..$5.80..**8.45%**

55.CCD..Calamos Dynamic..$23.75..**8.44%**

56.BAP..Credicorp Ltd..$132.41..**8.43%**

33.HYT..Blackrock Co…$11.11..**8.42%**

62.OHI...Omega Healthcare..$31.91..**8.4%**

47.OCSL..Oaktree Specialty..$4.99..**8.4%**

36.BPYUP..Brookfield Pr..$18.95..**8.4%**

52.DK..Delek US Hold…$14.80..**8.38%**

46.GPM..Guggenheim En..$5.77..**8.32%**

30.HTD..John Hancock..$19.86...**8.34%**

31.ROI..Cohen & Steers..$11.63...**8.3%**

30.AOD..Aberdeen Total..$8.33..**8.28%**

46.MAIN..Main Street C..$29.76..**8.27%**

44.SRV..The Cushing..$17.45...**8.25%**

57.FTAI..Fortress Trans..$16.01..**8.24%**

27.BSL..Blackstone GS..$13.54..**8.24%**

25.BGR..BlackRock Eng..6.87..**8.21%**

30.SZC...Cushing Re..31.20…..**8.20%**

20.WTREP..Watford H..$24.50...**8.2%**

41.MRLN..Marlin Busine.. 6.87..**8.15%**

25.KMF..Kayne Anderso..4.42..**8.14%**

27.MCR..MFS Charter ...8.62..**8.14%**

28.EHI..Western Asset G..9.89..**8.13%**

38.FSP..Franklin Street P..4.43..**8.13%**

28.MMT..MFS Multim..$6.09...**8.13%**

53.IRM..Iron Mountain …$30.50..**8.11%**

49.CODI..Compass Div..17.78...**8.10%**

48.CHY..Calamos Conv..$12.61..**8.09%**

41.SPKE..Spark Ener.$14.54….**8.08%**

33.CHI..Calamos Conv..$11.29..**8.07%**

39.FRA..Blackrock Float..$11.74..**8.05%**

32.HPF..John Hancock ..$18.34..**8.04%**

40.TEAF..Tortoise Essen..$11.19..**8.04%**

52.BLX..Banco Lainoa..$12.44..**8.04%**

42.IID..Voya International..$4.49...**8.02%**

23.PIHPP..1347 Property Ins24.95..**8.02%**

46.CMRE..Costamare Inc...$4.99..**8.02%**

42.LMRKP..Landmark Infr.$24.95..**8.02%**

30.LMRKO..Landmark Inf..$24.66..**8.01%**

27.AGD..Aberdeen Glob..$9.74..**8.01%**

29.AFINP..American Fin..$23.43….**8.00%**

8

28.JHIJohn Hancock Invest..$16.58..**7.99%**

32.LGI..Lazard Global Tota..16.00..**7.98%**

25.BGT.Blackrock floating ..$11.51..**7.97%**

54.TOT..Total SE………$48.95……**7.95%**

45.GOOD..Gladstone Com..18.98..**7.95%**

48.LMRK..Landmark Infra..$10.07...**7.94%**

29.HPS..John Hancock Prefer..16.54..**7.9%**

19.HTLFP..Heartland Financi..26.88..**7.88%**

33.FAX..Aberdeen Asia-pa..$4.19..**7.88%**

30.BDJ..BlackRock Enhanc..7.62…..**7.87%**

48.MO..Altria Group Inc..$43.76….**7.86%**

50.HYI……Western Asset Hi..14.45..**7.85%**

49.EVA….Enviva Partners ..$38.98..**7.85%**

70.PBA..Pembina Pipeline..$24.53..**7.83%**

26.BOE..Blackrock Enhanced..9.67..**7.82%**

54.NVEC..NVE Corp…….$51.81..**7.82%**

59.DIAX..Nuveen Dow 30sm ..13.99..**7.81%**

39.VGR...Vector Group Ltd..$10.24..**7.81%**

37.UTF..Cohen & Steers Infa..23.72...**7.8%**

58.FSLF...First Eagle Senior ..$12.29..**7.8%**

31.GUT..Babelli Utility Trust...$12.29..**7.8%**

54.KMI..Kinder Morgan Inc..$13.51...**7.77%**

24.EVG..Eaton Vance Short ..11.60..**7.76%**

26.FIF…..First Trust Energy ..9.68..**7.75%**

29.HIO..Western Asset Hig ..5.03..**7.75%**

31.BLW..Blackrock Ltd Dur..15.20..**7.74%**

50.WMB..Williams Compani...$20.69..**7.73**

48.DNP..DNP Select Inco ..10.11..**7.72%**

45.NYMT..New York Mortg.2.59..**7.72%**

35.CSQ..Calamos Strate...$14.40….**7.71%**

19.ECCB..Eagle Point Cr.25.17…..**7.70%**

48.ACV..AllianzGI Divers..26.04..**7.70%**

47.BBDC..Barings BDC ...$8.30...**7.7%**

57.EC..Ecopetrol SA….$11.56….**7.68%**

60.SBRA..Sabra Health Ca..$15.65..**7.67%**

34.ETO..Eaton Vance Ta..$22.30...**7.67%**

72.VLO..Valero Energy..51.23..**7.65%**

55.NTG..Tortoise Midstream..16.24..**7.64%**

17.ESGRP..Enstar Group..$224.65..**7.6%**

19.IHIT..Invesco High Incom..$7.84..**7.6%**

25.HIE..Miller/Howard High..$6.33..***7.58%***

39.OCSI..Oaktree Strategic..$6.61..**7.58%**

28.BGY..Blackrock Enhanced..5.36..**7.57%**

33.RNP..Cohen & Steers RE..19.74..**7.54%**

26.EFR..Eaton Vance Sen..$11.81..**7.53%**

45.BFS..Saul Centers Inc…$28.17...**7.53%**

56.ENB..Enbridge Inc..$31.58….**7.53%**

60.GLU..Gabelli Global Util..15.95..**7.52%**

52.RFI..Cohen & Steers To..12.77..**7.52%**

47.BCX..BlackRock Resour ..6.39..**7.51%**

56.AJX..Great Ajax ....9.07...**7.50%**

49THQ..Tekla Healthcare...$18.01..**7.50%**

29.HPI..John Hancock Prefe.$19.77..**7.50**%

56.DFP..Flaherty & Crumri..$26.58..**7.5%**

54.TYGTortoise Energy Infr..16.03..**7.49%**

21.MGF..MFS Government..4.65..**7.49%**

23.MCI..Barings Corporat..$12.81..**7.49%**

29.FFA..First Trust Enhan..$15.26..**7.47%**

26.BxMX..Nuveen S&P...$11.52..**7.47%**

55.CQP..Cheniere Energ..$34.60..**7.46%**

35.BPYPP..Brookfield Pro.$21.85..**7.44%**

44.CIO..City Office Reit I...$8.08..**7.43%**

45.MFA..MFA Financial Inc....$2.70..**7.42**

57.SPG..Simon Property Gr 70.23..**7.40%**

35..BPYPO..Brookfield Pr...$21.43..**7.4%**

38.AKO.B..Embotelladora ...$13.8..**7.39%**

53.NWBI..Northwest Ba..$10.29..**7.39%**

29.NFJ..ANuveen Senior In.$4.96..**7.39%**

48.NGHCP..National Gene..$25.43..**7.37%**

29.NGHCO..National Gene.$25.47..**7.36%**

62.NYCB..New York Comm..$9.24..**7.36%**

43.BRMK..Broadmark Real….$9.79..**7.36%**

18.AGNCM..AGNC Investm.$23.37..**7.35%**

71.CEO..CNOOC Ltd..$113.93….**7.35%**

30.ASRVP..Ameriserv Finan..$28.82..**7.33%**

14.DCF……BNY Mellon Alcen..8.20..**7.32%**

50.HTBK…Heritage Commerc.$9.00..**7.30%**

18.RILYP..B. Riley Financial..$23.60..**7.3%**

25.AWF..Alliancebernstein...$10.74..**7.3%**

15.IHTA..Invesco High Incom..$7.64..**7.3%**

24.JPC..Nuveen Preferred …$8.72...**7.3%**

46.ENIA..Enel Americas SA$7.26...**7.29%**

30.ASG..Liberty All Star Gro..$7.13..**7.29%**

23.MPV..Barings Participati..$10.99..**7.28%**

56.MAC..Macerich Co...$8.27….**7.26%**

26.PHD..Pioneer Floating …10.35..**7.25%**

47.HYB..New America High …$8.29..**7.24%**

38.AKO.A..Embotelladora..$11.68..**7.24%**

49.VOD..Vodafone Group…$14.18..**7.24%**

17.OCFCP..OceanFirst Fin...$26.37..**7.23%**

62.APAM..Artisan Partners..$37.05..**7.23%**

59.JGH...Nuveen Global High..$14.19..**7.23%**

17.LMRKN..Landmark Infrastr..24.52..**7.22%**

44.PEI..Pennsylvania Real ...$1.11…**7.21%**

36.DSWL..Deswell Industries ..$2.50..**7.20%**

35.BPYPN..Brookfield Prop..$19.97..**7.20**

41.BTZ..Blackrock Credit Allo.$13.94..**7.2%**

53.FPF..First Trust Inter Dur..$21.93...**7.2%**

17.FINS..Angel Oak Financi ..16.78..**7.2%**

71.SLG..St. Green Realty C..$49.21..**7.19%**

60.LDP..Cohen & Steers Lt…23.86..**7.19%**

18.AGNCN..AGNC Invest..$24.33..**7.19%**

47.EOI..Eaton Vance Enhan..$14.99..**7.19%**

48.IFS.Intercorp Financia..$24.37….**7.18%**

17.TSCAP..TriState Capital..$23.52..**7.17%**

59.UVV..Universal Corp….$43.03….**7.16%**

30.NGHCN..National Gen..$26.20..**7.16%**

22.AVA..Grupo Aval Accio..$5.10..**7.15%**

32.FLC..Flaherty & Crumri ..$22.16..**7.15%**

38.ENIC..Enel Chile SA$3.69…**7.15%**

30.CEE…Central & Eastern..$20.49..**7.14%**

21.DCUE..Dominion Energy..$101.75..**7.13%**

26.ERH..Wells Fargo Utilities..$12.18..**7.13%**

17.OXLCM..Oxford Lane Cap..$23.67..**7.1%**

44.MSBI..Midland States Banc..$14.92..**7.1%**

47.UBFO..United Security Bank..$6.21..**7.09%**

25.DVD..Dover Motorsports .$1.41..**7.09%**

33.FFC..Flaherty & Crumrine ...$21.86..**7.08%**

25.EFT..Eaton Vance Floating..$12.17..**7.07%**

25.EVF..Eaton Vance Senior …$5.94...**7.07%**

39.TFSL..TFS Financial Corp...$15.84..**7.07%**

59.T..AT & T……...……$29.42..**7.07%**

45.JHG..Janus Henderson ..$20.41..**7.06%**

28.SPXX..Nuveen S&P 500 ..$13.88..**7.06%**

30.CHSCO..CHS Inc……$27.95….**7.04%**

28.GDO..Western Asset G..$17.24…..**7.03%**

29.PSF...Cohen & Steers E..$26.83….**7.02%**

22.GNT..Gamco Natural Res..$5.13….**7.02**

28.GOODM..Gladstone Comm..$25.00..**7.00%**

7

16.JCO..Nuveen Credit Opport..$8.09..**6.97%**

18.AGNCO..AGNC Invest.$23.39..**6.95%**

60.NAVI..Navient Corp....$9.21….**6.95%**

25.JSD..Nuveen Short Dur…$12.18..**6.95%**

38.TKC..Turkecell Iletisim ..$4.85..**6.94%**

46.RWT..Redwood Trust I....$7.21..**6.93%**

16.BGIO..BlackRock 2022…8.67...**6.92%**

46.FDEU..First Trust Dyn..$10.41..**6.91%**

27.CHSCP..CHS Inc..…$28.93….**6.91%**

26.DBL..Doubleline Opp...$19.11..**6.91%**

57.NHI...National Health .63.88...**6.90%**

61.MPC..Marathon Petro $33.63..**9.90%**

17.UCBIO..United Commu..26.27..**6.9%**

45.CXP..Columbia Property..$12.19..**6.89%**

45.NTB..Bank.N.T. Butterfield..25.60..**6.88%**

19.OXLCP...Oxford Lane Capi..$22.70..**6.88%**

36.UTG..Reaves Utility Fu..$31.45..**6.87%**

18.GOODN..Gladstone Com..$24.11..**6.87%**

47.BCBP..BCB Bancorp I.…$8.15….**6.87%**

61.JPI...Nuveen Preferred.…$22.81….**6.87%**

49.HRB..H&R Block..$15.15….**6.87%**

27.JCE..Nuveen Core Equi.$13.11..**6.86%**

52.SRC..Spirit Realty Capit..$36.49..**6.85%**

56.CIT..CIT Group Inc..$20.43…**6.83%**

26.CHSCN..CHS Inc…..$26.03….**6.82%**

29.CPAC..Cementos Pacas..$7.90..**6.8%**

58.MGP..MGM Growth Prop..$28.55..**6.8%**

42.BDN..Brandywine Realty..$11.19..**6.8%**

33.CII..Blackrock Enhance..$15.48...**6.78%**

50.ALX..Alexander's Inc..$266.17...**6.76%**

17.TSCBP..TriState Capital..$23.56..**6.76%**

53.BWG..BrandywineGlob..$12.45..**6.75%**

49.CLP..Capital Product Par..$5.93..**6.75%**

39.HIHO..Highway Holdin..$2.67..**6.74%**

27.JPS..Nuveen Preferred &..8.99..**6.74%**

44.FCBP..First Choice Banc..$14.86..**6.73%**

56.PFS..Provident Finan..$13.68...**6.73%**

27.PFO..Flaherty & Crumri..$12.41..**6.72%**

19.AGNCP..AGNC Investme..$22.62..**6.7%**

30.CHSCL..CHS Inc……$27.97….**6.7%**

17.MBINP..Merchants Banc..$26.15..**6.69%**

56.FFIC..Flushing Financial ..12.61...**6.66%**

52.BKT..Blackrock Income Tru..6.20...**6.66%**

17.FMBIP..First Midwest Banc...$26.33..**6.65%**

49.OLN..Olin Corp…………$12.09..**6.62%**

33EVC..Entravision Communi..$1.51..**6.62%**

24.JFR..Nuveen Floating Rate..$8.35..**6.61%**

45.UNB..Union Bankshares..$19.35..**6.61%**

18.ESGRO..Enstar Group..$26.22..**6.61%**

58.CNQ..Canadian Natural..$25.71..**6.61%**

29.BUI..BlackRock Utility..$22.01..**6.60%**

37.SXC..Suncoke Energy ..$3.64..**6.59%**

18.GAINL..Gladstone Inve..$24.25..**6.57%**

22.TPZ..Tortoise Power &...$9.13..**6.57%**

26.CHSCM..CHS Inc……..$25.70….**6.57%**

70.CMA..Comerica Inc…..$41.47…**6.56%**

24.JRO..Nuveen Floating Rate ..$8.26..**6.54%**

35.KFFB..Kentucky First Feder..$6.12..**6.54%**

62.PBCT...People's United Fin..$11.03..**6.53%**

57.FFBC..First Financial Banc..$14.09..**6.53%**

23.DUC..Duff & Phelps Utility..$9.22..**6.51%**

59.TX..Ternium SA……….$18.44…..**6.51%**

22.VVR..Invesco Senior Inco...$3.70…..**6.50%**

66.BNS..Bank of Nova Scotia..$42.39...**6.50%**

32.SEL..Global Self Storage….$4.01….**6.45%**

28.TCBIP..Texas Captial Bank...$25.35..**6.41%**

57.HOPE..Hope Bancorp Inc.….$8.72….**6.4%**

18.PNEPP..Pinnacle Financial ..$26.36..**6.4%**

24.AIF..Apollo Tactical Income..$12.76..**6.39%**

25.WTFC..Wintrust Financial ..$25.66...**6.39%**

35.PFD..Flaherty & Crumrine..$16.17...**6.38%**

51.WSR...Whitestone RE…$6.60…..**6.36%**

50.CZNC..Citizens & North..$16.98..**6.36%**

29.BANFP..BFC Capital Tr.$28.30..**6.36%**

33.BPOPN..Popular Capital$26.36….**6.35%**

32.GBAB..Guggenheim Taxa..$23.80..**6.34%**

48.WDR..Waddell & Reed Fin..$15.78...**6.34%**

50.BGS..B&G Foods Inc…$29.99…**6.34%**

44.GGZ..The Gabelli Global S.$10.10...**6.34%**

50.EOS..Eaton Vance Enhanc..$18.72...**6.33%**

39.BRT..BRT Apartments C..$13.93..**6.32%**

60.PRU..Prudential Financial ...$69.71..**6.31%**

46.ESRT..Empire State Realty...$6.67..**6.30%**

18GAINM..Gladstone Investmen.$24.82..**6.3%**

59.QQQX..Nuveen NASDAQ ..$24.82..**6.29%**

17.HTIA..Healthcare Trust Inc...$21.79..**6.28%**

20.AVGOP..Broadcom Inc..$1,275.89..**6.27%**

61.FNB..F N B Corp……..$7.68……**6.25%**

54.VALE..Vale SA………..$11.38…..**6.20%**

26.TSI..Tcw Strategic Income ..5.76….**6.2%**

18.JPT..Nuveen Preferred ..$22.82….**6.2%**

61.PEBO..Peoples Bancorp...$21.71..**6.2%**

61.NIE..AllianzGI Equity..$24.56..**6.19%**

25.AFT..Apollo Senior Fl..$12.84..**6.17%**

18.DCOMP..Dime Commu..$22.35..**6.15%**

19.BHFAP..Brighthouse Fin..$26.82..**6.15%**

44.GLIBP..GCI Liberty Inc..$28.49..**6.14**

52.LTC..LTC Properties Inc..$37.24..**6.12%**

30.HBANO..Huntington Ban..$25.60..**6.1%**

28.AIO..Allianz Artificial..$21.39..**6.08%**

46.HNNA..Hennessy Advisor..$9.05..**6.08%**

33.FITBI..Fifth Third Bancorp..$27.38..**6.05%**

29.LANDP..Gladstone Land .$26.34..**6.05%**

43.CLI..Mack-Cali Realty ..$13.23..**6.05%**

42.ILPT..Industrial Logistics..$21.84..**6.04%**

62.HBAN..Huntington Bancs..$9.94..**6.04%**

18.MBINO..Merchants Banco..$24.90.. **6.02%**

62.FHN..First Horizon Nation...$9.95..**6%**

36.BPOPM..Popular Capital Tr...$25.46...**6%**

6

44.KW..Kennedy-Wilson Ho..$14.69..**5.99%**

51.PWOD..Penns Woods Banc..$21.42..**5.98%**

48.GMRE..Global Medical R…$14.25..**5.97%**

19.AUBAP..Atlantic Union B…$26.31..**5.93%**

39.TSE..Trinseo SA………….$27.09..**5.91%**

62.LYB..LyondellBasell Indus..$72.06..**5.83%**

68.SNV..Synovus Financial ..$22.75...**5.80%**

35.ETH..Ethan Allen Interior..$14.52..**5.79%**

61.VNO..Vornado Realty Tr..$36.76..**5.77%**

37.DOW..Dow Inc….$48.57..**5.76%**

65.UNM..Unum Group..$19.90..**5.73%**

63.TRTN..Triton Internation..$36.41..**5.71%**

77.CFG..Cititzens Financial..$27.36..**5.70%**

46.ATAX..America First Mul.$4.37..**5.49%**

16.JEMD..Nuveen Emergi..$7.64..**5.26%**

21.SWZ..Swiss Helvetia Fu..$8.52..**5.11%**

5

18.CEPU..Central Puerto SA..$2.51..**4.72%**

35.TEO..Telecom Agrentina SA..$7.11..**4.58%**

70.OMF..OneMain Holdings .$30.00..**4.40%**

32.STK..Columbia Seligman ..23.22..**4.15%**

4

35.IRCP..IRSA Propiedades ..$8.00..**3.95%**

49.HAFC..Hanmi Financial C..$9.68...**3.31%**

22.CMCTP..CIM Commercial .$26.24..**1.94%**

29.GECC..Great Elm Capital ...$5.25..**1.90%**

30.TDF..Templeton Dragon .$24.97..**1.83%**

54.CBSH..Commerce Bancs..$60.03..**1.80%**

59.GLPI..Gaming and Leisure...$37.65..**1.27%**

29.GRF..Eagle Capital Growth ...$7.08..**1.05%**

38.SVC.. Service Properties Tr...$8.90.. **0.49%**

41.RLJ...RLJ Lodging Trust…$10.05….**0.40%**

30.IGT..International Game...$11.38….**0%**

26.RESI..Front Yard Residential…$9.88..**0%**

48.CUK.. Carnival PLC………...$12.95..**0%**

19.MURR.. Medalist Diversified..$8.37**...0%**

28.CDOR..Condor Hospitality T....$4.40...**0%**

36.DBI..Designer Brands Inc……$7.43..**0%**

23.TGA..TransGlobe Energy C….$0.55….**0%**

34.BSMX..Banco Santander……..$3.28..**0%**

27.TEF...Telefonica SA……….$4.02……**0%**

27.CIG.C..Energy Company of .$1.92…..**0%**

39.AKR...Acadia Realty Trust..$11.30…..**0%**

32.TIGO..Millicom Internat…$29.73..**0%**

21.SCU..Sculptor Capital Ma..$12.81..**0%**

23.TPCO..Tribune Publishing..$11.35..**0%**

22.BWL.A..Bowl America Inc..$9.50….**0%**

15.ATV..Acorn International..$0.15……**0%**

12.FLNG..Flex LNG Ltd……$6.02….**0%**

41.TS..Tenaris SA…………..$11.43….**0%**

55.CCEP..Coca-Cola European..44.35..**0%**

16.LND..Brasilagro – Cia Bras ..$4.39..**0%**

CHAPTER 17

U.S. Stocks

With A Dividend Yield of 6% or Greater

BY STOCK SCORE

Stocks are sorted by descending stock score. There are 143 stocks with a score exceeding 50. I avoid stocks scoring below 50.

Score/Stock Symbol/Company Name/.Stock price/Dividend%

77.CFG..Cititzens Financial ..$27.36..5.70%

72.VLO...Valero Energy C..51.23..7.65%

71.CEO…CNOOC Ltd..$113.93..7.35%

71.SLG...St. Green Realty .$49.21..7.19%

70.CMA..Comerica Inc..$41.47..6.56%

70.OMF..OneMain Hold...$30.00..4.40%

70.RIO..Rio Tinto PLc..$61.50….8.73%

70.PBA..Pembina Pipeline..$24.53..7.83%

60

68.SNV..Synovus Financial ..$22.75..5.80%

67.BTI..British American Toba..$34.48...9.62%

66.BNS..Bank of Nova Scotia..$42.39..6.50%

66..SAR...Saratoga Investment .$17.19...9.31%

65.UNM..Unum Group..$19.90….5.73%

64.AB..AllianceBernstein Hold..$28.91..9.44%

64.PKO..PIMCO Income Oppo..$23.20...9.83%

64.DX..Dynex Capital Inc...$15.82….9.8%

63.XOM..Exxon Mobil Corp..$39.18…..8.88%

63.EPD..Enterprise Product..$17.60**..**10.12%

63.SNP..China Petroleum & C..$45.77..9.59%

63.TRTN..Triton International ..$36.41..5.71%

62.NYCB..New York Communit..$9.24..7.36%

62.APAM..Artisan Partners Ass.$37.05..7.23%

62.TSLX..Sixth Street Specialt..$17.60...9.32%

62.PBCT..People's United Fin..$11.03..6.53%

62.OHI..Omega Healthcare Inv..$31.91..8.4%

62.LYB..LyondellBasell Industr.$72.06..5.83%

62.OPI..Office Properties Inco.$23.84..9.23%

62.HBAN..Huntington Bancshar..$9.94..6.04%

62.FHN..First Horizon National C..$9.95..6%

61.VNO..Vornado Realty Trust..$36.76..5.77%

61..JPI..Nuveen Preferred .$22.81..6.87%

61.MPC..Marathon Petroleum ..$33.63..9.90%

61.PEBO..Peoples Bancorp Inc..$21.71….6.2%

61.NIE..AllianzGI Equity & C..$24.56…6.19%

61.FNB..F N B Corp….$7.68……6.25%

60.SBRA..Sabra Health Care RE..$15.65..7.67%

60.PRU..Prudential Financial..$69.71….6.31%

60.GLU..Gabelli Global Utility..15.95…..7.52%.

60.LDP..Cohen & Steers Ltd .$23.86….7.19%

60.NAVI..Navient Corp…...$9.21….6.95%

50

59.SMFG..Sumitomo Mistui Fin..$5.95..8.86%

59.QQQX..Nuveen NASDAQ ..$24.82..6.29%

59.T..AT & T……$29.42….7.07%

59.UVV..Universal Corp…$43.03….7.16%

59.CTL..CenturyLink Inc…..$10.91…..9.17%

59.GLPI..Gaming and Leisure..$37.65….1.27%

59.PCN..PIMCO Corporate & Inc..$15.79..8.5%

59.TCP..TC Pipelines LP..$29.65…..8.77%

59.BXMT..Blackstone Mortgage $24.08..10.30%

59.PDI..PIMCO Dynamic Income.$26.64…11%

59.DIAX..Nuveen Dow 30sm D.$13.99….7.81%

59.TX..Ternium SA….$18.44…..6.51%

59.JGH...Nuveen Global High ..$14.19..7.23%

58.NCV..AllianzGI Convertible ...$4.88….10%

58.LADR..Ladder Capital Corp..$7.77..10.30%

58.PMT..PennyMac Mortgage …$17.15….9.33

58.EMD..Western Asset Emergi.$12.98….8.78%

58.MGP..MGM Growth Properties..$28.55..6.8%

58.DHT..DHT Holdings Ltd....$6.12**......**31%

58.FSLF..First Eagle Senior $12.29..7.8%

58.ORCC..Owl Rock Capital $13.31..10%

58.TGP..Teekay LNG Partner..$10.96..9.12%

58.CNQ..Canadian Natural Res..$25.71**..**6.61%

57.EC..Ecopetrol SA.$11.56….7.68%

57.HOPE..Hope Bancorp Inc..$8.72….6.4%

57.FTAI..Fortress Transportat..$16.01..8.24%

57.FFBC..First Financial Banc..$14.09..6.53%

57.GHY..PGIM Global High Yie..$13.45..9.3%

57.PCI..PIMCO Dynamic Credit..$18.88….11%

57.SPG..Simon Property Group..$70.23..7.40%

57.NHS..Neuberger Berman H..$11.30..9.61%

57.NHI..National Health Investors..$63.88..6.90%

56.PFS..Provident Financial Serv..$13.68….6.73%

56.CIT..CIT Group Inc…$20.43…6.83

56.AJX..Great Ajax Corp..$9.07….7.50%

56.ENB..Enbridge Inc..$31.58….7.53%

56.MAC..Macerich Co..$8.27..7.26%

56.BAP..Credicorp Ltd..$132.41..8.43%

56.FFIC..Flushing Financial..$12.61.6.66%

56.BGB..Blackstone / GSO Str..$11.95..9.44%

56.DFP..Flaherty & Crumrine P..$26.58..7.5%

55.NTG.Tortoise Midstream En..$16.24..7.64%

55.CCEP..Coca-Cola European Part..$44.35..0%

55.PCM..Pcm Fund Inc….$9.94…..9.66%

55.CQP..Cheniere Energy Partne..$34.60..7.46%

55.GFNCP..General Finance ..$100.00..9.20%

55.CCD..Calamos Dynamic Con..$23.75…..8.44%

55.WF..Woori Franklin Group Inc..$21.37..16.09%

55.SUNS..Solar Senior Capital Ltd..$13.34. .9.00%

54.VALE….Vale SA…..$11.38…..6.20%

54.TOT..Total SE..$48.95……7.95%

54.NVEC..NVE Corp..$51.81….7.82%

54.PAA..Plains All American Pipe..$7.12..10.12%

54.ARCC..Ares Capital Corp…$14.19…..10.82%

54.NCZ..AllianzGI Convertible ..$4.35….10.34%

54.TPVG..TriplePoint Venture Gro..$11.78..12%

54.CBSH..Commerce Bancshares..$60.03..1.80%

54.KMI..Kinder Morgan Inc.…$13.51….7.77%

54.TYG..Tortoise Energy Infras…$16.03**.**7.49%

53.STWD..Starwood Property Tru..$16.01..12%

53.ET..Energy Transfer LP...$6.64......19%

53.BWG..BrandywineGlobal .$12.45….6.75%

53.ENBL..Enable Midstream P…$5.90…..11.21%

53.BIT..BlackRock Multi-Sect…$16.O2…9.22%

53.FPF..First Trust Inter Dur Pr..$21.93..7.2%

53.EFC.Ellington Financial Inc..$12.47..8.6%

53.NWBI..Northwest Bancshares .$10.29….7.39%

53.IRM..Iron Mountain Inc..$30.50……8.11%

52.BLX..Banco Lainoamericano…$12.44...8.04%

52.RFI..Cohen & Steers Total Ret..$12.77..7.52%

52.DK..Delek US Holdings Inc…$14.80….8.38%

52.RVT..Royce Value Trust Inc..$13.36….9.88%

52.MMP..Magellan Midstream Par..$38.61..10.67%

52.WHF..Whitehorse Finance Inc..$10.52..13.50%

52.SRC..Spirit Realty Capital Inc..$36.49..6.85%

52.LTC..LTC Properties Inc..$37.24..6.12%

52.MPLX..MPLX LP...$18.22.....15.09%

52.HMLP..Hoegh LNG Pa..$10.50..16.76%

52.EURN..Euronav NV...$9.64....16%

52.PSXP..Phillips 66 Partners LP..$26.52..13%

52.LTC..LTC Properties I..$37.24….6.12%

52.BKT..Blackrock Income Trust..$6.20..6.66%

52.BSM..Black Stone Minerals LP..$6.75..8.89%

52.GNL..Global Net Lease Inc…$17.52…9.13%

51.FDUS..Fidus Investment ..$10.47…..11.46%

51.RCS..PIMCO Strategic Global …$6.39..9.58%

51.CIK..Credit Suisse Asset Mgm..$2.85…..9.47%

51.PWOD..Penns Woods Bancorp ..$21.42..5.98%

51.GAIN..Gladstone Investment Co..$9.39..8.95

51.SLRC..Solar Capital Ltd..$16.97….9.8%

51.WSR..Whitestone REIT…$6.60…..6.36%

51.SHI..Sinopec Shanghai Petr..$20.00..8.45

51.PFN..PIMCO Income Strate..$11.28..11%

50.ALX..Alexander's Inc…$266.17..6.76%

50.BGS..B&G Foods Inc…$29.99…6.34%

50.EOS..Eaton Vance Enhanc..$18.72..6.33%

50.CZNC..Citizens & Northern..$16.98...6.36%

50.WMB..Williams Companies ..$20.69..7.73

50.ETJ..Eaton Vance Risk-Man....$10.26..8.89%

50.HTBK..Heritage Commerce..$9.00..7.30%

50.HYI..Western Asset High Yield..$14.45..7.85%

50.NHF..Nexpoint Strategic Oppor..$9.63..12.46%

50.MCN..Madison Covrd Call & Eq..$6.06..12%

50.RC..Ready Capital Corp….$10.49…..10%

50.HTBK..Heritage Commerce..$9.00...7.30%

40

49.OKE..ONEOK Inc..$28.07...13%

49.CLP..Capital Product Partn.$5.93..6.75%

49.OLN…..Olin Corp….$12.09…..6.62%

49.EARN..Ellington Residential .$11.62..10%

49.THQ..Tekla Healthcare..$18.01..7.50%

49.FRO.. Frontline Ltd......$8.37......32%

49.OLP..One Liberty Properti ..$19.14..9.40%

49.HFRO..Highland Income ...$8.90..10.38%

49.TWO..Two Harbors Investm..$5.47..10.24%

49.BPY..Brookfield Property..$23.23..11%

49.HAFC..Hanmi Financial Corp..$9.68..3.31%

49.ABR..Arbor Realty Trust Inc..$11.62..10.67%

49.EVA..Enviva Partners LP..$38.98..7.85%

49.ITCB..Itau Corpbanca..$4.43..9.74%

49.VOD..Vodafone Group ..$14.18..7.24%

49.HRB..H&R Block..$15.15….6.87%

49.GBDC..Golub Capital .$13.13..8.83%

49.CODI..Compass Diversif..$17.78..8.10%

48.CHY..Calamos Convertib..$12.61..8.09%

48.WDR..Waddell & Reed Fin..$15.78..6.34%

48.MO..Altria Group Inc…$43.76..7.86%

48.GMRE..Global Medical RE $14.25..5.97%

48.NGHCP..National General..$25.43..7.37%

48.DNP..DNP Select Income Fu..$10.11..7.72%

48.BHLB..Berkshire Hill Banc..$9.35..10.27%

48.KNOP.. KNOT Offshore Par..$12.81..16%

48.HTGC..Hercules Capital .$11.20….11.43%

48.LMRK..Landmark Infrastruc.$10.07..7.94%

48.CUK..Carnival PLC....$12.95.....0%

48.BGFV..Big 5 Sporting Good ..$5.72….6.99%

48.ACV..AllianzGI Diversi..$26.04..7.70%

48.FSK.. FS KKR Capital Co..$15.80..15%

48.PER..Sandridge Permian Tr.$0.45..36.34%

48.BGFV..Big 5 Sporting G$5.72..6.99%

48.IFS..Intercorp Financial S.$24.37….7.18%

47.UMPQ..Umpqua Holdings .$12.05..6.97%

47.UMPQ..Umpqua Holdin…$12.05**…**6.97%

47.NEWT..Newtek Business Se..$19.00..12%

47.BBDC..Barings BDC Inc….$8.30….7.7%

47.SPH..Suburban Propane Par..$12.75..9.41%

47.OCSL..Oaktree Specialty Lend..$4.99..8.4%

47.UBFO..United Security Banks..$6.21..7.09%

47.WLKP..Westlake Chemical P..$20.17..9.35%

47.IVH..Ivy High Income Opp.$11.99..9.07%

47.ETV..Eaton Vance Tax-Man..$15.07..9.04%

47.NAT..Nordic American Tank.$4.34..9.92%

47.NBLX..Noble Midstream Part..$8.67..8.65%

47.MVC..MVC Capital Inc..$8.04……8.46%

47.BCX..BlackRock Resources ….$6.39..7.51%

47.BCBP..BCB Bancorp Inc..$8.15..6.87%

47.EOI..Eaton Vance Enhanced..$14.99..7.19%

47.DHY..Credit Suisse High Yield..$2.09..9.47%

47.HYB.New America High In.$8.29..7.24%

47.EVV..Eaton Vance Ltd Duratio..$11.7..10%

46.CVI..CVR Energy Inc..$17.21..9.30%

46.ATAX..America First Multifa…$4.37..5.49%

46.BRG..Bluerock Residential G..$7.57…..8.5%

46.CMRE..Costamare Inc..$4.99..8.02%

46.ESRT..Empire State Realty T..$6.67…..6.30%

46.EMO.. ClearBridge Energy Mid..$2.90..10%

46.HNNA..Hennessy Advisors..$9.05. .6.08%

46.RWT..Redwood Trust Inc..$7.21.6.93%

46.FDEU..First Trust Dynamic E..$10.41..6.91%

46.GPM..Guggenheim Enhance..E.$5.77..8.32%

46.MAIN..Main Street Capital Co..$29.76..8.27%

46.ENI..Enel Americas SA...$7.26…..7.29%

45.HRZN..Horizon Technology F.$12.09..9.9%

45.WES..Western Midstream Pa$9.03..13.85%

45.SACH..Sachern Capital C..$3.48..13.78%

45.CXP..Columbia Property Tr..$12.19..6.89%

45.NTB..Bank of N.T. Butterfield..25.60..6.88%

45.IFN..The India Fund Inc..$17.07…..12.54%

45.UNB..Union Bankshares Inc..$19.35..6.61%

45.BFS..Saul Centers Inc..$28.17..7.53%

45.CEQP..Crestwood Equity ..$14.20..17.61%

45.GOOD..Gladstone Commer..$18.98..7.95%

45.JHG..Janus Henderson Group..$20.41..7.06%

45.ENLC..EnLink Midstream .$3.03..12.38%

45.NYMT..New York Mortgage ..$2.59.....7.72%

45.MFA..MFA Financial Inc..$2.70.. 7.42%

45.E..Eni SpA....$18.98....9.97%

44.HQH..Tekla Healthcare In...$20.06..8.87%

44.KW..Kennedy-Wilson Holdings..$14.69..5.99%

44.EDD..Morgan Stanley Emerging..$5.80..8.45%

44.MBT..Mobile TeleSystems ..$9.5..15.84%

44.GER..Goldman Sachs MLP...$7.12..8.71%

44.PEI..Pennsylvania Real Estate..$1.11..7.21%

44.MSBI..Midland States Banc..$14.92..7.1%

44.FCBP..First Choice Banc..$14.86..6.73%

44.SCM..Stellus Capital Invest..$8.20..12%

44.DSL..DoubleLIne Income S..$16.14..11%

44.DCP..DCP Midstream LP..$13.13..11.88%

44.CSWC..Capital Southwest ..$14.98..11%

44.KREF..KKR Real Estate Fin..$18.11..9.50%

44.CIO..City Office Reit Inc..$8.08..7.43%

44.GGZ..The Gabelli Global .$10.10..6.34%

44.GLIBP..GCI Liberty Inc..$28.49..6.14

44.SRV..The Cushing MLP..$17.45..8.25%

44.ETB..Eaton Vance Tax-Ma..$14.20..9.13%

44.FUND..Sprott Focus Trust..$6.24..8.98%

44.MFD..Macquarie/First Trust..7.93..10.04%

43.AGNC..AGNC Investment ..$14.14..10%

43.GLAD..Gladstone Capital..$7.64..10%

43.AINV..Apollo Investment ..$9.18..13.51%

43.DKL..Delek Logistics Part..$32.36..11%

43.CLI..Mack-Cali Realty..$13.23..6.05%

43.GEO..The GEO Group..10.81..17.76%

43.GMZ..Goldman Sachs M..$9.33..8.79%

43.BRMK..Broadmark Realty..$9.79..7.36%

43.EAD..Wells Fargo Income..$7.52..9.35%

43.GSBD..Goldman Sachs B$15.82..11%

43.LOAN..Manhattan Bridge..$4.20..9.52%

42.KYN..Kayne Anderson...$4.93..12%

42.IID..Voya International Hi..D$4.49..8.02%

42.LMRKP..Landmark Infrastr..$24.95..8.02%

42.ILPT..Industrial Logistics ..$21.84..6.04%

42.BDN..Brandywine Realty Tr..$11.19….6.8%

42.CNXM..CNX Midstream Part..$10.26..13.62%

42.RIV..Rivernorth Opportunities..$15.06.14%

41.ACRE..Ares Commearcial Res..$9.81..13%

41.MRLN..Marlin Business Services...$6.87..8.15%

41.NS..NuStar Engergy LP..$13.48….11.87

41.NMFC..New Mountain Finance..$10.11..12%

41.TS..Tenaris SA..$11.43..0%

41.BTZ..Blackrock Credit Alloc..$13.94..7.2%

41.RLJ..RLJ Lodging Trust..$10.05….0.40%

41.SPKE..Spark Energy Inc...$14.54….8.08%

41.RVI..Retail Value Inc..$12.77..16.05%

40.TEAF..Tortoise Essential A.$11.19..8.04%

40.HNW..Pioneer Diversified..$13.65..9.01%

40.AROC..Archrock Inc...$6.51….8.91%

40.CIM..Chimera Investment..$8.96..13.39%

40.MNDO..MIND C.T.I. Ltd..$2.32..10.34%

40.CMO..Capstead Mortgage..$6.29..9.55%

40.THW..Tekla World Healthcare..$14.39..9.73%

40.PAGP..Plains GP Holdings..$7.31..9.85%

30

39.SHLX..Shell Midstream P..$10.61..17.34%

39.GOF..Guggenheim Strategic..$18.02..12%

39.HQL..Tekla Life Sciences I..$16.93..9.69

39.FRA..Blackrock Floating Ra..$11.74..8.05%

39.TRTX..TPG RE Finance Trust..$8.82..9.07%

39.BRT..BRT Apartments..$13.93..6.32%

39.VGR..Vector Group Ltd..$10.24..7.81%

39.CGBD..TCG BDC..$8.76..14.61%

39.NCMI..National CineMedia..$3.13..8.95%

39.GLP..Global Partners..$12.75..14%

39.AKR..Acadia Realty Trust..$11.30..0%

39.HIHO..Highway Holdings..$2.67..6.74%

39.TSE..Trinseo SA…$27.09….5.91%

39.OCSI..Oaktree Strategic In.$6.61..7.58%

39.TFSL..TFS Financial Corp$15.84….7.07%

39.ARDC..Ares Dynamic Credit..$12.58..9.30%

38.ENIC..Enel Chile SA…$3.69…7.15%

38.SUN..Sunoco LP..$26.94…12.49%

38.PHT..Pioneer High Income.$8.05..10.06%

38.AKO.A..Embotelladora An$11.68..7.24%

38.NNA..Navios Maritime Acq..$5.22..23%

38.DPG..Duff & Phelps Global..$11.19..12.51%

38.FSP..Franklin Street Prop..$4.43..8.13%

38.ARI..Apollo Commercial Rea..$9.01..15.55%

38.DMLP..Dorchester Minerals ..$10.63.14.72%

38.PBF..PBF Logistics LP..$9.94..12%

38.FTF..Franklin Limited Dur..$12.06..10.92%

38.SVC..Service Properties Trust..$8.90..0.49%

38.TKC..Turkecell Iletisim Hizm..$4.85..6.94%

38.SCD..Lmp Capital Incom..$10.98…..11%

38.AKO.B..Embotelladora Andin..$13.8..7.39%

37.CHMI..Cherry Hill Mortgage In..$9.77..11%

37.SXC..Suncoke Energy Inc..$3.64…..6.59%

37.UTF..Cohen & Steers Infast.$23.72…..7.8%

37.MRCC..Monroe Capital Corp...$6.96...14%

37.ARR..Armour Residential R…$9.86….12%

37.TCPC..BlackRock TCP Cap..$9.90..12%

37.DOW..Dow ..Inc..$48.57….5.76%

37.HESM..Hesse Midstream ..$17.66..9.88%

36.UTG..Reaves Utility Fur..$31.45…..6.87%

36.NGL..NGL Energy Partners..$4.16..19%

36.PFLT..Pennant Park Floating $8..14.74%

36.PSEC..Prospect Capital Corp..$5.11..14%

36.IGD..Voya Global Equity Div.$5.04..9.52%

36.DSWL..Deswell Industries .$2.50….7.20%

36.EDF..Stone Harbor Emer..$7.09..13.54%

36.BPYUP..Brookfield Property..$18.95..8.4%

36.USAC..USA Compression.$11.78..17.83%

36.DBI..Designer Brands..$7.43..0%

36.NRGX..PIMCO Energy..$7.37..9.23%

36.BPOPM..Popular Capital..$25.46..6%

35.JRI..Nuveen Real Asset..$12.34..9.41%

35.PFD..Flaherty & Crumri..$16.17..6.38%

35.CSQ..Calamos Strategic..$14.40..7.71

35.NRP..Natural Resources.$10.55..17.06%

35..BKCC..BlackRock Capital..$2.71..14.76%

35.IEP..Icahn Enterprises LP..$49.68..16.10%

35.HCFT..Hunt companies Fin..$2.47..12%

35.GLOP..Gaslog Partners..$3.97…..12%

35.BPYPN..Brookfield Property..$19.97..7.20

35.MVO..MV Oil Trust..$2.95..30%

35.GEL..Genesis Energy.$5.51.,10.93%

35.APTS..Preferred Apartme.$6.61..10.61%

35.ETH..Ethan Allen Inte..$14.52..5.79%

35.BSBR..Banco Santander..$7.00..20.24%

35.KFFB..Kentucky First Fed..$6.12..6.54%

35.BPYPP..Brookfield Prope..$21.85..7.44%

35.BPYPO..Brookfield Prope..$21.43..7.4%

35.TEO..Telecom Agrentina..$7.11..4.58%

35.IRCP..IRSA Propiedades C..$8.00..3.95%

34.ETO..Eaton Vance Tax-ad..$22.30..7.67%

34.KRP..Kimbell Royalty Pa..$8.31..17.91%

34.CINR..Ciner Resources..$10.01..13.59%

34.BBVA..Banco Bilbao Vizcay..$2.97..16%

34.CRT..Cross Timbers Roya..$6.11..14.71%

34.SIM..Grupo Simec SAB de C..$6.13..9.9%

34.VEON..VEON Ltd..$1.53..19%

34.CAPL..CrossAmerica Partne..$15.73..13%

34.CDMOP..Avid Bioservices I..$**27**.88..10%

34.FEI..First Trust MLP and E..$5.34..11%

34.EVT..Eaton Vance Tax Adv..$20.42..8.5%

34.BSMX..Banco Santander Mexic..$3.28..0%

33.ITBI..Fifth Third Banco..$27.38..6.05%

33.POPN..Popular Capital T..$26.36..6.35%

33.CHI..Calamos Convertibl..$11.29..8.07%

33.PNNT..Pennant Park Inv..$3.27..14.70%

33.ETY..Eaton Vance Tax-mgd..$11.49..8.8%

33.HYT..Blackrock Corporat..$11.11..8.42%

33.OFS..OFS Capital Corp..$4.79..14%

33.FAX..Aberdeen Asia-pacif..$4.19..7.88%

33.BCSF..Bain Capital Specia..$10.48..13%

33.USA..Liberty All Star Equi..$6.21..10%

33.CII..Blackrock Enhance..$15.48..6.78%

33.VC..Entravision Communic..$1.51..6.62%

33.RNP..Cohen & Steers REI..$19.74..7.54%

33.FFC..Flaherty & Crumrin..$21.86..7.08%

32.OXSQ..Oxford Square Capit..$2.62..16%

32.PTY..PIMCO Corporate &..$16.18..9.64%

32.CHW..Calamos Global Dyn..$8.45..9.94%

32.HPF..John Hancock Prefe..$18.34..8.04%

32.SELF..Global Self Storag..$4.01..6.45%

32.FLC..Flaherty & Crumrin..$22.16..7.15%

32.ICMB..Investcorp Credi..$3.46..17.34%

32.PTMN..Portman Ridge Finan..$1.17..20%

32.CCA..Crescent Capital BDC..$12.24..13%

32.TIGO..Millicom Internation..$29.73..0%

32.LGI..Lazard Global Tota..$16.00..7.98%

32.SFL..SFL Corp Ltd..$8.91..11.23%

32.GBAB..Guggenheim Taxabl..$23.80..6.34%

32.STK..Columbia Seligman..$23.22..4.15%

31.GUT..Babelli Utility Tru..$12.29..7.8%

31.BLW..Blackrock Ltd Dura..$15.20..7.74%

31.NLY..Annaly Capital Manage..$7.47..12%

31.NRT..North European Oi..$3.29..20.76%

31.RTLR..Rattler Midstrea..$8.50..13.68%

31.BPMP..BP Midstream Partne..$11.74..12%

31.NYMTO..New York Mortga..$21.18..9.30%

31.ROI..Cohen & Steers Qual..$11.63..8.3%

30.ORC..Orchid Island Cap..$5.10..15.28%

30.ASG..Liberty All Star Gr..$7.13..7.29%

30.NGHCN..National Genera..$26.20..7.16%

30.CEE..Central & Eastern E..$20.49..7.14%

30.SZC..Cushing Renaissanc..$31.20..8.20%

30.AFIN..American Finance Tru..$6.97..12%

30.BDJ..BlackRock Enhanced..$7.62..7.87%

30.HBANO..Huntington Bancsh..$25.60..6.1%

30.IGT..International Game Te..$11.38..0%

30.CHSCO..CHS Inc..$27.95..7.04%

30.LMRKO..Landmark Infrast..$24.66..8.01%

30.OXLCO..Oxford Lane Capit..$24.65..7.6%

30.PIM..Putnam Master Interm..$4.24..8.5%

30.CHSCL..CHS Inc..$27.97..6.7%

30.SRLP..Sprague Resourc..$15.08..17.71%

30.SLMBP..SLM Corp..$33.05..9.20%

30.HTD..John Hancock Tax-a..$19.86..8.34%

30.AOD..Aberdeen Total Dyna..$8.33..8.28%

30.TDF..Templeton Dragon F..$24.97..1.83%

30.ASRVP..Ameriserv Financ..$28.82..7.33%

20

29.NFJ..Allianzgi NFJ Divi..$12.18..7.39%

29.NGHCO..National General..$25.47..7.36%

29.RMT..Royce Micro-Cap Tru..$7.93..9.96%

29.HPS..John Hancock Prefer..$16.54..7.9%

29.MARPS..Marine Petroleu..$2.03..14.95%

29.CPAC..Cementos Pacasmayo..$7.90..6.8%

29.HPI..John Hancock Pref..$19.77..7.50%

29.FFA..First Trust Enhanc..$15.26..7.47%

29.BANFP..BFC Capital Trus..$28.30..6.36%

29.GECC..Great Elm Capital..$5.25..1.90%

29.LANDP..Gladstone Land C..$26.34..6.05%

29.OXLC..Oxford Lane Capital..$4.24..19%

29.BPYU..Brookfield Property..$11.95..11%

29.FPL..First Trust New Oppor..$4.05..11%

29.MTBCP..MTBC Inc..$25.66..11%

29.AVK..Advent Claymore Co..$14.43..9.73%

29.AFINP..American Finance..$23.43..8.00%

29.HIO..Western Asset Hig I..$5.03..7.75%

29.PSF..Cohen & Steers Enh..$26.83..7.02%

29.GRF..Eagle Capital Growt..$7.05..1.05%

29.DMO..Western Asset Mor..$12.96..10.24%

29.BUI..BlackRock Utility..$22.01..6.60%

29.FOF..Cohen & Steers Clo..$11.86..8.80%

28.TCBIP..Texas Captial Ba..$25.35..6.41%

28.EHI..Western Asset Globa..$9.89..8.13%

28.MMT..MFS Multimarket Inc..$6.09..8.13%

28.BGY..Blackrock Enhanced..$5.36..7.57%

28.CDOR..Condor Hospitality T..$4.40..0%

28.CGO..Calamos Global Tot..$12.73..9.43%

28.AIO..Allianz Artificial..$21.39..6.08%

28.SPXX..Nuveen S&P 500 Dy..$13.88..7.06%

28.GMLPP..Golar LNG Partners..$19.24..11%

28.GCV..Gabelli Convertib ..$5.63..8.53%

28.GDO..Western Asset Glob..$17.24..7.03%

28.HIX..Western Asset High..$6.61..8.90%

28.GOODM..Gladstone Commer..$25.00..7.00%

28.JHI..John Hancock Inves..$16.58..7.99%

28.PDT..John Hancock Premi..$13.21..8.86%

27.JPS..Nuveen Preferred &..$8.99..6.74%

27.PFO..Flaherty & Crumrin..$12.41..6.72%

27.ISD..PGIM High Yield Fu..$14.06..9.19%

27.FCRD..First Eagle Alte..$3.34..11.98%

27.CHSCP..CHS Inc..$28.93..6.91%

27.JCE..Nuveen Core Equity..$13.11..6.86%

27.AGD..Aberdeen Global Dyn..$9.74..8.01%

27.AGD..Aberdeen Global Dyn..$9.74..8.01%

27.BSL..Blackstone/ GSO Se..$13.54..8.24%

27.MCR..MFS Charter Income..$8.62..8.14%

27.TEF..Telefonica SA..$4.02..0%

27.CIG.C..Energy Company of Mi..$1.92..0%

27.DDT..Dillard's Capital T..$21.44..8.7%

27.BTO..John Hancock Financ..$23.27..9.5%

27.CYCCP..Cyclacel Pharmace..$5.50..10.91

27.DNI..Dividend and Inco..$11.40..10.09%

26.JRS..Nuveen Real Estate..$8.02..9.48%

26.CHSCM..CHS Inc..$25.70..6.57%

26.CHSCN..CHS Inc..$26.03..6.82%

26.DBL..Doubleline Opportu..$19.11..6.91%

26.OE.. Blackrock Enhanced..$9.67..7.82%

26.HTC..Natural Health Trends..$5.78..14%

26.ERH..Wells Fargo Utilit..$12.18..7.13%

26.PHD..Pioneer Floating R..$10.35..7.25%

26.MXF..Mexico Fund Inc..$10.29..9.04%

26.EFR..Eaton Vance Senior..$11.81..7.53%

26.BxMX..Nuveen S&P 500 Bu..$11.52..7.47%

26.RESI..Front Yard Residentia..$9.88..0%

26.ANH..Anworth Mortgage Asse..$1.76..11%

26.IGR..CBRE Clarion Global..$6.18..9.69%

26.PPT..Putnam Premier Inco..$4.58..9.18%

26.FIF..First Trust Energy..$9.68..7.75%

26.VTA..Invesco Dynamic Cred..$9.10..9.9%

26.TSI..Tcw Strategic Income..$5.76..6.2%

26.MIE..Cohen & Steers MLP..$1.92..9.38%

26.ETW..Eaton Vance Tax-mang..$9.02..9.6%

26.EXG..Eaton Vance Tax-Mgd..$7.85..9.42%

25.FSD..First Trust High I..$14.09..9.37%

25.DHF..BNY Mellon High Yiel..$2.75..9.3%

25.DVD..Dover Motorsports I..$1.41..7.09%

25.JSD..Nuveen Short Durat..$12.18..6.95%

25.AWF..Alliancebernstein G..$10.74..7.3%

25.HIE..Miller/Howard High..$6.33..7.58%

25.AFT..Apollo Senior Floa..$12.84..6.17%

25.VGI..Virtus Global Mul..$11.64..10.31%

25.BGR..BlackRock Engergy &..$6.87..8.21%

25.KMF..Kayne Anderson Mids..$4.42..8.14%

25.BGT..Blackrock floating..$11.51..7.97%

25.EFT..Eaton Vance Float..$12.17..7.07%

25.EVF..Eaton Vance Senior..$5.94..7.07%

25.BGX..Blackstone / GSO L..$12.55..9.56%

25.BGH..Barings Global Sho..$13.31..9.52%

25.HEQ..John Hancock Hedged..$11.33..10%

25.GGN..GAMCO Global Gold N..$3.65..9.89%

25.WTFCM..Wintrust Financi..$25.66..6.39%

24.MIN..MFS Intermediate In..$3.84..8.88%

24.SPE..Special Opportunit..$12.82..8.81%

24.AIF..Apollo Tactical In..$12.76..6.39%

24.TLI..Western Asset Corpo..$9.20..8.61%

24.AWP..Aberdeen Global Pre..$4.87..9.85%

24.FSKR..FS KKR Capital Cor..$49.19..15%

24.JPC..Nuveen Preferred & I..$8.72..7.3%

24.JRO..Nuveen Floating Rat..$8.26..6.54%

24.EVG..Eaton Vance Short..$11.60..7.76%

24.JFR..Nuveen Floating Inc..$8.35..6.61%

24.JTA..Nuveen Tax Advantag..$8.59..8.94%

24.EXD..Eaton Vance Tax-Man..$9.54..8.91%

24.ERC..Wells Fargo Multi..$11.26..10.94%

24.MFV..MFS Special Value..$5.35..10.05%

23.NYMTN..New York Mortga..$21.12..9.47%

23.MPV..Barings Participat..$10.99..7.28%

23.MCI..Barings Corporate..$12.81..7.49%

23.TGA..TransGlobe Energy Corp..$0.55..0%

23.IDE..Voya Infrastructure..$9.49..9.7%

23.DUC..Duff & Phelps Utili..$9.22..6.51%

23.TPCO..Tribune Publishing C..$11.35..0%

23.PGP..PIMCO Global Stocksp..$8.49..9.9%

23.MNKP..Medallion Bank..$18.50..10.81%

23.PIHPP..1347 Property In..$24.95..8.02%

23.FAM..First Trust / Aberd..$10.10..9.5%

22.WL.A..Bowl America Inc..$9.50..0%

22.VVR..Invesco Senior Inco..$3.70..6.50%

22.NSL..Nuveen Senior Incom..$4.96..7.39%

22.OCCI..OFS Credit Co Inc..$10.74..20%

22.TPZ..Tortoise Power & En..$9.13..6.57%

22.AM..Antero Midstrea C..$7.22..17.04%

22.PHK..PIMCO High Income Fun..$5.43..11%

22.AIRTP..Air T Inc..$20.54..9.74%

22.AVAL..Grupo Aval Accione..$5.10..7.15%

22.GNT..Gamco Natural Resour..$5.13..7.02%

22.CMCTP..CIM Commercial T..$26.24..1.94%

22.IGA..Voya Global Advantag..$8.39..9.3%

21.GAB..Gabelli Equity Trust..$5.48..11%

21.PFL..PIMCO Floating Rate..$10.04..11%

21.CLM..Cornerstone Strateg..$11.02..20%

21.SWZ..Swiss Helvetia Fund..$8.52..5.11%

21.DCUE..Dominion Energy..$101.75..7.13%

21.MGF..MFS Government Mark..$4.65..7.49%

21.SCU..Sculptor Capital Mana..$12.81..0%

21.IAF..Aberdeen Australia E..$4.82..9.9%

21.CTR..Clearbridge Ener..$14.34..11.16%

21.GLQ..Clough Global Equity..$11.86..11%

20.MINDP..Mind Technology..$17.86..12.53%

20.GGT..Gabelli Multimedia Tr..$7.20..12%

20.ECC..Eagle Point Credit Co..$7.79..12%

20.RA..Brookfield Real Asse..$16.96..14%

20.CEN..Center Coast Brook..$8.45..31.95%

20.CRF..Cornerstone Total R..$10.81..20%

20.FMO..Fiduciary/Claymore En..$8.61..11%

20.AHC..A H Belo Corp..$1.55..10.32%

20.WTREP..Watford Holdings..$24.50..8.2%

20.NYMTM..New York Mortga..$20.60..9.56%

20.AVGOP..Broadcom Inc..$1,275.89..6.27%

20.CIF..Mfs Intermediate H..$2.31..10.08%

10

19.FCT..First Trust Senior F..$11.22..11%

19.MURR..Medalist Diversified..$8.37..0%

19.ECCB..Eagle Point Credi..$25.17..7.70%

19.GLO..Clough Global Opportu..$9.58..11%

19.KIO..KKR Income Opportuni..$13.34..11%

19.IHIT..Invesco High Income..$7.84..7.6%

19.BHFAP..Brighthouse Fina..$26.82..6.15%

19.OXLCP..Oxford Lane Capi..$22.70..6.88%

19.AUBAP..Atlantic Union B..$26.31..5.93%

19.GGM..Guggenheim Credit Al..$18.14..12%

19.SPKEP..Spark Energy Inc..$22.05..9.92%

19.HTLFP..Heartland Financ..$26.88..7.88%

19.FEN..First Trust Energy I..$10.02..12%

19.AGNCP..AGNC Investment C..$22.62..6.7%

18.OPP..RiverNorth/DoubleL..$14.23..15%

18.GOODN..Gladstone Commer..$24.11..6.87%

18.AGNCM..AGNC Investment..$23.37..7.35%

18.ESGRO..Enstar Group Ltd..$26.22..6.61%

18.PNEPP..Pinnacle Financi..$26.36..6.4%

18.RILYP..B. Riley Financia..$23.60..7.3%

18.AGNCO..AGNC Investment..$23.39..6.95%

18.AGNCN..AGNC Investment..$24.33..7.19%

18.MBINO..Merchants Bancor..$24.90..6.02%

18.JPT..Nuveen Preferred an..$22.82..6.2%

18.DCOMP..Dime Community B..$22.35..6.15%

18.GAINM..Gladstone Investm..$24.82..6.3%

18.CEPU..Central Puerto SA..$2.51..4.72%

18.PCF..High Income Securitie..$8.10..12%

18.AINL..Gladstone Investm..$24.25..6.57%

17.EDI..Stone Harbor Emg Mkts..$7.93..12%

17.HTIA..Healthcare Trust..$21.79..6.28%

17.UCBIO..United Community..$26.27..6.9%

17.OXLCM..Oxford Lane Capit..$23.67..7.1%

17.LMRKN..Landmark Infrast..$24.52..7.22%

17.JOC..Nuveen Credit Strate..$6.07..16%

17.FINS..Angel Oak Financia..$16.78..7.2%

17.TSCBP..TriState Capital..$23.56..6.76%

17.MBINP..Merchants Bancor..$26.15..6.69%

17.FMBIP..First Midwest Ba..$26.33..6.65%

17.TSCAP..TriState Capital..$23.52..7.17%

17.ESGRP..Enstar Group Ltd..$26.39..7.64%

17.OCFCP..OceanFirst Finan..$26.37..7.23%

17.CSSEP..Chicken Soup for th..$0.00..11%

17.NRO..Neuberger Berman Re..$3.90..12%

17.PGZ..Principal Real Estat..$11.63..11%

16.TECTP..Tectonic Financial..$9.00..10%

16.FEO..First Trust/Aberdeen..$13.28..11%

16.JCO..Nuveen Credit Oppor..$8.09..6.97%

16.BGIO..BlackRock 2022 Glo..$8.67..6.92%

16.EOD..Wells Fargo Global..$4.57..12.49%

16.USDP..USD Parnters LP..$3.57..12.44%

16.JEMD..Nuveen Emerging Ma..$7.64..5.26%

16.IHD..Voya Emerging Markets..$6.77..11%

16.LND..Brasilagro – Cia Bras..$4.39..0%

15.DEX..Delaware Enhanced..$8.96..10.98%

15.IHTA..Invesco High Income..$7.64..7.3%

15.HTY..John Hancock Tax-Adv..$11.04..12%

15.FGB..First Trust Specia..$2.66..12.41%

15.FCO..Aberdeen Global In..$6.82..12.32%

15.DDF..Delaware Investmen..$8.37..12.05%

15.GLV..Clough Global Dividen..$9.87..12%

15.ATV..Acorn International In..$0.15..0%

14.EGI..Eagle Growth and I..$5.03..20.28%

14.IRR..Voya Natural Resource..$2.61..12%

14.RSF..RiverNorth Marketpal..$14.73..12%

14.DCF..BNY Mellon Alcentra..$8.20..7.32%

13.BKEP..Blueknight Ener..$1.50..10.65%..

13.IAE..Voya Asia Pacific Hig..$9.63..11%

13.FBIOP..Fortress Biotec..$18.37..12.76%

12.FLNG..Flex LNG Ltd..$6.02..0%

12.MDRRP..Medalist Diversif..$12.50..16%

12.CUBA..Herzfeld Caribbean ..$3.83..16%

12.WTFCP..Wintrust Financial..$26.59..11%

11.NREE..NexPoint Real Es..$14.99..10.67%

10.HGLB..Highland Global All..$6.56..15%

9

9.XFLT..XAI Octagon FR & Alt..$6.02..12%

8.GDV..Gabelli Dividend &..$9.76..12.30%

8.BKEPP..Blueknight Energy P..$5.93..12%

CHAPTER 18

U.S. Stocks

With A Dividend Yield of 6% or Greater

Alpha Sort

Score/Stock Symbol/Company Name/.Stock price/Dividend%

A

33.FAX..**Aberdeen Asia-pacif**..$4.19..7.88%

21.IAF..**Aberdeen Australia E**..$4.82..9.9%

24.AWP..**Aberdeen Global Pr**..$4.87..9.85%

15.FCO..**Aberdeen Global In**..$6.82..12.32%

27.AGD..**Aberdeen Global Dyn**..$9.74..8.01%

30.AOD..**Aberdeen Total Dyna**..$8.33..8.28%

39.AKR..**Acadia Realty Trust**..$11.30..0%

29.AVK..**Advent Claymore Co**..$14.43..9.73%

43.AGNC..**AGNC Investment Cor**..$14.14..10%

19.AGNCP..**AGNC Investment C**..$22.62..**6.7%**

18.AGNCM..**AGNC Investment**..$23.37..7.35%

18.AGNCO..**AGNC Investment**..$23.39..6.95%

18.AGNCN..**AGNC Investment**..$24.33..7.19%

20.AHC..**A H Belo Corp**..$1.55..10.32%

22.AIRTP..**Air T Inc**..$20.54..9.74

50.ALX..**Alexander's Inc**..$266.17..6.76%

25.AWF..**Alliancebernstein G**..$10.74..7.3%

64.AB..**AllianceBernstein H**..$28.91..9.44%

28.AIO..**Allianz Artificial**..$21.39..6.08%

58.NCV..**AllianzGI Convertible**..$4.88..10%

54.NCZ..**AllianzGI Converti**..$4.35..10.34%

48.ACV..**AllianzGI Diversiv**..$26.04..7.70%

61.NIE..**AllianzGI Equity**..$24.56..6.19%

29.NFJ..**Allianzgi NFJ Divi**..$12.18..7.39%

48.MO..**Altria Group Inc**..$43.76..7.86%

46.ATAX..**America First Mult**..$4.37..5.49%

30.AFIN..**American Finance Tru**..$6.97..12%

30.ASRVP..**Ameriserv Financ**..$28.82..7.33%

29.AFINP..**American Finance**..$23.43..8.00%

17.FINS..**Angel Oak Financia**..$16.78..7.2%

31.NLY..**Annaly Capital Manage**..$7.47..12%

22.AM..**Antero Midstrea**..$7.22..17.04%

26.ANH..**Anworth Mortgage Asse**..$1.76..11%

38.ARI..**Apollo Commercial**..$9.01..15.55%

43.AINV..**Apollo Investment**..$9.18..13.51%

25.AFT..**Apollo Senior Floa**..$12.84..6.17%

24.AIF..**Apollo Tactical In**..$12.76..6.39%

40.AROC..**Archrock Inc**..$6.51..8.91%

41.ACRE..**Ares Commearcial Res**..$9.81..13%

39.ARDC..**Ares Dynamic Cred**..$12.58..9.30%

37.ARR..**Armour Residential RE**..$9.86..12%

62.APAM..**Artisan Partners**..$37.05..7.23%

19.AUBAP..**Atlantic Union B**..$26.31..5.93%

49.ABR..**Arbor Realty Tru**..$11.62..10.67%

54.ARCC..**Ares Capital Co**..$14.19..10.82%

59.T..**AT & T**..$29.42..7.07%

15.ATV..**Acorn International In**..$0.15..0%

34.CDMOP..**Avid Bioservices I**..$27.88..10%

B

50.BGS..**B&G Foods Inc**..$29.99..6.34%

31.GUT..**Babelli Utility Tru**..$12.29..7.8%

33.BCSF..**Bain Capital Speci**..$10.48..13%

34.BBVA..**Banco Bilbao Vizca**..$2.97..16%

52.BLX..**Banco Lainoamerica**..$12.44..8.04%

35.BSBR..**Banco Santander**..$7.00..20.24%

34.BSMX..**Banco Santander Mexic**..$3.28..0%

66.BNS..**Bank of Nova Scoti**..$42.39..6.50%

45.NTB..**Bank of N.T. Butter**..25.60..6.88%

47.BBDC..**Barings BDC Inc**..$8.30..7.7%

23.MCI..**Barings Corporate**..$12.81..7.49%

25.BGH..**Barings Global Sho**..$13.31..9.52%

23.MPV..**Barings Participat**..$10.99..7.28%

47.BCBP..**BCB Bancorp Inc**..$8.15..6.87

48.BHLB..**Berkshire Hill Ba**..$9.35..10.27%

29.BANFP..**BFC Capital Trus**..$28.30..6.36%

48.BGFV..**Big 5 Sporting Goo**..$5.72..6.99%

35.BKCC..**BlackRock Capita**..$2.71..14.76%

33.HYT..**Blackrock Corporat**..$11.11..8.42%

41.BTZ..**Blackrock Credit Al**..$13.94..7.2%

25.BGR..**BlackRock Energy &**..$6.87..8.21%

33.CII..**Blackrock Enhanced**..$15.48..6.78%

30.BDJ..**BlackRock Enhanced**..$7.62..7.87%

26.BOE.. **Blackrock Enhanced**..$9.67..7.82%

39.FRA..**Blackrock Floating**..$11.74..8.05%

25.BGT..**Blackrock floating**..$11.51..7.97%

52.BKT..**Blackrock Income Tr**..$6.20..6.66%

31.BLW..**Blackrock Ltd Dura**..$15.20..7.74%

53.BIT..**BlackRock Multi-Se**..$16.02..9.22%

47.BCX..**BlackRock Resources**..$6.39..7.51%

16.BGIO..**BlackRock 2022 Glo**..$8.67..6.92%

37.TCPC..**BlackRock TCP Capita**..$9.90..12%

29.BUI..**BlackRock Utility**..$22.01..6.60%

27.BSL..**Blackstone/GSO Sen**..$13.54..8.24%

25.BGX..**Blackstone/GSO Lon**..$12.55..9.56%

56.BGB..**Blackstone/GSO Stra**..$11.95..9.44

52.BSM..**Black Stone Mineral**..$6.75..8.89%

59.BXMT..**Blackstone Mortg**..$24.08..10.30%

25.BGX..**Blackstone/GSO Lon**..$12.55..9.56%

13.BKEP..**Blueknight Ener**..$1.50..10.65%..

8.BKEPP..**Blueknight Engergy P**..$5.93..12%

46.BRG..**Bluerock Residential**..$7.57..8.5%

14.DCF..**BNY Mellon Alcentra**..$8.20..7.32%

25.DHF..**BNY Mellon High Yiel**..$2.75..9.3%

22.BWL.A..**Bowl America Inc**..$9.50..0%

31.BPMP..**BP Midstream Partne**..$11.74..12%

53.BWG..**BrandywineGlobal G**..$12.45..6.75%

42.BDN..**Brandywine Realty T**..$11.19..6.8%

16.LND..**Brasilagro–Cia Bras de**..$4.39..0%

19.BHFAP..**Brighthouse Fina**..$26.82..6.15%

18.RILYP..**B. Riley Financia**..$23.60..7.3%

67.BTI..**British American T**..$34.48..9.62%

20.AVGOP..**Broadcom Inc**..$1,275.89..6.27%

43.BRMK..**Broadmark Realty C**..$9.79..7.36%

49.BPY..**Brookfield Property**..$23.23..11%

36.BPYUP..**Brookfield Proper**..$18.95..8.4%

29.BPYU..**Brookfield Property**..$11.95..11%

35.BPYPN..**Brookfield Proper**..$19.97..7.20

35.BPYPP..**Brookfield Prope**..$21.85..7.44%

35.BPYPO..**Brookfield Proper**..$21.43..7.4%

20.RA..**Brookfield Real Asse**..$16.96..14%

39.BRT..**BRT Apartments Cor**..$13.93..6.32%

C

33.CHI..**Calamos Convertibl**..$11.29..8.07%

48.CHY..**Calamos Convertibl**..$12.61..8.09%

55.CCD..**Calamos Dynamic Co**..$23.75..8.44%

28.CGO..**Calamos Global Tot**..$12.73..9.43%

32.CHW..**Calamos Global Dyna**..$8.45..9.94%

58.CNQ..**Canadian Natural R**..$25.71..6.61%

49.CLP..**Capital Product Pa**..$5.93..6.75%

44.CSWC..**Capital Southwest C**..$14.98..11%

40.CMO..**Capstead Mortgage C**..$6.29..9.55%

48.CUK..**Carnival PLC**..$12.95..0%

26.IGR..**CBRE Clarion Global**..$6.18..9.69%

29.CPAC..**Cementos Pacasmayo**..$7.90..6.8%

20.CEN..**Center Coast Brook**..$8.45..31.95%

30.CEE..**Central & Eastern E**..$20.49..7.14%

18.CEPU..**Central Puerto SA**..$2.51..4.72%

59.CTL..**CenturyLink Inc**..$10.91..9.17%

55.CQP..**Cheniere Energy Pa**..$34.60..7.46%

37.CHMI..**Cherry Hill Mortgage**..$9.77..11%

17.CSSEP..**Chicken Soup for th**..$0.00..11%

40.CIM..**Chimera Investmen**..$8.96..13.39%

63.SNP..**China Petroleum &**..$45.77..9.59%

30.CHSCL..**CHS Inc**..$27.97..6.7%

26.CHSCM..**CHS Inc**..$25.70..6.57%

26.CHSCN..**CHS Inc**..$26.03..6.82%

30.CHSCO..**CHS Inc**..$27.95..7.04%

27.CHSCP..**CHS Inc**..$28.93..6.91%

22.CMCTP..**CIM Commercial T**..$26.24..1.94%

34.CINR..**Ciner Resources**..$10.01..13.59%

56.CIT..**CIT Group Inc**..$20.43..6.83%

50.CZNC..**Citizens & Northe**..$16.98..6.36%

77.CFG..**Cititzens Financia**..$27.36..5.70%

44.CIO..**City Office Reit In**..$8.08..7.43%

46.EMO..**ClearBridge Energy Mi**..$2.90..10%

21.CTR..**Clearbridge Ener**..$14.34..11.16%

15.GLV..**Clough Global Dividen**..$9.87..12%

21.GLQ..**Clough Global Equity**..$11.86..11%

19.GLO..**Clough Global Opportu**..$9.58..11%

71.CEO..**CNOOC Ltd**..$113.93..7.35%

42.CNXM..**CNX Midstream Par**..$10.26..13.62%

55.CCEP..**Coca-Cola European P**..$44.35..0%

29.FOF..**Cohen & Steers Clo**..$11.86..8.80%

29.PSF..**Cohen & Steers Enh**..$26.83..7.02%

37.UTF..**Cohen & Steers Infa**..$23.72..7.8%

60.LDP..**Cohen & Steers Ltd**..$23.86..7.19%

26.MIE..**Cohen & Steers MLP**..$1.92..9.38%

31.ROI..**Cohen & Steers Qual**..$11.63..8.3%

33.RNP..**Cohen & Steers REI**..$19.74..7.54%

52.RFI..**Cohen & Steers Tot**..$12.77..7.52%

45.CXP..**Columbia Property**..$12.19..6.89%

32.STK..**Columbia Seligman**..$23.22..4.15%

70.CMA..**Comerica Inc**..$41.47..6.56%

54.CBSH..**Commerce Bancshar**..$60.03..1.80%

49.CODI..**Compass Diversifi**..$17.78..8.10%

28.CDOR..**Condor Hospitality T**..$4.40..0%

21.CLM..**Cornerstone Strateg**..$11.02..20%

20.CRF..**Cornerstone Total R**..$10.81..20%

46.CMRE..**Costamare Inc**..$4.99..8.02%

56.BAP..**Credicorp Ltd**..$132.41..8.43%

51.CIK..**Credit Suisse Asset**..$2.85..9.47%

47.DHY..**Credit Suisse High**..$2.09..9.47%

32.CCA..**Crescent Capital BDC**..$12.24..13%

45.CEQP..**Crestwood Equit**..$14.20..17.61%

34.CAPL..**CrossAmerica Partne**..$15.73..13%

34.CRT..**Cross Timbers Roya**..$6.11..14.71%

30.SZC..**Cushing Renaissanc**..$31.20..8.20%

46.CVI..**CVR Energy Inc**..$17.21..9.30%

27.CYCCP..**Cyclacel Pharmac**..$5.50..10.91%

D

52.DK..**Delek US Holdings I**..$14.80..8.38%

44.DCP..**DCP Midstream LP**..$13.13..11.88%

15.DEX..**Delaware Enhanced**..$8.96..10.98%

15.DDF..**Delaware Investmen**..$8.37..12.05%

43.DKL..**Delek Logistics Part**..$32.36..11%

36.DBI..**Designer Brands Inc**..$7.43..0%

36.DSWL..**Deswell Industries**..$2.50..7.20%

58.DHT..**DHT Holdings Ltd**..$6.12..31%

27.DDT..**Dillard's Capital T**..$21.44..8.7%

18.DCOMP..**Dime Community B**..$22.35..6.15%

27.DNI..**Dividend and Inco**..$11.40..10.09%

48.DNP..**DNP Select Income**..$10.11..7.72%

21.DCUE..**Dominion Energy**..$101.75..7.13%

38.DMLP..**Dorchester Miner**..$10.63..14.72%

44.DSL..**DoubleLIne Income So**..$16.14..11%

26.DBL..**Doubleline Opportu**..$19.11..6.91%

25.DVD..**Dover Motorsports I**..$1.41..7.09%

37.DOW..**Dow Inc**..$48.57..5.76%

38.DPG..**Duff & Phelps Glo**..$11.19..12.51%

23.DUC..Duff & Phelps Utili..$9.22..6.51%

64.DX..**Dynex Capital Inc**..$15.82..9.8%

E

29.GRF..**Eagle Capital Growt**..$7.05..1.05%

14.EGI..**Eagle Growth and I**..$5.03..20.28%

19.ECCB..**Eagle Point Credi**..$25.17..7.70%

20.ECC..**Eagle Point Credit Co**..$7.79..12%

50.EOS..**Eaton Vance Enhanc**..$18.72..6.33%

26.EFR..**Eaton Vance Senior**..$11.81..7.53%

25.EFT..**Eaton Vance Floatin**..$12.17..7.07%

25.EVF..**Eaton Vance Senior**..$5.94..7.07%

24.EVG..**Eaton Vance Short**..$11.60..7.76%

34.EVT..**Eaton Vance Tax Adv**..$20.42..8.5%

34.ETO..**Eaton Vance Tax-ad**..$22.30..7.67%

24.EXD..**Eaton Vance Tax-Man**..$9.54..8.91%

47.ETV..**Eaton Vance Tax-Ma**..$15.07..9.04%

47.EOI..**Eaton Vance Enhanc**..$14.99..7.19%

47.EVV..**Eaton Vance Ltd Dura**..$11.70..10%

50.ETJ..**Eaton Vance Risk-M**..$10.26..8.89%

33.ETY..**Eaton Vance Tax-mgd**..$11.49..8.8%

44.ETB..**Eaton Vance Tax-Ma**..$14.20..9.13%

26.ETW..**Eaton Vance Tax-mang**..$9.02..9.6%

26.EXG..**Eaton Vance Tax-Mgd**..$7.85..9.42%

57.EC..**Ecopetrol SA**..$11.56..7.68%

53.EFC..**Ellington Financial**..$12.47..8.6%

49.EARN..**Ellington Residenti**..$11.62..10%

38.AKO.A..**Embotelladora An**..$11.68..7.24%

38.AKO.B..**Embotelladora An**..$13.80..7.39%

46.ESRT..**Empire State Realt**..$6.67..6.30%

53.ENBL..**Enable Midstream**..$5.90..11.21%

56.ENB..**Enbridge Inc**..$31.58..7.53%

46..ENIA..**Enel Americas SA**..$7.26..7.29%

38..ENIC..**Enel Chile SA**..$3.69..7.15%

27..CIG.C..**Energy Company of M**..$1.92..0%

53.ET..**Energy Transfer LP**..$6.64..19%

45.E..**Eni SpA**..$18.98..9.97%

45..ENLC..**EnLink Midstream**..$3.03..12.38%

18.ESGRO..**Enstar Group Ltd**..$26.22..6.61%

17.ESGRP..**Enstar Group Ltd**..$26.39..7.64%

63.EPD..**Enterprise Produc**..$17.60..10.12%

33.EVC..**Entravision Communi**..$1.51..6.62%

49.EVA..**Enviva Partners LP**..$38.98..7.85%

35.ETH..**Ethan Allen Interi**..$14.52..5.79%

52.EURN..**Euronav NV**..$9.64..16%

63.XOM..**Exxon Mobil Corp**..$39.18..8.88%

F

20.FMO..**Fiduciary/Claymore En**..$8.61..11%

51.FDUS..**Fidus Investment**..$10.47..11.46%

33.FITBI..**Fifth Third Banc**..$27.38..6.05%

44.FCBP..**First Choice Banc**..$14.86..6.73%

27.FCRD..**First Eagle Alter**..$3.34..11.98%

58.FSLF..**First Eagle Senior**..$12.29..7.8%

57.FFBC..**First Financial B**..$14.09..6.53%

62.FHN..**First Horizon National**..$9.95..6%

17.FMBIP..**First Midwest Ba**..$26.33..6.65%

23.FAM..**First Trust / Aberd**..$10.10..9.5%

26.FIF..**First Trust Energy**..$9.68..7.75%

19.FEN..**First Trust Energy I**..$10.02..12%

29.FFA..**First Trust Enhanc**..$15.26..7.47%

25.FSD..**First Trust High I**..$14.09..9.37%

53.FPF..**First Trust Inter D**..$21.93..7.2%

34.FEI..**First Trust MLP and E**..$5.34..11%

29.FPL..**First Trust New Oppor**..$4.05..11%

19.FCT..**First Trust Senior F**..$11.22..11%

33.FFC..**Flaherty & Crumrine**..$21.86..7.08%

56.DFP..**Flaherty & Crumrine**..$26.58..7.5%

35.PFD..**Flaherty & Crumrin**..$16.17..6.38%

27.PFO..**Flaherty & Crumrin**..$12.41..6.72%

32.FLC..**Flaherty & Crumrin**..$22.16..7.15%

56.FFIC..**Flushing Financia**..$12.61..6.66%

61.FNB..**F N B Corp**..$7.68..6.25%

57.FTAI..**Fortress Transpor**..$16.01..8.24%

38.FTF..**Franklin Limited**..$12.06..10.92%

38.FSP..**Franklin Street Pro**..$4.43..8.13%

49.FRO..**Frontline Ltd**..$8.37..32%

26.RESI..**Front Yard Residential Co**..$9.88%

48.FSK..**FS KKR Capital Corp**..$15.80..15%

24.FSKR..**FS KKR Capital Corp**..$49.19..15%

16.FEO..**First Trust/Aberdeen**..$13.28..11%

15.FGB..**First Trust Specia**..$2.66..12.41%

13.FBIOP..**Fortress Biotec**..$18.37..12.76%

12.FLNG..**Flex LNG Ltd**..$6.02..0%

G

28.GCV..**Gabelli Convertible**..$5.63..8.53%

8.GDV..**Gabelli Dividend & I**..$9.76..12.30

21.GAB..**Gabelli Equity Trust**..$5.48..11%

60.GLU..**Gabelli Global Ut**..$15.95..7.52%.

20.GGT..**Gabelli Multimedia Tr**..$7.20..12%

25.GGN..**GAMCO Global Gold** N..$3.65..9.89%

22.GNT..**Gamco Natural Resou**..$5.13..7.02%

59.GLPI..**Gaming and Leisur**..$37.65..1.27%

35.GLOP..**Gaslog Partners LP**..$3.97..12%

44.GLIBP..**GCI Liberty Inc**..$28.49..6.14%

55.GFNCP..**General Finance**..$100.00..9.20%

35.GEL..**Genesis Energy LP**..$5.51..10.93%

43.GLAD..**Gladstone Capital Co**..$7.64..10%

45.GOOD..**Gladstone Commerc**..$18.98..7.95%

18.GOODN..**Gladstone Commer**..$24.11..6.87%

28.GOODM..**Gladstone Commer**..$25.00..7.00%

18.GAINM..**Gladstone Investm**..$24.82..6.3%

51.GAIN..**Gladstone Investmen**..$9.39..8.95%

29.LANDP..**Gladstone Land C**..$26.34..6.05%

18.GAINL..**Gladstone Invest**..$24.25..6.57%

48.GMRE..**Global Medical RE**..$14.25..5.97%

52.GNL..**Global Net Lease I**..$17.52..9.13%

39.GLP..**Global Partners LP**..$12.75..14%

32.SELF..**Global Self Storag**..$4.01..6.45%

28.GMLPP..**Golar LNG Partners**..$19.24..11%

44.GER..**Goldman Sachs MLP**..$7.12..8.71%

43.GSBD..**Goldman Sachs BDC I**..$15.82..11%

43.GMZ..**Goldman Sachs MLP I**..$9.33..8.79%

49.GBDC..**Golub Capital BDC**..$13.13..8.83%

56.AJX..**Great Ajax Corp**..$9.07..7.50%

29.GECC..**Great Elm Capital**..$5.25..1.90%

22.AVAL..**Grupo Aval Accione**..$5.10..7.15%

34.SIM..**Grupo Simec SAB de C**..$6.13..9.9%

19.GGM..**Guggenheim Credit Al**..$18.14..12%

46.GPM..**Guggenheim Enhanced**..$5.77..8.32%

39.GOF..**Guggenheim Strategic**..$18.02..12%

32.GBAB..**Guggenheim Taxabl**..$23.80..6.34%

H

49.HRB..**H&R Block**..$15.15..6.87%

49.HAFC..**Hanmi Financial Co**..$9.68..3.31%

17.HTIA..**Healthcare Trust**..$21.79..6.28%

19.HTLFP..**Heartland Financ**..$26.88..7.88%

46.HNNA..**Hennessy Advisors**..$9.05..6.08%

48.HTGC..**Hercules Capital**..$11.20..11.43%

12.CUBA..**Herzfeld Caribbean**..$3.83..16%

50.HTBK..**Heritage Commerce**..$9.00..7.30%

50.HTBK..**Heritage Commerce**..$9.00..7.30%

37.HESM..**Hesse Midstream L**..$17.66..9.88%

18.PCF..**High Income Securitie**..$8.10..12%

49.HFRO..**Highland Income F**..$8.90..10.38%

39.HIHO..**Highway Holdings**..$2.67..6.74%

52.HMLP..**Hoegh LNG Partn**..$10.50..16.76%

48.HEP..**Holly Energy Patn**..$12.59..11.18%

57.HOPE..**Hope Bancorp Inc**..$8.72..6.4%

45.HRZN..**Horizon Technology**..$12.09..9.9%

35.HCFT..**Hunt companies Finan**..$2.47..12%

48.HEP..**Holly Energy Patn**..$12.59..11.18%

30.HBANO..**Huntington Bancsh**..$25.60..6.1%

62.HBAN..**Huntington Bancsha**..$9.94..6.04%

10.HGLB..**Highland Global All**..$6.56..15%

I

35.IEP..**Icahn Enterpris**..$49.68..16.10%

42.ILPT..**Industrial Logis**..$21.84..6.04%

48.IFS..**Intercorp Financia**..$24.37..7.18%

30.IGT..**International Game Te**..$11.38..0%

26.VTA..**Invesco Dynamic Cred**..$9.10..9.9%

15.IHTA..**Invesco High Income**..$7.64..7.3%

19.IHIT..**Invesco High Income**..$7.84..7.6%

22.VVR..**Invesco Senior Inco**..$3.70..6.50%

32.ICMB..**Investcorp Credi**..$3.46..17.34%

53.IRM..**Iron Mountain Inc**..$30.50..8.11%

35.IRCP..**IRSA Propiedades C**..$8.00..3.95%

49.ITCB..**Itau Corpbanca**..$4.43..9.74%

47.IVH..**Ivy High Income Op**..$11.99..9.07%

J

45.JHG..**Janus Henderson Gr**..$20.41..7.06%

27.BTO..**John Hancock Financ**..$23.27..9.5%

25.HEQ..**John Hancock Hedged**..$11.33..10%

28.JHI..**John Hancock Inves**..$16.58..7.99%

32.HPF..**John Hancock Prefe**..$18.34..8.04%

29.HPI..**John Hancock Prefe**..$19.77..7.50%

29.HPS..**John Hancock Prefer**..$16.54..7.9%

28.PDT..**John Hancock Premi**..$13.21..8.86%

30.HTD..**John Hancock Tax-a**..$19.86..8.34%

15.HTY..**John Hancock Tax-Adv**..$11.04..12%

K

25.KMF..**Kayne Anderson Mids**..$4.42..8.14%

42.KYN..**Kayne Anderson MLP/M**..$4.93..12%

44.KW..**Kennedy-Wilson Hold**..$14.69..5.99%

35.KFFB..**Kentucky First Fed**..$6.12..6.54%

34.KRP..**Kimbell Royalty Pa**..$8.31..17.91%

19.KIO..**KKR Income Opportuni**..$13.34..11%

54.KMI..**Kinder Morgan Inc**..$13.51..7.77%

44.KREF..**KKR Real Estate F**..$18.11..9.50%

48.KNOP..**KNOT Offshore Part**..$12.81..16%

L

58.LADR..**Ladder Capital Co**..$7.77..10.30%

48.LMRK..**Landmark Infrastr**..$10.07..7.94%

17.LMRKN..**Landmark Infrast**..$24.52..7.22%

30.LMRKO..**Landmark Infrast**..$24.66..8.01%

42.LMRKP..**Landmark Infras**..$24.95..8.02%

32.LGI..**Lazard Global Tota**..$16.00..7.98%

33.USA..**Liberty All Star Equi**..$6.21..10%

30.ASG..**Liberty All Star Gr**..$7.13..7.29%

38.SCD..**Lmp Capital Income F**..$10.98..11%

52.LTC..**LTC Properties Inc**..$37.24..6.12%

62.LYB..**LyondellBasell Ind**..$72.06..5.83%

M

56.MAC..**Macerich Co**..$8.27..7.26%

43.CLI..**Mack-Cali Realty C**..$13.23..6.05%

44.MFD..**Macquarie/First Tr**..$7.93..10.04%

50.MCN..**Madison Covrd Call &**..$6.06..12%

52.MMP..**Magellan Midstrea**..$38.61..10.67%

46.MAIN..**Main Street Capit**..$29.76..8.27%

43.LOAN..**Manhattan Bridge C**..$4.20..9.52%

61.MPC..**Marathon Petroleum**..$33.63..9.90%

29.MARPS..**Marine Petroleu**..$2.03..14.95%

41.MRLN..**Marlin Business Se**..$6.87..8.15%

23.MBNKP..**Medallion Bank**..$18.50..10.81%

12.MDRRP..**Medalist Diversi**..$12.50..16%

19.MURR..**Medalist Diversified**..$8.37..0%

18.MBINO..**Merchants Banco**..$24.90..6.02%

17.MBINP..**Merchants Banco**..$26.15..6.69%

26.MXF..**Mexico Fund Inc**..$10.29..9.04%

45.MFA..**MFA Financial Inc**..$2.70..7.42%

27.MCR..**MFS Charter Income**..$8.62..8.14%

21.MGF..**MFS Government Mark**..$4.65..7.49%

20.CIF..**Mfs Intermediate H**..$2.31..10.08%

24.MIN..**MFS Intermediate In**..$3.84..8.88%

28.MMT..**MFS Multimarket Inc**..$6.09..8.13%

24.MFV..**MFS Special Value**..$5.35..10.05%

58.MGP..**MGM Growth Properti**..$28.55..6.8%

44.MSBI..**Midland States Ban**..$14.92..7.1%

25.HIE..**Miller/Howard High**..$6.33..7.58%

32.TIGO..**Millicom Internation**..$29.73..0%

20.MINDP..**Mind Technology**..$17.86..12.53%

44.MBT..**Mobile TeleSystems**..$9.55..15.84%

37.MRCC..**Monroe Capital**..$6.96..14%

44.EDD..**Morgan Stanley Emer**..$5.80..8.45%

52.MPLX..**MPLX LP**..$18.22..15.09%

9..MTBCP..**MTBC Inc**..$25.66..11%

47.MVC..**MVC Capital Inc**..$8.04..8.46%

35.MVO..**MV Oil Trust**..$2.95..30%

N

39.NCMI..**National CineMedi**..$3.13..8.95%

30.NGHCN..**National General**..$26.20..7.16%

29.NGHCO..**National General**..$25.47..7.36%

48.NGHCP..**National General**..$25.43..7.37%

57.NHI..**National Health In**..$63.88..6.90%

26.NHTC..**Natural Health Trend**..$5.78..14%

35.NRP..**Natural Resource**..$10.55..17.06%

60.NAVI..**Navient Corp**..$9.21..6.95%

38.NNA..**Navios Maritime Acqu**..$5.22..23%

17.NRO..**Neuberger Berman Re**..$3.90..12%

57.NHS..**Neuberger Berman H**..$11.30..9.61%

47.HYB..**New America High In**..$8.29..7.24%

41.NMFC..**New Mountain Financ**..$10.11..12%

47.NEWT..**Newtek Business Ser**..$19.00..12%

62.NYCB..**New York Community**..$9.24..7.36%

45.NYMT..**New York Mortgage**..$2.59..7.72%

20.NYMTM..**New York Mortga**..$20.60..9.56%

23.NYMTN..**New York Mortga**..$21.12..9.47%

31.NYMTO..**New York Mortga**..$21.18..9.30%

11.NREE..**NexPoint Real Es**..$14.99..10.67%

50.NHF..**Nexpoint Strategic**..$9.63..12.46%

36.NGL..**NGL Energy Partners**..$4.16..19%

47.NBLX..**Noble Midstream Pa**..$8.67..8.65%

47.NAT..**Nordic American Tan**..$4.34..9.92%

31.NRT..**North European Oi**..$3.29..20.76%

53.NWBI..**Northwest Bancsha**..$10.29..7.39%

41.NS..**NuStar Engergy LP**..$13.48..11.87%

27.JCE..**Nuveen Core Equity**..$13.11..6.86%

16.JCO..**Nuveen Credit Oppor**..$8.09..6.97%

17.JOC..**Nuveen Credit Strate**..$6.07..16%

59.DIAX..**Nuveen Dow 30sm D**..$13.99..7.81%

16.JEMD..**Nuveen Emerging Ma**..$7.64..5.26%

24.JFR..**Nuveen Floating Rat**..$8.35..6.61%

24.JRO..**Nuveen Floating Rat**..$8.26..6.54%

59.JGH..**Nuveen Global High**..$14.19..7.23%

59.QQQX..**Nuveen NASDAQ 100**..$24.82..6.29%

24.JPC..**Nuveen Preferred & I**..$8.72..7.3%

61.JPI..**Nuveen Preferred**..$22.81..6.87%

27.JPS..**Nuveen Preferred &**..$8.99..6.74%

18.JPT..**Nuveen Preferred an**..$22.82..6.2%

35.JRI..**Nuveen Real Asset**..$12.34..9.41%

26.JRS..**Nuveen Real Estate**..$8.02..9.48%

28.SPXX..**Nuveen S&P 500 Dy**..$13.88..7.06%

26.BxMX..**Nuveen S&P 500 Bu**..$11.52..7.47%

22.NSL..**Nuveen Senior Incom**..$4.96..7.39%

25.JSD..**Nuveen Short Durat**..$12.18..6.95%

24.JTA..**Nuveen Tax Advantag**..$8.59..8.94%

54.NVEC..**NVE Corp**..$51.81..7.82%

O

39.OCSI..**Oaktree Strategic**..$6.61..7.58%

47.OCSL..**Oaktree Specialty L**..$4.99..8.4%

17.OCFCP..**OceanFirst Finan**..$26.37..7.23%

62.OPI..**Office Properties**..$23.84..9.23%

33.OFS..**OFS Capital Corp**..$4.79..14%

22.OCCI..**OFS Credit Co Inc**..$10.74..20%

49.OLN..**Olin Corp**..$12.09..6.62%

62.OHI..**Omega Healthcare In**..$31.91..8.4%

23.PIHPP..**1347 Property In**..$24.95..8.02%

49.OLP..**One Liberty Proper**..$19.14..9.40%

70.OMF..**OneMain Holdings I**..$30.00..4.40%

49.OKE..**ONEOK Inc**..$28.07..13%

30.ORC..**Orchid Island Cap**..$5.10..15.28%

58.ORCC..**Owl Rock Capital Co**..$13.31..10%

29.OXLC..**Oxford Lane Capital**..$4.24..19%

17.OXLCM..**Oxford Lane Capit**..$23.67..7.1%

30.OXLCO..**Oxford Lane Capit**..$24.65..7.6%

19.OXLCP..**Oxford Lane Capi**..$22.70..6.88%

32.OXSQ..**Oxford Square Capit**..$2.62..16%

P

38.PBFX..**PBF Logistics LP**..$9.94..12%

55.PCM..**Pcm Fund Inc**..$9.94..9.66%

70.PBA..**Pembina Pipeline C**..$24.53..7.83%

51.PWOD..**Penns Woods Banco**..$21.42..5.98%

44.PEI..**Pennsylvania Real**..$1.11..7.21%

36.PFLT..**Pennant Park Floatin**..$8..14.74%

33.PNNT..**Pennant Park Inv**..$3.27..14.70%

58.PMT..**PennyMac Mortgage I**..$17.15..9.33%

61.PEBO..**Peoples Bancorp In**..$21.71..6.2%

62.PBCT..**People's United F**..$11.03..6.53%

57.GHY..**PGIM Global High Yi**..$13.45..9.3%

27.ISD..**PGIM High Yield Fu**..$14.06..9.19%

52.PSXP..**Phillips 66 Partner**..$26.52..13%

59.PCN..**PIMCO Corporate & I**..$15.79..8.5%

32.PTY..**PIMCO Corporate &**..$16.18..9.64%

59.PDI..**PIMCO Dynamic Income**..$26.64..11%

57.PCI..**PIMCO Dynamic Credit**..$18.88..11%

36.NRGX..**PIMCO Energy & Tac**..$7.37..9.23%

21.PFL..**PIMCO Floating Rate**..$10.04..11%

23.PGP..**PIMCO Global Stocksp**..$8.49..9.9%

22.PHK..**PIMCO High Income Fun**..$5.43..11%

64.PKO..**PIMCO Income Oppor**..$23.20..9.83%

51.PFN..**PIMCO Income Strateg**..$11.28..11%

51.RCS..**PIMCO Strategic Glo**..$6.39..9.58%

18.PNEPP..**Pinnacle Financia**..$26.36..6.4%

40.HNW..**Pioneer Diversifie**..$13.65..9.01%

26.PHD..**Pioneer Floating R**..$10.35..7.25%

38.PHT..**Pioneer High Incom**..$8.05..10.06%

54.PAA..**Plains All America**..$7.12..10.12%

40.PAGP..**Plains GP Holdings**..$7.31..9.85%

36.BPOPM..**Popular Capital Tru**..$25.46..6%

33.BPOPN..**Popular Capital**..$26.36..6.35%

32.PTMN..**Portman Ridge Finan**..$1.17..20%

35.APTS..**Preferred Apartmen**..$6.61..10.61%

17.PGZ..**Principal Real Estat**..$11.63..11%

36.PSEC..**Prospect Capital Co**..$5.11..14%

56.PFS..**Provident Financia**..$13.68..6.73%

60.PRU..**Prudential Financi**..$69.71..6.31%

30.PIM..**Putnam Master Interm**..$4.24..8.5%

26.PPT..**Putnam Premier Inco**..$4.58..9.18%

Q

R

31.RTLR..**Rattler Midstrea**..$8.50..13.68%

50.RC..**Ready Capital Corp**..$10.49..10%

36.UTG..**Reaves Utility Fur**..$31.45..6.87%

46.RWT..**Redwood Trust Inc**..$7.21..6.93%

41.RVI..**Retail Value Inc**..$12.77..16.05%

70.RIO..**Rio Tinto PLc**..$61.50..8.73%

18.OPP..**RiverNorth/DoubleLi**..$14.23..15%

14.RSF..**RiverNorth Marketpal**..$14.73..14%

42.RIV..**Rivernorth Opportun**..$15.06..14%

41.RLJ..**RLJ Lodging Trust**..$10.05..0.40%

29.RMT..**Royce Micro-Cap Tru**..$7.93..9.96%

52.RVT..**Royce Value Trust**..$13.36..9.88%

S

60.SBRA..**Sabra Health Care**..$15.65..7.67%

45.SACH..**Sachern Capital C**..$3.48..13.78%

71.SLG..**St. Green Realty C**..$49.21..7.19%

48.PER..**Sandridge Permian T**..$0.45..36.34%

66.SAR..**Saratoga Investmen**..$17.19..9.31%

45.BFS..**Saul Centers Inc**..$28.17..7.53%

21.SCU..**Sculptor Capital Mana**..$12.81..0%

38.SVC..**Service Properties**..$8.90..0.49%

32.SFL..**SFL Corp Ltd**..$8.91..11.23%

39.SHLX..**Shell Midstream**..$10.61..17.34%

57.SPG..**Simon Property Gro**..$70.23..7.40%

51.SHI..**Sinopec Shanghai Pe**..$20.00..8.45%

62.TSLX..**Sixth Street Spec**..$17.60..9.32%

30.SLMBP..**SLM Corp**..$33.05..9.20%

51.SLRC..**Solar Capital Ltd**..$16.97..9.8%

55.SUNS..**Solar Senior Capi**..$13.34..9.00%

41.SPKE..**Spark Energy Inc**..$14.54..8.08%

19.SPKEP..**Spark Energy Inc**..$22.05..9.92%

24.SPE..**Special Opportunit**..$12.82..8.81%

52.SRC..**Spirit Realty Capi**..$36.49..6.85%

30.SRLP..**Sprague Resourc**..$15.08..17.71%

44.FUND..**Sprott Focus Trust**..$6.24..8.98%

36.EDF..**Stone Harbor Emerg**..$7.09..13.54%

53.STWD..**Starwood Property T**..$16.01..12%

44.SCM..**Stellus Capital Inves**..$8.20..12%

17.EDI..**Stone Harbor Emg Mkts**..$7.93..12%

47.SPH..**Suburban Propane P**..$12.75..9.41%

59.SMFG..**Sumitomo Mistui Fi**..$5.95..8.86%

37.SXC..**Suncoke Energy Inc**..$3.64..6.59%

38.SUN..**Sunoco LP**..$26.94..12.49%

21.SWZ..**Swiss Helvetia Fund**..$8.52..5.11%

68.SNV..**Synovus Financial**..$22.75..5.80%

T

59.TCP..**TC Pipelines LP**..$29.65..8.77%

26.TSI..**Tcw Strategic Income**..$5.76..6.2%

39.CGBD..**TCG BDC Inc**..$8.76..14.61%

16.TECTP..**Tectonic Financial**..$9.00..10%

58.TGP..**Teekay LNG Partner**..$10.96..9.12%

49.THQ..**Tekla Healthcare**..$18.01..7.50%

44.HQH..**Tekla Healthcare I**..$20.06..8.87%

39.HQL ..**Tekla Life Science**..$16.93..9.69%

40.THW..**Tekla World Health**..$14.39..9.73%

35.TEO..**Telecom Agrentina**..$7.11..4.58%

27.TEF..**Telefonica SA**..$4.02..0%

30.TDF..**Templeton Dragon F**..$24.97..1.83%

41.TS..**Tenaris SA**..$11.43..0%

59.TX..**Ternium SA**..$18.44..6.51%

28.TCBIP..**Texas Capital Ba**..$25.35..6.41%

39.TFSL..**TFS Financial Cor**..$15.84..7.07%

44.SRV..**The Cushing MLP &**..$17.45..8.25%

44.GGZ..**The Gabelli Global**..$10.10..6.34%

43.GEO..**The GEO Group In**..$10.81..17.76%

45.IFN..**The India Fund Inc**..$17.07..12.54%

54.TYG..**Tortoise Energy In**..$16.03..7.49%

40.TEAF..**Tortoise Essentia**..$11.19..8.04%

55.NTG..**Tortoise Midstream**..$16.24..7.64%

22.TPZ..**Tortoise Power & En**..$9.13..6.57%

54.TOT..**Total SE**..$48.95..7.95%

39.TRTX..**TPG RE Finance Tru**..$8.82..9.07%

23.TGA..**TransGlobe Energy Corp**..$0.55..0%

23.TPCO..**Tribune Publishing C**..$11.35..0%

39.TSE..**Trinseo SA**..$27.09..5.91%

54.TPVG..**TriplePoint Venture**..$11.78..12%

63.TRTN..**Triton Internatio**..$36.41..5.71%

17.TSCAP..**TriState Capita**..$23.52..7.17%

17.TSCBP..**TriState Capita**..$23.56..6.76%

38.TKC..**Turkecell Iletisim**..$4.85..6.94%

49.TWO..**Two Harbors Inves**..$5.47..10.24%

U

47.UMPQ..**Umpqua Holdings C**..$12.05..6.97%

45.UNB..**Union Bankshares I**..$19.35..6.61%

17.UCBIO..**United Community**..$26.27..6.9%

47.UBFO..**United Security Ba**..$6.21..7.09%

59.UVV..**Universal Corp**..$43.03..7.16%

65.UNM..**Unum Group**..$19.90..5.73%

36.USAC..**USA Compression**..$11.78..17.83%

16.USDP..**USD Parnters LP**..$3.57..12.44%

V

72.VLO..**Valero Energy Corp**..51.23..7.65%

54.VALE..**Vale SA**..$11.38..6.20%

39.VGR..**Vector Group Ltd**..$10.24..7.81%

34.VEON..**VEON Ltd**..$1.53..19%

25.VGI..**Virtus Global Mul**..$11.64..10.31%

49.VOD..**Vodafone Group PLC**..$14.18..7.24%

61.VNO..**Vornado Realty Tru**..$36.76..5.77%

13.IAE..**Voya Asia Pacific Hig**..$9.63..11%

16.IHD..**Voya Emerging Markets**..8.39..9.3%

36.IGD..**Voya Global Equity**..$5.04..9.52%

23.IDE..**Voya Infrastructure**..$9.49..9.7%

42.IID..**Voya International**..$4.49..8.02%

14.IRR..**Voya Natural Resource**..$2.61..12%

W

48.WDR..**Waddell & Reed Fin**..$15.78..6.34%

20.WTREP..**Watford Holdings**..$24.50..8.2%

24.ERC..**Wells Fargo Multi**..$11.26..10.94%

16.EOD..**Wells Fargo Global**..$4.57..12.49%

43.EAD..**Wells Fargo Income**..$7.52..9.35%

26.ERH..**Wells Fargo Utilit**..$12.18..7.13%

28.HIX..**Western Asset High**..$6.61..8.90%

24.TLI..**Western Asset Corpo**..$9.20..8.61%

28.GDO..**Western Asset Glob**..$17.24..7.03%

28.EHI..**Western Asset Globa**..$9.89..8.13%

29.HIO..**Western Asset Hig I**..$5.03..7.75%

58.EMD..**Western Asset Emer**..$12.98..8.78%

50.HYI..**Western Asset High**..$14.45..7.85%

29.DMO..**Western Asset Mor**..$12.96..10.24%

45.WES..**Western Midstream**..$9.03..13.85%

47.WLKP..**Westlake Chemical**..$20.17..9.35%

52.WHF..**Whitehorse Finana**..$10.52..13.50%

51.WSR..**Whitestone REIT**..$6.60..6.36%

50.WMB..**Williams Companies**..$20.69..7.73%

25.WTFCM..**Wintrust Financi**..$25.66..6.39%

12.WTFCP..**Wintrust Financial**..$26.59..11%

55.WF..**Woori Franklin Gro**..$21.37..16.09%

X

9.XFLT..**XAI Octagon FR & Alt**..$6.02..12%

Y

7.YGYIP..**Youngevity Interna**..$14.34..17%

Z

CHAPTER 19

U.S. Stocks

With A Dividend Yield of 6% or Greater

SORTED BY PRICE

Score/Stock Symbol/Company Name/.Stock price/Dividend%

20.AVGOP..Broadcom Inc..**$1,275.89**..6.27%

50.ALX..Alexander's Inc..**$266.17**..6.76%

56.BAP..Credicorp Ltd..**$132.41**..8.43%

21.DCUE..Dominion Energy..**$101.75**..7.13%

71.CEO..CNOOC Ltd..**$113.93**..7.3%

55.GFNCP..General Finance..**$100.00**..9.20%

62.LYB..LyondellBasell Ind..**$72.06**..5.83%

57.SPG..Simon Property Gro..**$70.23**..7.40%

60.PRU..Prudential Financi..**$69.71**..6.31%

57.NHI..National Health In..**$63.88**..6.90%

70.RIO..Rio Tinto PLc..**$61.50**..8.73%

54.CBSH..Commerce Bancshar..**$60.03**..1.80%

54.NVEC..NVE Corp..**$51.81**..7.82%

72.VLO..Valero Energy Corp..**$51.23**..7.65%

$50^

35.IEP..Icahn Enterprises..**$49.68**..16.10%

24.SKR..FS KKR Capital Cor..**$49.19**..15%

54.TOT..Total SE..**$48.95**..7.95%

55.CCEP..Coca-Cola European..**$44.35**..0%

37.DOW..Dow Inc..**$48.57**..5.76%

71.SLG..St. Green Realty C..**$49.21**..7.19%

63.SNP..China Petroleum &..**$45.77**..9.59%

48.MO..Altria Group Inc..**$43.76**..7.86%

59.UVV..Universal Corp..**$43.03**..7.16%

66.BNS..Bank of Nova Scoti..**$42.39**..6.50%

70.CMA..Comerica Inc..**$41.47**..6.56%

$40^

49.EVA..Enviva Partners LP..**$38.98**..7.85%

63.XOM..Exxon Mobil Corp..**$39.18**..8.88%

52.MMP..Magellan Midstrea..**$38.61**..10.67%

59.GLPI..Gaming and Leisur..**$37.65**..1.27%

52.LTC..LTC Properties Inc..**$37.24**..6.12%

62.APAM..Artisan Partners..**$37.05**..7.23%

61.VNO..Vornado Realty Tru..**$36.76**..5.77%

52.SRC..Spirit Realty Capi..**$36.49**..6.85%

63.TRTN..Triton Internatio..**$36.41**..5.71%

55.CQP..Cheniere Energy Pa..**$34.60**..7.46%

67.BTI..British American T..**$34.48**..9.62%

61.MPC..Marathon Petroleum..**$33.63**..9.90%

30.SLMBP..SLM Corp..**$33.05**..9.20%

43.DKL..Delek Logistics Part..**$32.36**..11%

62.OHI..Omega Healthcare In..**$31.91**..8.4%

56.ENB..Enbridge Inc..**$31.58**..7.53%

36.UTG..Reaves Utility Fur..**$31.45**..6.87%

30.SZC..Cushing Renaissanc..**$31.20**..8.20%

53.IRM..Iron Mountain Inc..**$30.50**..8.11%

70.OMF..OneMain Holdings In..**$30.00**..4.40%

$30^

50.BGS..B&G Foods Inc..**$29.99**..6.34%

46.MAIN..Main Street Capit..**$29.76**..8.27%

32.TIGO..Millicom Internation..**$29.73**..0%

59.TCP..TC Pipelines LP..**$29.65**..8.77%

59.T..AT & T..**$29.42**..7.07%

$29^

27.CHSCP..CHS Inc..**$28.93**..6.91%

64.AB..AllianceBernstein H..**$28.91**..9.44%

30.ASRVP..Ameriserv Financ..**$28.82**..7.33%

58.MGP..MGM Growth Properti..**$28.55**..6.8%

44.GLIBP..GCI Liberty Inc..**$28.49**..6.14%

29.BANFP..BFC Capital Trus..**$28.30**..6.36%

45.BFS..Saul Centers Inc..**$28.17**..7.53%

49.OKE..ONEOK Inc..**$28.07**..13%

$28^

30.CHSCL..CHS Inc..**$27.97**..6.7%

30.CHSCO..CHS Inc..**$27.95**..7.04%

34.CDMOP..Avid Bioservices I..**$27.88**..10%

33.FITBI..Fifth Third Banc..**$27.38**..6.05%

7.CFG..Cititzens Financial..**$27.36**..5.70%

39.TSE..Trinseo SA..**$27.09**..5.91%

$27^

38.SUN..Sunoco LP..**$26.94**..12.49%

19.HTLFP..Heartland Finana..**$26.88**..7.88%

29.PSF..Cohen & Steers Enh..**$26.83**..7.02%

19.BHFAP..Brighthouse Fina..**$26.82**..6.15%

59.PDI..PIMCO Dynamic Income..**$26.64**..11%

12.WTFCP..Wintrust Financial..**$26.59**..11%

56.DFP..Flaherty & Crumrine..**$26.58**..7.5%

52.PSXP..Phillips 66 Partner..**$26.52**..13%

17.ESGRP..Enstar Group Ltd..**$26.39**..7.64%

17.OCFCP..OceanFirst Finan..**$26.37**..7.23%

18.PNEPP..Pinnacle Financia..**$26.36**..6.4%

33.BPOPN..Popular Capital..**$26.36**..6.35%

29.LANDP..Gladstone Land C..**$26.34**..6.05%

17.FMBIP..First Midwest Ba..**$26.33**..6.65%

19.AUBAP..Atlantic Union B..**$26.31**..5.93%

17.UCBIO..United Community..**$26.27**..6.9%

22.CMCTP..CIM Commercial T..**$26.24**..1.94%

18.ESGRO..Enstar Group Ltd..**$26.22**..6.61%

30.NGHCN..National General..**$26.20**..7.16%

17.MBINP..Merchants Bancor..**$26.15**..6.69%

48.ACV..AllianzGI Diversiv..**$26.04**..7.70%

26.CHSCN..CHS Inc..**$26.03**..6.82%

26^

58.CNQ..Canadian Natural R..**$25.71**..6.61%

26.CHSCM..CHS Inc..**$25.70**..6.57%

29.MTBCP..MTBC Inc..**$25.66**..11%

25.WTFCM..Wintrust Financi..**$25.66**..6.39%

45.NTB..Bank of N.T. Butte..**$25.60**..6.88%

30.HBANO..Huntington Bancsh..**$25.60**..6.1%

29.NGHCO..National General..**$25.47**..7.36%

36.BPOPM..Popular Capital Tru..**$25.46**..6%

48.NGHCP..National General..**$25.43**..7.37%

28.TCBIP..Texas Captial Ba..**$25.35**..6.41%

19.ECCB..Eagle Point Credi..**$25.17**..7.70%

28.GOODM..Gladstone Commer..**$25.00**..7.00%

$25^

30.TDF..Templeton Dragon F..**$24.97**..1.83%

23.PIHPP..1347 Property In..**$24.95**..8.02%

42.LMRKP..Landmark Infrast..**$24.95**..8.02%

23.PIHPP..1347 Property In..**$24.95**..8.02%

18.MBINO..Merchants Bancor..**$24.90**..6.02%

18.GAINM..Gladstone Investm..**$24.82**..6.3%

59.QQQX..Nuveen NASDAQ 100..**$24.82**..6.29%

30.LMRKO..Landmark Infrast..**$24.66**..8.01%

30.OXLCO..Oxford Lane Capit..**$24.65**..7.6%

61.NIE..AllianzGI Equity &..**$24.56**..6.19%

70.PBA..Pembina Pipeline C..**$24.53**..7.83%

7.LMRKN..Landmark Infrastr..**$24.52**..7.22%

20.WTREP..Watford Holdings..**$24.50**..8.2%

20.WTREP..Watford Holdings..**$24.50**..8.2%

48.IFS..Intercorp Financia..**$24.37**..7.18%

18.AGNCN..AGNC Investment..**$24.33**..7.19%

18.GAINL..Gladstone Invest..**$24.25**..6.57%

18.GOODN..Gladstone Commer..**$24.11**..6.87%

59.BXMT..Blackstone Mortg..**$24.08**..10.30%

$24^

60.LDP..Cohen & Steers Ltd..**$23.86**..7.19%

62.OPI..Office Properties..**$23.84**..9.23%

32.GBAB..Guggenheim Taxabl..**$23.80**..6.34%

55.CCD..Calamos Dynamic Co..**$23.75**..8.44%

37.UTF..Cohen & Steers Infa..**$23.72**..7.8%

17.OXLCM..Oxford Lane Capit..**$23.67**..7.1%

18.RILYP..B. Riley Financia..**$23.60**..7.3%

17.TSCBP..TriState Capital..**$23.56**..6.76%

17.TSCAP..TriState Capital..**$23.52**..7.17%

29.AFINP..American Finance..**$23.43**..8.00%

18.AGNCO..AGNC Investment..**$23.39**..6.95%

18.AGNCM..AGNC Investment..**$23.37**..7.35%

27.BTO..John Hancock Financ..**$23.27**..9.5%

49.BPY..Brookfield Property..**$23.23**..11%

32.STK..Columbia Seligman..**$23.22**..4.15%

64.PKO..PIMCO Income Oppor..**$23.20**..9.83%

$23^

18.JPT..Nuveen Preferred an..**$22.82**..6.2%

61.JPI..Nuveen Preferred a..**$22.81**..6.87%

68.SNV..Synovus Financial..**$22.75**..5.80%

19.OXLCP..Oxford Lane Capi..**$22.70**..6.88%

19.AGNCP..AGNC Investment C..**$22.62**..6.7%

18.DCOMP..Dime Community B..**$22.35**..6.15%

34.ETO..Eaton Vance Tax-ad..**$22.30**..7.67%

32.FLC..Flaherty & Crumrin..**$22.16**..7.15%

19.SPKEP..Spark Energy Inc..**$22.05**..9.92%

29.BUI..BlackRock Utility..**$22.01**..6.60%

$22^

53.FPF..First Trust Inter D..**$21.93**..7.2%

33.FFC..Flaherty & Crumrin..**$21.86**..7.08%

35.BPYPP..Brookfield Prope..**$21.85**..7.44%

42.ILPT..Industrial Logist..**$21.84**..6.04%

17.HTIA..Healthcare Trust ..**$21.79**..6.28%

61.PEBO..Peoples Bancorp In..**$21.71**..6.2%

27.DDT..Dillard's Capital T..**$21.44**..8.7%

35.BPYPO..Brookfield Proper..**$21.43**..7.4%

51.PWOD..Penns Woods Banco..**$21.42**..5.98%

28.AIO..Allianz Artificial..**$21.39**..6.08%

55.WF..Woori Franklin Gro..**$21.37**..16.09%

31.NYMTO..New York Mortga..**$21.18**..9.30%

23.NYMTN..New York Mortga..**$21.12**..9.47%

$21^

50.WMB..Williams Companies..**$20.69**..7.73%

20.NYMTM..New York Mortga..**$20.60**..9.56%

22.AIRTP..Air T Inc..**$20.54**..9.74%

30.CEE..Central & Eastern..**$20.49**..7.14%

56.CIT..CIT Group Inc..**$20.43**..6.83%

34.EVT..Eaton Vance Tax Adv..**$20.42**..8.5%

45.JHG..Janus Henderson Gro..**$20.41**..7.06%

47.WLKP..Westlake Chemical..**$20.17**..9.35%

44.HQH..Tekla Healthcare I..**$20.06**..8.87%

51.SHI..Sinopec Shanghai P..**$20.00**..8.45%

$20^

35.BPYPN..Brookfield Proper..**$19.97**..7.20%

65.UNM..Unum Group..**$19.90**..5.73%

30.HTD..John Hancock Tax-a..**$19.86**..8.34%

29.HPI..John Hancock Prefe..**$19.77**..7.50%

33.RNP..Cohen & Steers REI..**$19.74**..7.54%

45.UNB..Union Bankshares I..**$19.35**..6.61%

28.GMLPP..Golar LNG Partners..**$19.24**..11%

49.OLP..One Liberty Proper..**$19.14**..9.40%

26.DBL..Doubleline Opportu..**$19.11**..6.91%

7.NEWT..Newtek Business Serv..**$19.00**..12%

$19^

45.E..Eni SpA..**$18.98**..9.97%

45.GOOD..Gladstone Commerc..**$18.98**..7.95%

36.BPYUP..Brookfield Proper..**$18.95**..8.4%

57.PCI..PIMCO Dynamic Credit..**$18.88**..11%

50.EOS..Eaton Vance Enhanc..**$18.72**..6.33%

23.MBNKP..Medallion Bank..**$18.50**..10.81%

59.TX..Ternium SA..**$18.44**..6.51%

13.FBIOP..Fortress Biotec..**$18.37**..12.76%

32.HPF..John Hancock Prefe..**$18.34**..8.04%

52.MPLX..MPLX LP..**$18.22**..15.09%

19.GGM..Guggenheim Credit Al..**$18.14**..12%

44.KREF..KKR Real Estate F..**$18.11**..9.50%

39.GOF..Guggenheim Strategic..**$18.02**..12%

49.THQ..Tekla Healthcare..**$18.01**..7.50%

$18^

20.MINDP..Mind Technology..**$17.86**..12.53%

49.CODI..Compass Diversifi..**$17.78**..8.10%

37.HESM..Hesse Midstream L..**$17.66**..9.88%

63.EPD..Enterprise Produc..**$17.60**..10.12%

62.TSLX..Sixth Street Spec..**$17.60**..9.32%

52.GNL..Global Net Lease I..**$17.52**..9.13%

44.SRV..The Cushing MLP &..**$17.45**..8.25%

28.GDO..Western Asset Glob..**$17.24**..7.03%

46.CVI..CVR Energy Inc..**$17.21**..9.30

66.SAR..Saratoga Investmen..**$17.19**..9.31%

58.PMT..PennyMac Mortgage I..**$17.15**..9.33

45.IFN..The India Fund In..**$17.07**..12.54%

$17^

50.CZNC..Citizens & Northe..**$16.98**..6.36%

51.SLRC..Solar Capital Ltd..**$16.97**..9.8%

20.RA..Brookfield Real Asse..**$16.96**..14%

39.HQL ..Tekla Life Science..**$16.93**..9.69%

17.FINS..Angel Oak Financia..**$16.78**..7.2%

28.JHI..John Hancock Inves..**$16.58**..7.99%

29.HPS..John Hancock Prefer..**$16.54**..7.9%

55.NTG..Tortoise Midstream..**$16.24**..7.64%

32.PTY..PIMCO Corporate &..**$16.18**..9.64%

35.PFD..Flaherty & Crumrin..**$16.17**..6.38%

44.DSL..DoubleLIne Income So..**$16.14**..11%

54.TYG..Tortoise Energy In..**$16.03**..7.49%

57.FTAI..Fortress Transpor..**$16.01**..8.24%

53.BIT..BlackRock Multi-Se..**$16.O2**..9.22%

53.STWD..Starwood Property T..**$16.01**..12%

32.LGI..Lazard Global Tota..**$16.00**..7.98%

$16^

60.GLU..Gabelli Global Uti..**$15.95**..7.52%

39.TFSL..TFS Financial Cor..**$15.84**..7.07%

64.DX..Dynex Capital Inc..**$15.82**..9.8%

43.GSBD..Goldman Sachs BDC I..**$15.82**..11%

48.FSK..FS KKR Capital Corp..**$15.80**..15%

59.PCN..PIMCO Corporate & I..**$15.79**..8.5%

48.WDR..Waddell & Reed Fin..**$15.78**..6.34%

34.CAPL..CrossAmerica Partne..**$15.73**..13%

60.SBRA..Sabra Health Care..**$15.65**..7.67%

33.CII..Blackrock Enhanced..**$15.48**..6.78%

29.FFA..First Trust Enhanc..**$15.26**..7.47%

31.BLW..Blackrock Ltd Dura..**$15.20**..7.74%

49.HRB..H&R Block..**$15.15**..6.87%

30.SRLP..Sprague Resourc..**$15.08**..17.71%

47.ETV..Eaton Vance Tax-Ma..**$15.07**..9.04%

42.RIV..Rivernorth Opportun..**$15.06**..14%

$15^

47.EOI..Eaton Vance Enhanc..**$14.99**..7.19%

11.NREE..NexPoint Real Es..**$14.99**..10.67%

44.CSWC..Capital Southwest C..**$14.98**..11%

44.MSBI..Midland States Ban..**$14.92**..7.1%

44.FCBP..First Choice Banc..**$14.86**..6.73%

52.DK..Delek US Holdings I..**$14.80**..8.38%

14.RSF..RiverNorth Marketpal..**$14.73**..12%

44.KW..Kennedy-Wilson Hold..**$14.69**..5.99%

41.PKE..Spark Energy Inc..**$14.54**..8.08%

35.ETH..Ethan Allen Interi..**$14.52**..5.79%

50.HYI..Western Asset High..**$14.45**..7.85%

29.AVK..Advent Claymore Co..**$14.43**..9.73%

35.CSQ..Calamos Strategic..**$14.40**..7.71%

40.THW..Tekla World Health..**$14.39**..9.73%

21.CTR..Clearbridge Ener..**$14.34**..11.16%

7.YGYIP..Youngevity Intern..**$14.34**..17%

48.GMRE..Global Medical RE..**$14.25**..5.97%

18..OPP..RiverNorth/Doubl..**$14.23**..15%

45.CEQP..Crestwood Equit..**$14.20**..17.61%

44.ETB..Eaton Vance Tax-Ma..**$14.20**..9.13%

54.ARCC..Ares Capital Cor..**$14.19**..10.82%

59.JGH..Nuveen Global High..**$14.19**..7.23%

49.VOD..Vodafone Group PLC..**$14.18**..7.24%

43.AGNC..AGNC Investment Cor..**$14.14**..10%

57.FFBC..First Financial B..**$14.09**..6.53%

25.FSD..First Trust High I..**$14.09**..9.37%

27.ISD..PGIM High Yield Fu..**$14.06**..8.96%

$14^

59.DIAX..Nuveen Dow 30sm D..**$13.99**..7.81%

41.BTZ..Blackrock Credit Al..**$13.94**..7.2%

39.BRT..BRT Apartments Cor..**$13.93**..6.32%

28.SPXX..Nuveen S&P 500 Dy..**$13.88**..7.06%

38.AKO.B..Embotelladora..**$13.80**..7.39%

56.PFS..Provident Financia..**$13.68**..6.73%

40.HNW..Pioneer Diversifie..**$13.65**..9.01%

25.JTD..Nuveen Tax-advanta..**$13.63**..8.64%

27.BSL..Blackstone/ GSO Se..**$13.54**..8.24%

54.KMI..Kinder Morgan Inc..**$13.51**..7.77%

41.NS..NuStar Energy LP..**$13.48**..11.87%

52.RVT..Royce Value Trust..**$13.36**..9.88%

55.SUNS..Solar Senior Capi..**$13.34**..9.00%

19.KIO..KKR Income Opportuni..**$13.34**..11%

25.BGH..Barings Global Sho..**$13.31**..9.52%

16.FEO..First Trust/Aberdeen..**$13.28**..11%

43.CLI..Mack-Cali Realty C..**$13.23**..6.05%

28.PDT..John Hancock Premi..**$13.21**..8.86%

49.GBDC..Golub Capital BDC..**$13.13**..8.83%

57.GHY..PGIM Global High Yi..**$13.45**..9.3%

44.DCP..DCP Midstream LP..**$13.13**..11.88%

27.JCE..Nuveen Core Equity..**$13.11**..6.86%

$13^

58.EMD..Western Asset Emer..**$12.98**..8.78%

29.DMO..Western Asset Mor..**$12.96**..10.24%

48.CUK..Carnival PLC..**$12.95**..0%

25.AFT..Apollo Senior Floa..**$12.84**..6.17%

24.SPE..Special Opportunit..**$12.82**..8.81%

23.MCI..Barings Corporate..**$12.81**..7.49%

48.KNOP..KNOT Offshore Part..**$12.81**..16%

21.SCU..Sculptor Capital Mana..**$12.81**..0%

41.RVI..Retail Value Inc..**$12.77**..16.05%

52.RFI..Cohen & Steers Tot..**$12.77**..7.52%

24.AIF..Apollo Tactical In..**$12.76**..6.39%

39.GLP..Global Partners LP..**$12.75**..14%

47.SPH..Suburban Propane P..**$12.75**..9.41%

28.CGO..Calamos Global Tot..**$12.73**..9.43%

24.VLT..Invesco High Incom..**$12.67**..9.13%

48.CHY..Calamos Convertibl..**$12.61**..8.09%

56.FFIC..Flushing Financia..**$12.61**..6.66%

48.HEP..Holly Energy Parn..**$12.59**..11.18%

39.ARDC..Ares Dynamic Cred..**$12.58**..9.30%

25.BGX..Blackstone / GSO L..**$12.55**..9.56%

12.MDRRP..Medalist Diversif..**$12.50**..16%

53.EFC..Ellington Financial..**$12.47**..8.6%

53.BWG..BrandywineGlobal..**$12.45**..6.75%

52.BLX..Banco Lainoamerica..**$12.44**..8.04%

27.PFO..Flaherty & Crumrin..**$12.41**..6.72%

35.JRI..Nuveen Real Asset..**$12.34**..9.41%

31.GUT..Babelli Utility Tru..**$12.29**..7.8%

58.FSLF..First Eagle Senior..**$12.29**..7.8%

32.CCAP..Crescent Capital BD..**$12.24**..13%

45.CXP..Columbia Property..**$12.19**..6.89%

29.NFJ..Allianzgi NFJ Divi..**$12.18**..7.39%

25.JSD..Nuveen Short Durat..**$12.18**..6.95%

26.ERH..Wells Fargo Utilit..**$12.18**..7.13%

25.EFT..Eaton Vance Floati..**$12.17**..7.07%

45.HRZN..Horizon Technology..**$12.09**..9.9%

49.OLN..Olin Corp..**$12.09**..6.62%

38.FTF..Franklin Limited..**$12.06**..10.92%

$12^

47.IVH..Ivy High Income Op..**$11.99**..9.07%

29.BPYU..Brookfield Property..**$11.95**..11%

56.BGB..Blackstone / GSO..**$11.95**..9.44%

29.FOF..Cohen & Steers Clo..**$11.86**..8.80%

21.GLQ..Clough Global Equity..**$11.86**..11%

26.EFR..Eaton Vance Senior..**$11.81**..7.53%

54.TPVG..TriplePoint Venture..**$11.78**..12%

36.USAC..USA Compression..**$11.78**..17.83%

39.FRA..Blackrock Floating..**$11.74**..8.05%

31.BPMP..BP Midstream Partne..**$11.74**..12%

47.EVV..Eaton Vance Ltd Dura..**$11.70**..10%

38.AKO.A..Embotelladora An..**$11.68**..7.24%

25.VGI..Virtus Global Mul..**$11.64**..10.31%

31.ROI..Cohen & Steers Qual..**$11.63**..8.3%

17.PGZ..Principal Real Estat..**$11.63**..11%

49.EARN..Ellington Residenti..**$11.62**..10%

49.ABR..Arbor Realty Trus..**$11.62**..10.67%

24.EVG..Eaton Vance Short..**$11.60**..7.76%

57.EC..Ecopetrol SA..**$11.56**..7.68%

26.BxMX..Nuveen S&P 500 Bu..**$11.52**..7.47%

25.BGT..Blackrock floating..**$11.51**..7.97%

33.ETY..Eaton Vance Tax-mgd..**$11.49**..8.8%

41.TS..Tenaris SA..**$11.43**..0%

27.DNI..Dividend and Inco..**$11.40**..10.09%

30.IGT..International Game Te..**$11.38**..0%

54.VALE..Vale SA..**$11.38**..6.20%

23.TPCO..Tribune Publishing C..**$11.35**..0%

25.HEQ..John Hancock Hedged..**$11.33**..10%

39.AKR..Acadia Realty Trust..**$11.30**..0%

57.NHS..Neuberger Berman H..**$11.30**..9.61%

33.CHI..Calamos Convertibl..**$11.29**..8.07%

51.PFN..PIMCO Income Strateg..**$11.28**..11%

24.ERC..Wells Fargo Multi..**$11.26**..10.94%

19.FCT..First Trust Senior F..**$11.22**..11%

48.HTGC..Hercules Capital..**$11.20**..11.43%

40.TEAF..Tortoise Essentia..**$11.19**..8.04%

42.BDN..Brandywine Realty T..**$11.19**..6.8%

38.DPG..Duff & Phelps Glo..**$11.19**..12.51%

33.HYT..Blackrock Corporat..**$11.11**..8.42%

15.HTY..John Hancock Tax-Adv..**$11.04**..12%

62.PBCT..People's United F..**$11.03**..6.53%

21.CLM..Cornerstone Strategi..**$11.02**..20%

$11^

23.MPV..Barings Participat..**$10.99**..7.28%

38.SCD..Lmp Capital Income F..**$10.98**..11%

58.TGP..Teekay LNG Partner..**$10.96**..9.12%

59.CTL..CenturyLink Inc..**$10.91**..9.17%

20.CRF..Cornerstone Total Re..**$10.81**..20%

43.GEO..The GEO Group Inc..**$10.81**..17.76%

25.AWF..Alliancebernstein G..**$10.74**..7.3%

22.OCCI..OFS Credit Co Inc..**$10.74**..20%

38.DMLP..Dorchester Miner..**$10.63**..14.72%

39.SHLX..Shell Midstream..**$10.61**..17.34%

35.NRP..Natural Resources..**$10.55**..17.06%

52.WHF..Whitehorse Financ..**$10.52**..13.50%

52.HMLP..Hoegh LNG Partne..**$10.50**..16.76%

50.RC..Ready Capital Corp..**$10.49**..10%

51.FDUS..Fidus Investment..**$10.47**..11.46%

46.FDEU..First Trust Dynam..**$10.41**..6.91%

26.PHD..Pioneer Floating R..**$10.35**..7.25%

26.MXF..Mexico Fund Inc..**$10.29**..9.04%

53.NWBI..Northwest Bancsha..**$10.29**..7.39%

42.CNXM..CNX Midstream P..**$10.26**..13.62%

50.ETJ..Eaton Vance Risk-M..**$10.26**..8.89%

39.VGR..Vector Group Ltd..**$10.24**..7.81%

48.DNP..DNP Select Income..**$10.11**..7.72%

41.NMFC..New Mountain Financ..**$10.11**..12%

23.FAM..First Trust / Aberd..**$10.10**..9.5%

44.GGZ..The Gabelli Global..**$10.10**..6.34%

48.LMRK..Landmark Infrastr..**$10.07**..7.94%

41.RLJ..RLJ Lodging Trust..**$10.05**..0.40%

21.PFL..PIMCO Floating Rate..**$10.04**..11%

19.FEN..First Trust Energy I..**$10.02**..12%

34.CINR..Ciner Resources..**$10.01**..13.59%

$10^

62.FHN..First Horizon National..**$9.95**..6%

62.HBAN..Huntington Bancsha..**$9.94**..6.04%

38.PBFX..PBF Logistics LP..**$9.94**..12%

55.PCM..Pcm Fund Inc..**$9.94**..9.66%

37.TCPC..BlackRock TCP Capita..**$9.90**..12%

28.EHI..Western Asset Globa..**$9.89**..8.13%

26.RESI..Front Yard Residentia..**$9.88**..0%

15.GLV..Clough Global Dividen..**$9.87**..12%

37.ARR..Armour Residential RE..**$9.86**..12%

41.ACRE..Ares Commearcial Res..**$9.81**..13%

43.BRMK..Broadmark Realty C..**$9.79**..7.36%

37.CHMI..Cherry Hill Mortgage..**$9.77**..11%

8.GDV..Gabelli Dividend &..**$9.76**..12.30%

27.AGD..Aberdeen Global Dyn..**$9.74**..8.01%

49.HAFC..Hanmi Financial Co..**$9.68**..3.31%

26.FIF..First Trust Energy..**$9.68**..7.75%

26.BOE.. Blackrock Enhanced..**$9.67**..7.82%

52.EURN..Euronav NV..**$9.64**..16%

50.NHF..Nexpoint Strategic..**$9.63**..12.46%

13.IAE..Voya Asia Pacific Hig..**$9.63**..11%

19.GLO..Clough Global Opportu..**$9.58**..11%

44.MBT..Mobile TeleSystems..**$9.55**..15.84%

24.EXD..Eaton Vance Tax-Man..**$9.54**..8.91%

22.BWL.A..Bowl America Inc..**$9.50**..0%

23.IDE..Voya Infrastructure..**$9.49**..9.7%

51.GAIN..Gladstone Investmen..**$9.39**..8.95%

48.BHLB..Berkshire Hill Ba..**$9.35**..10.27%

43.GMZ..Goldman Sachs MLP I..**$9.33**..8.79%

62.NYCB..New York Community..**$9.24**..7.36%

23.DUC..Duff & Phelps Utili..**$9.22**..6.51%

60.NAVI..Navient Corp..**$9.21**..6.95%

24.TLI..Western Asset Corpo..**$9.20**..8.61%

43.AINV..Apollo Investment..**$9.18**..13.51%

22.TPZ..Tortoise Power & En..**$9.13**..6.57%

26.VTA..Invesco Dynamic Cred..**$9.10**..9.9%

6.AJX..Great Ajax Corp..**$9.07**..7.50%

46.HNNA..Hennessy Advisors..**$9.05**..6.08%

45.WES..Western Midstream..**$9.03**..13.85%

26.ETW..Eaton Vance Tax-mang..**$9.02**..9.6%

38.ARI..Apollo Commercial..**$9.01**..15.55%

16.TECTP..Tectonic Financial..**$9.00**..10%

50.HTBK..Heritage Commerce..**$9.00**..7.30%

$9^

27.JPS..Nuveen Preferred &..**$8.99**..6.74%

40.CIM..Chimera Investmen..**$8.96**..13.39%

15.DEX..Delaware Enhanced..**$8.96**..10.98%

32.SFL..SFL Corp Ltd..**$8.91**..11.23%

49.HFRO..Highland Income F..**$8.90**..10.38%

38.SVC..Service Properties..**$8.90**..0.49%

39.TRTX..TPG RE Finance Tru..**$8.82**..9.07%

39.CGBD..TCG BDC Inc..**$8.76**..14.61%

57.HOPE..Hope Bancorp Inc..**$8.72**..6.4%

24.JPC..Nuveen Preferred & I..**$8.72**..7.3%

47.NBLX..Noble Midstream Pa..**$8.67**..8.65%

16.BGIO..BlackRock 2022 Glo..**$8.67**..6.92%

27.MCR..MFS Charter Income T..**$8.62**..8.14%

20.FMO..Fiduciary/Claymore En..**$8.61**..11%

24.JTA..Nuveen Tax Advantag..**$8.59**..8.94%

21.SWZ..Swiss Helvetia Fund..**$8.52**..5.11%

31.RTLR..Rattler Midstrea..**$8.50**..13.68%

23.PGP..PIMCO Global Stocksp..**$8.49**..9.9%

32.CHW..Calamos Global Dyna..**$8.45**..9.94%

20.CEN..Center Coast Brook..**$8.45**..31.95%

22.IGA..Voya Global Advantage..**$8.39**..9.3%

15.DDF..Delaware Investmen..**$8.37**..12.05%

49.FRO..Frontline Ltd..**$8.37**..32%

19.MURR..Medalist Diversified..**$8.37**..0%

36.PFLT..Pennant Park Floa..**$8.37**..14.74%

24.JFR..Nuveen Floating Rat..**$8.35**..6.61%

30.AOD..Aberdeen Total Dyna..**$8.33**..8.28%

34.KRP..Kimbell Royalty Pa..**$8.31**..17.91%

47.BBDC..Barings BDC Inc..**$8.30**..7.7%

47.HYB..New America High In..**$8.29**..7.24%

56.MAC..Macerich Co..**$8.27**..7.26%

24.JRO..Nuveen Floating Rat..**$8.26**..6.54%

14.DCF..BNY Mellon Alcentra..**$8.20**..7.32%

44.SCM..Stellus Capital Inves..**$8.20**..12%

47.BCBP..BCB Bancorp Inc..**$8.15**..6.87%

18.PCF..High Income Securitie..**$8.10**..12%

16.JCO..Nuveen Credit Oppor..**$8.09**..6.97%

44.CIO..City Office Reit In..**$8.08**..7.43%

38.PHT..Pioneer High Incom..**$8.05**..10.06%

47.MVC..MVC Capital Inc..**$8.04**..8.46%

26.JRS..Nuveen Real Estate..**$8.02**..9.48%

35.IRCP..IRSA Propiedades C..**$8.00**..3.95%

$8^

22.JDD..Nuveen Diversified D..**$7.99**..9.9%

44.MFD..Macquarie/First Tr..**$7.93**..10.04%

29.RMT..Royce Micro-Cap Tru..**$7.93**..9.96%

17.EDI..Stone Harbor Emg Mkts..**$7.93**..12%

29.CPAC..Cementos Pacasmayo..**$7.90**..6.8%

26.EXG..Eaton Vance Tax-Mgd..**$7.85**..9.42%

19.IHIT..Invesco High Income..**$7.84**..7.6%

20.ECC..Eagle Point Credit Co..**$7.79**..12%

58.LADR..Ladder Capital Co..**$7.77**..10.30%

61.FNB..F N B Corp..**$7.68**..6.25%

43.GLAD..Gladstone Capital Co..**$7.64**..10%

16.JEMD..Nuveen Emerging Ma..**$7.64**..5.26%

15.IHTA..Invesco High Income..**$7.64**..7.3%

30.BDJ..BlackRock Enhanced..**$7.62**..7.87%

46.BRG..Bluerock Residential..**$7.57**..8.5%

43.EAD..Wells Fargo Income..**$7.52**..9.35%

31.NLY..Annaly Capital Manage..**$7.47**..12%

36.DBI..Designer Brands Inc..**$7.43**..0%

36.NRGX..PIMCO Energy & Tac..**$7.37**..9.23%

40.PAGP..Plains GP Holdings..**$7.31**..9.85%

46.ENIA..Enel Americas SA..**$7.26**..7.29%

22.AM..Antero Midstream C..**$7.22**..17.04%

46.RWT..Redwood Trust Inc..**$7.21**..6.93%

20.GGT..Gabelli Multimedia Tr..**$7.20**..12%

30.ASG..Liberty All Star Gr..**$7.13**..7.29%

44.GER..Goldman Sachs MLP a..**$7.12**..8.71%

54.PAA..Plains All America..**$7.12**..10.12%

35.TEO..Telecom Agrentina S..**$7.11**..4.58%

36.EDF..Stone Harbor Emerg..**$7.09**..13.54%

29.GRF..Eagle Capital Growt..**$7.05**..1.05%

35.BSBR..Banco Santander..**$7.00**..20.24%

$7^

30.AFIN..American Finance Tru..**$6.97**..12%

37.MRCC..Monroe Capital Corp..**$6.96**..14%

25.BGR..BlackRock Engergy &..**$6.87**..8.21%

15.FCO..Aberdeen Global In..**$6.82**..12.32%

16.IHD..Voya Emerging Markets..**$6.77**..11%

52.BSM..Black Stone Mineral..**$6.75**..8.89%

46.ESRT..Empire State Realt..**$6.67**..6.30%

53.ET..Energy Transfer LP..**$6.64**..19%

35.APTS..Preferred Apartmen..**$6.61**..10.61%

39.OCSI..Oaktree Strategic ..**$6.61**..7.58%

28.HIX..Western Asset High ..**$6.61**..8.90%

10.HGLB..Highland Global All..**$6.56**..15%

40.AROC..Archrock Inc..**$6.51**..8.91%

51.RCS..PIMCO Strategic Glo..**$6.39**..9.58%

47.BCX..BlackRock Resources..**$6.39**..7.51%

25.HIE..Miller/Howard High..**$6.33**..7.58%

40.CMO..Capstead Mortgage C..**$6.29**..9.55%

44.FUND..Sprott Focus Trust..**$6.24**..8.98%

33.USA..Liberty All Star Equi..**$6.21**..10%

47.UBFO..United Security Ba..**$6.21**..7.09%

52.BKT..Blackrock Income Tr..**$6.20**..6.66%

26.IGR..CBRE Clarion Global..**$6.18**..9.69%

34.SIM..Grupo Simec SAB de..**$6.13**..9.19%

58.DHT..DHT Holdings Ltd..**$6.12**..31%

35.KFFB..Kentucky First Fed..**$6.12**..6.54%

34.CRT..Cross Timbers Roya..**$6.11**..14.71%

28.MMT..MFS Multimarket Inc..**$6.09**..8.13%

17.JOC..Nuveen Credit Strate..**$6.07**..16%

50.MCN..Madison Covrd Call &..**$6.06**..12%

9.XFLT..XAI Octagon FR & Alt..**$6.02**..12%

$6^

59.SMFG..Sumitomo Mistui Fi..**$5.95**..8.86%

25.EVF..Eaton Vance Senior..**$5.94**..7.07%

8.BKEPP..Blueknight Engergy P..**$5.93**..12%

49.CLP..Capital Product Pa..**$5.93**..6.75%

53.ENBL..Enable Midstream..**$5.90**..11.21%

44.EDD..Morgan Stanley Emer..**$5.80**..8.45%

26.NHTC..Natural Health Trend..**$5.78**..14%

46.GPM..Guggenheim Enhanced..**$5.77**..8.32%

26.TSI..Tcw Strategic Income..**$5.76**..6.2%

28.GCV..Gabelli Convertible..**$5.63**..8.53%

34.FEI..First Trust MLP and E..**$5.34**..11%

35.GEL..Genesis Energy LP..**$5.51**..10.93%

27.CYCCP..Cyclacel Pharmace..**$5.50**..10.91%

21.GAB..Gabelli Equity Trust ..**$5.48**..11%

49.TWO..Two Harbors Inves..**$5.47**..10.24%

22.PHK..PIMCO High Income Fun..**$5.43**..11%

28.BGY..Blackrock Enhanced..**$5.36**..7.57%

24.MFV..MFS Special Value..**$5.35**..10.05%

29.GECC..Great Elm Capital..**$5.25**..1.90%

38.NNA..Navios Maritime Acqu..**$5.22**..23%

22.GNT..Gamco Natural Resour..**$5.13**..7.02%

36.PSEC..Prospect Capital Co..**$5.11**..14%

22.AVAL..Grupo Aval Accione..**$5.10**..7.15%

30.ORC..Orchid Island Cap..**$5.10**..15.28%

36.IGD..Voya Global Equity..**$5.04**..9.52%

14.EGI..Eagle Growth and I..**$5.03**..20.28%

29.HIO..Western Asset Hig I..**$5.03**..7.75%

$5^

46.CMRE..Costamare Inc..**$4.99**..8.02%

47.OCSL..Oaktree Specialty L..**$4.99**..8.4%

22.NSL..Nuveen Senior Incom..**$4.96**..7.39%

42.KYN..Kayne Anderson MLP/M..**$4.93**..12%

58.NCV..AllianzGI Convertible..**$4.88**..10%

24.AWP..Aberdeen Global Pre..**$4.87**..9.85%

38.TKC..Turkecell Iletisim..**$4.85**..6.94%

21.IAF..Abereen Australia Eq..**$4.82**..9.9%

33.OFS..OFS Capital Corp..**$4.79**..14%

21.MGF..MFS Government Mark..**$4.65**..7.49%

26.PPT..Putnam Premier Inco..**$4.58**..9.18%

16.EOD..Wells Fargo Global..**$4.57**..12.49%

42.IID..Voya International..**$4.49**..8.02%

38.FSP..Franklin Street Pro..**$4.43**..8.13%

49.ITCB..Itau Corpbanca..**$4.43**..9.74%

28.CDOR..Condor Hospitality T..**$4.40**..0%

16.LND..Brasilagro – Cia Bras..**$4.39**..0%

46.ATAX..America First Mult..**$4.37**..5.49%

54.NCZ..AllianzGI Converti..**$4.35**..10.34%

47.NAT..Nordic American Tan..**$4.34**..9.92%

29.OXLC..Oxford Lane Capital..**$4.24**..19%

30.PIM..Putnam Master Interm..**$4.24**..8.5%

43.LOAN..Manhattan Bridge C..**$4.20**..9.52%

33.FAX..Aberdeen Asia-pacif..**$4.19**..7.88%

36.NGL..NGL Energy Partners..**$4.16**..19%

29.FPL..First Trust New Oppor..**$4.05**..11%

27.TEF..Telefonica SA..**$4.02**..0%

32.SELF..Global Self Storag..**$4.01**..6.45%

$4^

35.GLOP..Gaslog Partners LP..**$3.97**..12%

17.NRO..Neuberger Berman Re..**$3.90**..12%

24.MIN..MFS Intermediate In..**$3.84**..8.88%

12.CUBA..Herzfeld Caribbean..**$3.83**..16%

22.VVR..Invesco Senior Inco..**$3.70**..6.50%

38.ENIC..Enel Chile SA..**$3.69**..7.15%

25.GGN..GAMCO Global Gold N..**$3.65**..9.89%

37.SXC..Suncoke Energy Inc..**$3.64**..6.59%

16.USDP..USD Parnters LP..**$3.57**..12.44%

45.SACH..Sachern Capital C..**$3.48**..13.78%

32.ICMB..Investcorp Credi..**$3.46**..17.34%

27.FCRD..First Eagle Alte..**$3.34**..11.98%

34.BSMX..Banco Santa..**$3.28**..0%

33.PNNT..Pennant Park Inv..**$3.27**..14.70%

39.NCMI..National CineMedi..**$3.13**..8.95%

45.ENLC..EnLink Midstream..**$3.03**..12.38%

$3^

34.BBVA..Banco Bilbao Vizcaya..**$2.97**..16%

35.MVO..MV Oil Trust..**$2.95**..30%

46.EMO..ClearBridge Energy M..**$2.90**..10%

51.CIK..Credit Suisse Asset..**$2.85**..9.47%

25.DHF..BNY Mellon High Yie..**$2.75**..9.30%

35.BKCC..BlackRock Capita..**$2.71**..14.76%

45.MFA..MFA Financial Inc..**$2.70**..7.42%

39.HIHO..Highway Holdings..**$2.67**..6.74%

15.FGB..First Trust Specia..**$2.66**..12.41%

32.OXSQ..Oxford Square Capit..**$2.62**..16%

14.IRR..Voya Natural Resource..**$2.61**..12%

45.NYMT..New York Mortgage..**$2.59**..7.72%

18.CEPU..Central Puerto SA..**$2.51**..4.72%

36.DSWL..Deswell Industries..**$2.50**..7.20%

35.HCFT..Hunt companies Finan..**$2.47**..12%

40.MNDO..MIND C.T.I. Ltd..**$2.32**..10.34%

20.CIF..Mfs Intermediate H..**$2.31**..10.08%

47.DHY..Credit Suisse High..**$2.09**..9.47%

29.MARPS..Marine Petroleu..**$2.03**..14.95%

$2^

27.CIG.C..Energy Company of Mi..**$1.92**..0%

26.MIE..Cohen & Steers MLP..**$1.92**.9..38%

26.ANH..Anworth Mortgage Asse..**$1.76**..11%

20.AHC..A H Belo Corp..**$1.55**..10.32%

34.VEON..VEON Ltd..**$1.53**..19%

33.EVC..Entravision Communi..**$1.51**..6.62%

13.BKEP..Blueknight Ener..**$1.50**..10.65%..

25.DVD..Dover Motorsports I..**$1.41**..7.09%

32.PTMN..Portman Ridge Finan..**$1.17**..20%

44.PEI..Pennsylvania Real E..**$1.11**..7.21%

$1^

23.TGA..TransGlobe Energy Corp..**$0.55**..0%

48.PER..Sandridge Permian..**$0.45**..36.34%

15.ATV..Acorn International In..**$0.15**..0%

17.CSSEP..Chicken Soup for th..**$0.00**..11%

CHAPTER 20
CANADIAN STOCKS

In last year's book, "Income and Wealth from Self-Directed Investing" I listed all Canadian stocks paying a dividend greater than 3.5%. In this year's book, "Safer Better Dividend Investing" you will find 199 Canadian common stocks listed that were paying 3.5% dividends. This year I removed are all preferred shares. They were included last year.

All the preferred shares last year had low scores. They are more loans than stocks. They lack operating margins, analyst recommendations and other data used in the scoring software. There was not much point in including them.

What has been added to the Canadian charts is a side-by-side comparison of the 2020 score with the 2019 score. Those with more than a 10-point difference between this year's and last year's score are highlighted along with those stocks paying a 3.5% for the first time. You will notice that there is an overall decline in scores from one year to the next which reflects the impact of the pandemic on most businesses. The charts also now highlight the shares of companies appearing for the first time. By comparing this book with last year's book, you can identify companies that did not meet the qualifications for the new book.

In addition to the score for each stock you will find the stock symbol, the company name, the price of the stock (in Canadian dollars) .and the dividend percent paid. These are all stocks traded on the Toronto Stock Exchange (TSX).

The TSX was incorporated in 1878. Recognizing the richness of Canada's natural resources, it is not surprising that the TSX became the largest trader of mining stocks in the world.

SORTED BY SCORE

<SCORE>
2020.(2019)..Symbol..Company..$Price..Dividend%

76.(76)..RY..Royal Bank of Ca..$93.08..4.64%
74.(70)..FTS..Fortis Inc……..$54.75..3.49%
73.(NEW)..AP.UN..Allied Prop ..$40.96..4.03%
72.(70)..CNQ..Canadian Natural Re.$23.93..7.10%
72.(72)..MIC..Genworth MI Cana.$33.09..6.53%
70.(60)..ENB..Enbridge Inc……...$40.70..7.96%
70.(75)..TRP..TransCanada Energ..$61.00..5.31%
70
69.(67)..MFC..Manulife Financ.$17.93..6%
69.(64)..REI.UN..Real Estate Invest..$14.76..10%
68.(58)..AL..AltaGas Ltd……$16.65..6.13%
67.(73)..CM..Can Imperial Bank…$91.12..6.41%
67.(NEW)..MG..Magna Internat$61.91..3.48%
67.(64)..MRG.UN..Morguard North$14.18..4.93%
67.(NEW)..QSR..Restaurant Brands .$54.17..3.80%
67.(59)..SRU.UN..Smartcentres..$20.18..9.17%
66.(74)..BMO..Bank of Montreal..$72.02..5.89%
66.(74)..BNS..Bank of Nova Scotia…$56.88..6.33%
66.(64)..NA..National Bank of …$62.09..4.57%
65.(NEW)..CWB..Can West Bank..$22.88..5.07%
65.(NEW)..CNU..CNOOC Ltd……$156.40..9%
65.(67)..PPL..Pembina Pipeline....$32.95..8%
65.(NEW)..RCI.B..Rogers Commu..$53.59..3.73%
64.(68)..SLF..Sun Life Financial …$48.96..6.49%

63.(57)..CU..Canadian Utilities L..$34.55..5.04%
63.(47)..CUF.UN..Cominar REIT..$8.14..8.85%
63.(NEW)..TOU..Tourmaline Oil ..$12.84..3.73%
62.(65)..EMA..Emera Inc.........$56.20..4.36%
62.(New)..FCR.UN..First Capital...$13.22..6.51%
61.(55)..AI..Atrium Mortgage Inv...$10.95..8.22%
61.(63)..LB..Laurentian Bank of C...$27.51..5.82%
61.(64)..NPI..Northland Power Inc..$34.96..3.43%
61.(56)..SJR.B..Shaw Communicat...$24.16..4.90%
60.(NEW)..CTC.A..Canadian Tire..$117.08..3.89%
60.(57)..DIR.UN..Dream Industrial ...$10.76..6.51%
60.(63)..D.UN..Dream Office REIT...$20.44..4.89%
60.(69)..GRT.UN...Granite REIT...$73.76..3.94%
60.(52)..GWO..Great-West Lifeco...$24.27..7.51%
60.(NEW)..IMO..Imperial Oil L...$22.76..3.82%
60.(54)..KEY..Keyera Corp.........$21.03..9.13%
60.(62)..POW..Power Corporati...$23.72..7.53%
60
59.(62)..ACO.X..AtcoLtd..............$41.71..4.17%
59.(69)..BCE...BCE Inc.................$56.77..6%
59.(NEW)..HBL.UN..Brand Leaders...$10.05..8%
59.(56)..BIP.UN..Brookfield Infrast...$55.71...6%
59.(62)..CPX...Capital Power Corp....$27.38..7.01%
59.(56)..KMP.UN...Killam Apt REI..$17.21..3.81%
59.(62)..NVU.UN..Northview Apt R.$34.96..4.66%
58.(59)...BPY.UN..Brookfield Property...$15.02..12%
58..(NEW)..IAG..IA Financial Corp..$45.87..5.15%
58..(NEW)..LIF..Labrador Iron Ore..$25.88...3.86%
58..(62)..PIF...Polaris Infrastructure ..$14.32..5.96%
57..(59)..AQN..Algonquin Power .$17.55....4.77%
57..(50)..FCA.U..Firm Capital Am..$6.21...3.80%
57..(64)..NXR.UN..Nexus Real Estate ..$1.54..10%
57..(64)..NPI..Northland Power Inc..$36.04..3.33%
57..(71)..SU..Suncor Energy Inc....$21.95...3.83%
57..(68)...T...Telus ....$23.05...5.05%
56...(50)..IGM..IGM Financial Inc....$33.49....7%

56..(NEW)..PKI…Parkland Corpo..$34.77..3.49%
56..(44)..TF…Timbercreek Financial….$8.26…8%
55..(50)..CU.X..Canadian Utilities...$34.99….4.98%
55..(26)..MBK.UN..Manulife US ..$6.48….7.70%
54..(57)..BEP.UN..Brookfield Renew..$66.91..4.44%
54..(47)..AGF.B....AGF Managem….$5.02…6.37%
54..(55)..ACO.Y…Atco Ltd.……$39.00….4.46
54..(61)..EIF...Exchange Income C..$26.94..8%
54..(48)..OLY..Olympia Finanl G..$32.00..8.63%
54..(46)..TCL.A...Transcontinental..$15.10…5.97%
53…(NEW)..FTT..Fining Internati..$19.11…4.29%
53..(62)..IPL...Inter Pipeline Ltd.……$11.81..4.06%
53..(51)..MRD..Melcor Develop……$7.70…4.16%
53..(56)..TNT.UN..True North REIT..$5.97….10%
52..(33)..HRR.UN..Australian REIT…$9.44..6.99%
52..(25)..RBN.UN..Blue Ribbon Inc…$6.27..7.66%
52..(21)..CIQ.UN..Canadian High Inc..$5.90..8.14%
52..(32)..CHP.UN..Choice Properties..$13.28.5.57%
52..(47)..GEI...Gibson Energy Inc….$21.95..6.20%
52..(43)..RCO.UN..Middlefield Can…$9.81…6.63%
52..(28)..MID.UN...Mint Income Fund..$5.05..9.50%
52..(57)..PZA..Pizza Pizza Royalty ...$8.17….6.91%
52..(62)..PRV.UN..Pro Real Estate Inv..$4.62…10%
51..(NEW)..ALC..Algoma Central Co..$10.06..4.77%
51..(52)..BEK.B..Becker Milk Co…$11.68....6.85%
51..(NEW)..FFH.U..Fairfax Financial..$254.74..3.93%
51..(NEW)..WTE..Westshore Term…$17.02…3.76%
50..(54)..BTB.UN..BTB REIT……….$3.10….10%
50..(NEW)..FCA.UN..Firm Capital Am..$6.00..5.37%
50..(NEW)..UFC…Urbanfund Corp….$0.65….4.62%
50
49..(51)..ADN..Acadian Timber Corp..$14.52...7.99%
49..(55)..CHR…Chorus Aviation.……$2.78…0.00%
49..(53)..CIX…CI Financial Corp……$18.09...3.98%
49..(59)..CRR.UN..Crombie REIT…$13.07…6.81%
49..(61)..UFS….Domtar Corp.……..$29.73…8.90%

49..(51)..FC……Firm Capital……….$11.47….8.16%
49..(NEW)..MAL..Magellan Aerosp...$6.67….6.30%
49...(49)..PLZ.UN..Plaza Retail REIT...$3.37..8.31%
49..(49)..RUS..Russel Metals Inc………$18.50...8%
49..(57)..SOT.UN…Slate Office REIT…$3.62…11%
49..(54)..SMU.UN..Summit Indust.REI.$11.26..4.80%
49..(49)..KEG.UN..The Keg Royalties….$8.85..4.75%
49..(46)..WJX….Wajax Corp………….$9.89….10%
48..(53)..AW.UN..A&W Revenue Roy..$28.10..4.27%
48..(25).EIT.UN…Canoe EIT Income …$9.11….13%
48..(57)..CRT.UN..CT REIT…$13.87….5.68%
48….(40)….FDI…Findev Inc………..$0.41…7.32%
48..(NEW)..HGI.UN...Global Telecom $8.40..8.57%
47..(65)..ARX..ARC Resources Ltd…$4.82…4.98%
47..(55)..AX.UN..Artis REIT… $7.82…6.91%
47..(61)..HR.UN…H&R REIT……$9.57….7%
47..(65)..INO.UN….Inovalis REIT...$7.61…..11%
47..(39)..SPS.A...Spotscene Group ..$3.25….9.23%
47..(50)..WCP..Whitecap . Inc……$4.99…4.01%
45..(44)..ISV...Information Servic..$16.50..4.85%
45..(46)..ITP..Intertape Polymer Gr.$15.22..5.38%
45..(50)..NWC..The North West Co ..$30.00..4.40%
45..(.52)..RNW..TransAlta Renew..$15.36...6.12%
44..(58)..AD..Alaris Royalty Corp...$12.95…9%
44..(NEW)..ADN..Aecon Group Inc..$14.76..4.34%
44..(59)..FCD...Firm Capital Propert..$4.70..10.64%
44..(New)..FCD.UN..Firm Capital P..$4.70…11%
44..(52)..FN..First National Financ..$29.46….6.62%
44..(47)..MR.UN…Melcor REIT…….$3.50…10%
44..(NEW)...ORC.B..Orca Explorati....$5.50..5.96%
43..(44…UP.U...Caribbean Utilities …15.56..4.52%
43..(36)...CRWN..Crown Capital Part..$3.26….18%
43..(42)..XTC..Exco Technologies …...$6.46…..6%
43..(38)..SJR.A...Shaw Communicat..$24.50….4.83%
43..(25)..SRT.U..Slate Retail REIT..…$6.94….12%
42..(36)..CWX..CanWel Building Mat..$5.02….10%

42..(43)..FRU...Freehold Royalties Ltd…$3.73..4.83%
42..(52)..MKP..McCan Mortgage Corp..$12.83..11%
41..(46)..HPS..Hammond Power Soluti..$6.47...5.26%
41..(NEW)..TII…Terra Firma Capital ..$23.05..5.05%
41..(66)..VET…Vermillion Energy….$5.61….0.00%
41..(44)..WFC…Wall Financial Corp…$18.50….11%
40..(30)..CEE…Centamin PLC…………$3.20…3.49%
40..(49)..ET…Evertz Technologies ….$13.29….2.71%
40..(34)..H…Hydro One Ltd………27.73….4%
40..(35)..ZZZ..Sleep Country Canada..$19.06..0.00%
40
39..(34)..FAP..Aberdeen Asia-Pacific ..$2.94...9.18%
39..(57)..AFN…AG Growth……..$27.20….2.21%
39..(39)..CSW.B...Corby Spirit …$13.87….5.77%
39..(40)..CSW.A...Corby Spirit …$15.90….5.03%
39..(26)..ENI.UN..Energy Income ..$1.20….10.00%
39..(NEW)..NEO...Neo Performance ..$8.66..4.62%
39..(47)..TCL.B..Transcontinental Inc..$15.10..5.96%
38..(59)..HRR.UN..Automotive Prop REI..$9.06..9%
38..(NEW)..GBT..BMTC Group Inc..$8.10..3.46%
38..(48)..BPF.UN..Boston Pizza Royal..$7.13..0.00%
38..(43)..CSH.UN..Chartwell Retirem…$9.36..6.30%
38..(19)..MMP.UN..Precious Metals ….$2.52...4.76%
37..(27)...BDT..Bird Construction Inc…$6.05...6.45%
37..(42)..CMG..Computer Modelling …$4.63...4.48%
37..(41)..PIC.A..Premium Income Corp..$3.37..12%
37...(27)..RAY.A..Stingray Group Inc...$4.95..6.06%
37..(49)..SPB..Superior Plus Group…$11.86...6.07%
36..(36)..FSZ…Fiera Capital Corp….$10.24..8%
36...(NEW)..KBL..K-Bro Linen Inc…$27.75..4.29%
36...(46)..LNF…Leon's Furniture Ltd...$13.50..3.56%
36..(33)..SXP……Supremex Inc………$1.13....23%
36..(57)..WIR.U..WPT Industrial REIT...$13.50..5.63%
35...(32)..EXE….Extendicare Inc….$5.64….8.51%
35...(35)..KPT…KP Tissue Inc………$11.85….6.08%
35..(22)..MFR.UN..Manulife Floating Rate ..$6.05..11%

35..(55)..MBN...MBN Corp…………..$6.07….5.27%
35..(NEW)..PSI..Parson Systems Inc…..$6.84….11%
34..(43)..ACD..Accord Financial Corp…$6.15..3.25%
34..(NEW)..BRE..Bridgemarq Real Est..$11.70..12%
34..(36)..SBC…Brompton Split Banc ….$8.20…..15%
34..(26)..BGI.UN..Brookfield Global In..$6.24...9.50%
34..(31)..ERE.UN..European Resid REI..$4.11..3.93%
34..(NEW)..TPX.B..Molson Coors Can..$48.75..6.15%
34..(NEW)..TPX.A..Molson Coors Can..$48.00..5.84%
34..(NEW)..QSP.UN..Restaurant Brands ..$75.3..3.70%
33..(NEW)..CNE...Canacol Energy Ltd..$3.86...5.39%
33..(41)..NEXA….Nexa Resources…….$6.29…6.00%
33..(NEW)..SFC..Sagicor Financial Co ..$6.65…4.78%
32..(19)..RAY.B…Stingray Group Inc…$4.89….6.13%
32..(20)..TXT.UN..Top 10 Split Trust….$1.48….15%
31..(40)..BCF..Builders Capital Mortg C..$8.60….9%
31..(36)..CHE.UN..Chemtrade Logistics..$5.44…11%
31..(52)..CGX……Cineplex……………$8.41…0.00%
31..(27)GMP..GMP Capital Inc..………$1.32…7.58%
31..(NEW)..MX….Methanex Corp……$26.15…0.76%
31..(33)..SWP…Swiss Water Decaf ….$2.68…0.00%
31..(47)..TOG…TORC Oil & Gas Ltd….$1.72…0.00%
30..(38)..AFCC...Automotive Finco Cor..$1.29....16%
30..(NEW)...ERF..Enerplus Corp……$3.44….3.49%
30..(47)..SIA..Sienna Senior Living ….$10.32…9%
30
29...(43)..CHW..Chesswood Group Ltd…$3.87…11%
29..(58)..MRT.UN…Morguard REIT…..$4.97….10%
29..(NEW)..SYZ……Sylogist Ltd……...$11.73..3.75%
29..(NEW)..Y……Yellow Pages Ltd…$8.10….5.43%
28...(48)..RME..Rocky Mountain Dealer..$4.35...1.38%
26..(57)..ESI……….. Ensign Energy…$0.73..32.88%
26..(40)..RSI………Rogers Sugar Inc…$4.80….7.50%
27..(NEW)..NWX…Newport Exploration ..$0.36..11%
27..(NEW)..TWM..Tidewater Midstream..$0.80..5.00%
26..(53)..IVQ………Invesque Inc……$3.00…0.00%

26..(31)..MKZ.UN..Mackenzie Master L…$0.82..14%
26..(23)..MCS……McChip Resources …$0.45..8.89%
24..(23)..CLR…Clearwater Seafoods I…$5.70…4%
24..(27)..INP……Input Captial Corp…..$0.78….5.13%
24..(38)..WEF…Western Forest Products..$1.06…0%
21.(19)..USF.UN..US Financials Income..$5.47..9.14%
20.(19)..CDD.UN..Core Canadian Divide..$4.07..8.19%
20..(28)..ELC…Elysee Development Corp..$0.34..12%
20..(22)..GMN….GobiMin Inc………….$0.26….4%
20..(20)..WBE…WestBond Enterprises..$0.31..3.23%
20
19..(NEW)..WIR.UN..WPT Indu.REIT.$18.13….5.81%
18..(16)..HOM.UN…BSR REIT…$14.36….4.63%
17..(17)..PRM…Big Pharma Split Corp….$13.44…..9%
17...(51)..TGL…TransGlobe Energy...$0.78….0%
17..(21)..TSL…Tree Island Steel Ltd…$2.05….3.90%
16..(24)..HOM.U…BSR REIT…$10.96….4.69%
13..(21)..DS…Dividend Select 15 Corp..$6.23..11.10%
13..(30)..DRA.UN..Dream Hard Asset A.$4.82..8.30%
13..(9)..GDV..Global Dividend Growth ..$9.39..13%
10..(9)..RE……RE Royalties Ltd……$1.03….3.88%
9..(NEW)..ENS..E Split Corp……$11.88…13%

CHAPTER 21
CANADIAN STOCKS ALPHA SORT

In Chapter 21 the same information is sorted alphabetically by company name. This can be useful for a quick stock risk on a company that you may have read about or been asked about.

<SCORE>
2020..(2019)..Symbol..Company..$Price..Dividend%
A
48..(53)..AW.UN..**A&W Revenue Roy..**$28.10..4.27%
39..(34)..FAP..**Aberdeen Asia-Pacific In**..$2.94..9.18%
49..(51)..ADN..**Acadian Timber Corp**..$14.52...7.99%
34..(43)..ACD..**Accord Financial Corp**..$6.55….3.10%
44..(NEW)..ADN..**Aecon Group Inc**..$14.76….4.34%
39..(57)..AFN…**AG Growth**……..$27.20….2.21%
54...(47)..AGF.B..**AGF Management**...$5.02..6.37%
44..(58)...AD..**Alaris Royalty Corp**…$12.95….9%
51..(NEW)..ALC..**Algoma Central Co..**$10.06..4.77%
57..(59)..AQN..**Algonquin Power & U**..$17.55..4.77%
73..(NEW)..AP.UN...**Allied Proper…**$40.96….4.03%
68..(58)..ALA…**AltaGas Ltd**………$16.65….6.13%
45..(NEW)..APY..**Anglo Pacific Gr**…$2.83….5.44%
47..(65)..ARX..**ARC Resources Ltd**...$4.82….4.98%
47..(55)..AX.UN..**Artis REIT**…. $7.82….6.91%
59...(62)....ACO.X…**Atco Ltd**…$41.71….4.17%
54….(55)….ACO.Y..**Atco Ltd**..$39.00….4.46%
61..(55)..AI..**Atrium Mortgage I**..$10.95..8.22%

52..(33)..HRR.UN..**Australian REIT**..$9.44..6.99%
30..(38)..AFCC..**Automotive Finco C**..$1.29...16%
38...(59)..HRR.UN..**Automotive Pro**...$9.06....9%
B
66..(74)..BMO..**Bank of Montreal**..$72.02..5.89%
66..(74)..BNS..**Bank of Nova Scotia**..$56.88..6.33%
59..(69)..BCE......**BCE Inc**...........$56.77..6%
51..(BEK.B...**Becker Milk Co**.........$11.68..6.85%
17...(17)..PRM..**Big Pharma Split Co**.$13.44..9.21%
37..(27)..BDT..**Bird Construction Inc**..$6.05..6.45%
52..(25)..RBN.UN..**Blue Ribbon Inc**..$6.27..7.66%
38..(NEW)..GBT..**BMTC Group Inc..**$8.10...3.46%
38..(48)..BPF.UN..**Boston Pizza Roya**..$7.13..0.00%
59..(NEW)..HBL.UN..**Brand Leaders In**..$10.05..8%
34..(NEW)..BRE..**Bridgemarq Real E..**$11.70....12%
34..(36)..SBC..**Brompton Split Banc**...$8.20....15%
59..(56)..BIP.UN..**Brookfield Infras**...$55.71...6%
58..(59)..BPY.UN..**Brookfield Prop**....$15.02..12%
34..(26)..BGI.UN..**Brookfield Global**..$6.24...9.50%
54..(57)..BEP.UN..**Brookfield Renew**..$66.91..4.44%
16..(24)..HOM.U...**BSR REIT**..$10.96....4.69%
18..(16)..HOM.UN..**BSR REIT**...$14.36....4.63%
50..(54)....BTB.UN..**BTB Real Estate .**$3.10...10%
31..(40)..BCF..**Builders Capital Mor..**$8.60...9%
C
33..(NEW)..CNE..**Canacol Energy..**$3.86..5.39%
52..(21)..CIQ.UN..**Canadian High I**..$5.90..8.14%
67...(73)...CM..**Canadian Imperial** ..$91.12..6.41%
72..(70)..CNQ..**Canadian Natural R..**$23.93..7.10%
60..(NEW..CTC.A..**Canadian Tire...**$117.08..3.89%
55..(50)..CU.X..**Canadian Utilities ..**$34.99..4.98%
63..(57)..CU..**Canadian Utilities** .....$34.55..5.04%
65..(NEW)..CWB..**Canadian W Bank**..$22.88..5.07%
48..(25)..EIT.UN..**Canoe EIT Income** ..$9.11..13%
42....(36)...CWX..**CanWel Building M..**$5.02..10%
59..(62)..CPX...**Capital Power Corp**..$27.38...7.01%

43..(44)..CUP.U..**Caribbean Utilities**..$15.56..4.52%
40..(30)..CEE......**Centamin P**..........$3.20...3.49%
38..(43)..CSH.UN..**Chartwell Retire**....$9.36..6.30%
31..(36)..CHE.UN..**Chemtrade Logis**....$5.44...11%
29..(43)..CHW..**Chesswood Group Ltd**...$3.87...11%
52..(32)..CHP.UN..**Choice Properties R**.$13.28...5.57%
49..(55)..CHR.......**Chorus Aviation**...$2.78....0.00%
31..(52)..CGX...........**Cineplex**.........$8.41....0.00%
49..(53)..CIX...**CI Financial Corp**.....$18.09....3.98%
24...(23)..CLR..**Clearwater Seafoods** ......$5.70....4%
65..(NEW)..CNU...**CNODC Ltd**.........$156.40....9%
63...(47)..CUF.UN...**Cominar REIT**....$8.14....8.85%
37..(42)..CMG..**Computer Modelling G**..$4.63..4.48%
39..(39)..CSW.B..**Corby Spirit and Win**..$13.87..5.77%
39..(40)..CSW.A..**Corby Spirit and Win**..$15.90..5.03%
20..(19)...CDD.UN..**Core Canadian Div**..$4.07....8.19%
46..(NEW)...CJR.B..**Corus Entertainm**...$2.56....9.38%
49..(59)..CRR.UN..**Crombie REIT**........$13.07...6.81%
43..(36)..CRWN..**Crown Capital Part**....$3.26....18%
48..(57)..CRT.UN..**CT REIT**...........$13.87....5.68%

D

!3...(21)..DS..**Dividend Select 15** .... $6.23..11.10%
49..(61)..UFS...**Domtar Corp**............$29.73....8.90%
13..(30)..DRA.UN...**Dream Hard Asset** ..$4.82..8.30%
60..(57)..DIR.UN..**Dream Industr REIT**..$10.76..6.51%
60..(63)..D.UN..**Dream Office REIT**.....$20.44.....4.89%

E

9..(NEW)..ENS..**E Split Corp**..$11.88..13%
20..(28)..ELC..**Elysee Develop** ...$0.34..12%
62..(65)..EMA...**Emera Inc**...$56.20....4.36%
70..(60)..ENB..**Enbridge Inc**...$40.70....7.96%
39..(26)..ENI.UN..**Energy Inc**..$1.20....10.00%
30..(NEW)..ERF..**Enerplus Co**..$3.44....3.49%
26..(57)..ESI.. **Ensign Energy**..$0.73..32.88%
34..(31)..ERE.UN..**European Resi**..$4.11.,3.93%
40..(49)..ET..**Evertz Technolog**....$13.29..2.71%

54..(61)..EIF..**Exchange Income** ..$26.94..8%
43...(42)..XTC..**Exco Technolog**...$6.46....6%
35..(32)..EXE..**Extendicare Inc**...$5.64....8.51%
F
51..(NEW)..FFH..**Fairfax Financi**..$254.74..3.93%
36..(36)..FSZ..**Fiera Capital Corp**..$10.24....8%
48..(40)..FDI..**Findev Inc**..............$0.41.....7.32%
53..(NEW)..FTT..**Fining Int**.........$19.11....4.29%
49..(51)...FC...**Firm Capital........**$11.47....8.16%
44..(59)..FC..**Firm Capital.........**$4.70....10.64%
57..(50)..FCA.U..**Firm Capital**.......$6.21..3.80%
50..(NEW)..FCA.UN..**Firm Capital..**$6.00..5.37%
49..(51)..FC..**Firm Capital Mort**......$11.47..8%
44..(New)..FCD.UN..**Firm Capital .....**$4.70..11%
62..(New)..FCR.UN..**First Capital** ....$13.22..6.51%
44..(52)..FN..**First National Fin**.......$29.46..6.62%
74..(70)..FTS...**Fortis Inc**..............$54.75....3.49%
42..(43)..FRU..**Freehold Royal**.........$3.73..4.83%
45..(NEW)..FRO.UN..**Fronsac R**.......$0.54...4.73%
G
72..(72)..MIC..**Genworth MI** $33.09....6.53%
52..(47)..GEI..**Gibson Energy** .$21.95....6.20%
13..(9)...GDV...**Global Dividend**..$9.39..13%
48..(NEW)..HGI.UN..**Global Tele**..$8.40..8.57%
31..(27)..GMP..**GMP Capital Inc**..$1.32..7.58%
20..(22)..GMN...**GobiMin Inc**........$0.26....4%
45..(NEW)..GDL..**Goodfellow ..**$4.99....4.01%
60...(69)..GRT.UN..**Granite REIT**..$73.76..3.94%
60..(52)..GWO..**Great-West Life**..$24.27..7.51%
H
47..(61)..HR.UN...**H&R REIT**......$9.57....7%
41..(46)...HPS.A..**Hammond Pow**..$6.47..5.26%
40..(34)..H...**Hydro One Ltd**...,,,,,27.73....4%
I
58..(NEW)..IAG...**IA Financial** ..$45.87..5.15%
56...(50)..IGM...**IGM Financial Inc**..$33.49..7%

60..(NEW)..IMO..**Imperial Oil Ltd**..$22.76..3.82
45..(44)..ISV..**Information Serv**..$16.50….4.85%
46..(48)..INE..**Innergex Ren**…...$22.00….3.27%
47..(65)..INO.UN..**Inovalis REIT...**$7.61....11%
24..(27)..INP…**Input Captial** …$0.78….5.13%
53..62)..IPL..**Inter Pipeline Ltd**...$11.81….4.06%
45..(46)..ITP..**Intertape Polymer**…$15.22.5.38%
26..(53)..IVQ..**Invesque Inc**…….$3.00….0.00%
J - K
36..(NEW)..KBL..**K-Bro Linen..**$27.75..4.29%
60..(54)..KEY…**Keyera Corp**…$21.03..…9.13%
59..(56)..KMP.UN..**Killam Apar..**$17.21….3.81%
35..(35)..KPT..**KP Tissue Inc**…$11.85….6.08%
L
58..(NEW)..LIF..**Labrador Iron** ..$25.88..3.86%
61..(63)..LB..**Laurentian Bank** ..$27.51…5.82%
36..(46)..LNF..**Leon's Furniture**...$13.50..3.56%
M
26..(31)..MKZ.UN..**Mackenzie** ..$0.82..14%
49..(NEW)..MAL..**Magellan Aer**..$6.67..6.30%
67..(NEW)..MG..**Magna Intern**..$61.91..3.48%
69..(67)..MFC..**Manulife Fin**…..$17.93….6%
35..(22)...MFR.UN..**Manulife Fl**..$6.05..11%
55..(26)..MBK.UN..**Manulife US..**$6.48..7.70%
35..(55)..MBN..**MBN Corp**…….$6.07….5.27%
42..(52)..MKP...**McCan Mort**…..$12.83..11%
26..(23)..MCS..**McChip Reso**...$0.45….8.89%
53...(51)..MRD..**Melcor Dev**….$7.70….4.16%
44..(47)..Mr.UN..**Melcor REIT**…..$3.50..10%
31..(NEW)...MX..**Methanex ….**$26.15….0.76%
52..(43)..RCO.UN...**Middlefield**..$9.81..6.63%
52..(28)..MID.UN..**Mint Income**..$5.05..9.50%
34..(NEW)..TPX.B..**Molson Coor..**$48.75..6.15%
34..(NEW)..TPX.A..**Molson Coor**..$48.00..5.84%
67.. (64)..MRG.UN..**Morguard N**...$14.18..4.93%
29..(58)..MRT.UN...**Morguard R**…$4.97….10%

N

66..(64)..NA...**National Bank** ...$62.09..4.57%
39..(NEW)..NEO..**Neo Perfor**....$8.66....4.62%
27..(NEW)..NWX..**Newport E**....$0.36....11%
33..(41)..NEXA..**Nexa Resources..**$6.29..6.00%
57..64)..NXR.UN..**Nexus Real E**...$1.54....10%
57..64)..NPI..**Northland Power** ..$36.04....3.33%
59..(62)..NVU.UN..**Northview Apa**..$34.96..4.66%
53..(47)..NWH.UN..**Northwest Hea**..$10.72..46%
61..(64)...NPI...**Northland ower Inc**...$34.96..3.43%

O

54..(48)..OLY..**Olympia Financl**..$32.00..8.63%
44..(NEW)..ORC.B..**Orca Explor**..$5.50...5.96%

P/Q

56..(NEW)..PK..**Parkland Corp**...$34.77..3.49%
35..(NEW)..PSI..**Parson System**....$6.84....11%
65..(67)..PPL..**Pembina Pipeline**.....$32.95..8%
52..(57)..PZA..**Pizza Pizza Roya**..$8.17..6.91%
49..(49)..PLZ.UN..**Plaza Retail** ...$3.37....8.31%
58..(62)..PIF..**Polaris Infrastru**..$14.32..5.96%
60..(62)..POW..**Power Corpor**...$23.72....7.53%
38..(19)..MMP.UN..**Precious Me**..$2.52....4.76%
37..(41)..PIC.A..**Premium Incom**..$3.37....12%
52..(62)..PRV.UN..**Pro Real Esta**..$4.62....10%

R

10.(9)..RE..**RE Royalties ....**$1.03....3.88%
67.(NEW)..QSR..**Restaurant Bra**..$54.17..3.80%
34.(NEW)..QSP.UN..**Restaurant Bra**..$75.33..3.70%
69.(64)..REI.UN..**Riocan Real Estate..**$14.76..10%
28..48)..RME...**Rocky Mountain Deal**..$4.35..1.38%
65..(NEW)..RCI.B..**Rogers Communic**..$53.59..3.73%
26..(40)..RSI..**Rogers Sugar Inc**.......$4.80....7.50%
76....(76)..RY...**Royal Bank** ....$93.08....4.64%
49..(49)..RUS..**Russel Metals Inc.........**$18.50..8%

S

33.(NEW)..SFC..**Sagicor Financial**..$6.65..4.78%

61.(56)..SJR.B..**Shaw Communica**.$24.16..4.90%
43.(38)..SJR.A..**Shaw Communica**..$24.5...83%
30.(47)..SIA..**Sienna Senior Living**..$10.32..9%
49.(57)..SOT.UN..**Slate Office RE**...$3.62..11%
46.(50)..SRT.UN..**Slate Retail RE**..$9.27….13%
43.(25)..SRT.U..**Slate Retail REIT**..$6.94..12%
40.(35)..ZZZ...**Sleep Country Can**..$19.06..0.00%
67.(59)..SRU.UN...**Smartcentres** ..$20.18..9.17%
47.(39)..SPS.A..**Spotscene Group**..$3.25..9.23%
32.(19)..RAY.B..**Stingray Group**..$4.89..6.13%
37.(27)..RAY.A..**Stingray Group...**$4.95..6.06%
49.(54)..SMU.UN..**Summit Indust**..$11.26..4.80%
64.(68)..SLF..**Sun Life Financial...**$48.96..6.49%
57.(71)..SU..**Suncor Energy Inc**...$21.95..3.83%
37.(49)..SPB..**Superior Plus Gr..**$11.86..6.07%
36.(33)..SXP..**Supremex Inc**……$1.13...23%
31.(33)..SWP..**Swiss Water Decaf..**$2.68..0.00%
29.(NEW)..SYZ..**Sylogist Ltd**….$11.73….3.75%

T

72.(NEW)..TRP..**TC Energy Corp**..$55.94..5.79%
57.(68)..T…….**Telus Corp**……..$23.05….5.05%
41.(NEW)..TII..**Terra Firma Capi**.$23.05….5.05%
49.(49)..KEG.UN..**The Keg Royalties**..$8.85..4.75%
45.(50)..NWC…**The North West Co**..$30.00...4.40%
72.(74)..TD..**The Toronto-Dom Bank**..$59.82...5.27%
27.(NEW)..TWM..**Tidewater Midstrm**..$0.80...5.00%
56.(44)..TF…**Timbercreek Financial**…$8.26….8%
32.(20)..TXT.UN..**Top 10 Split Trust**…$1.48…..15%
31.(47)..TOG..**TORC Oil & Gas Ltd**….$1.72….0.00%
63.(NEW)..TOU..**Tourmaline Oil Corp**..$12.84..3.73%
45.(.52)..RNW..**TransAlta Renewables**...$15.36..6.12%
70.(75)..TRP..**Transcanada Energy**….$61.00….5.31%
54.(46)..TCL.A...**Transcontinental Inc**...$15.10..5.97%
39.(47)..TCL.B..**Transcontinental Inc**..$15.10...5.96%
17..(51)..TGL..**TransGlobe Energy** …....$0.78….0%
17.(21)..TSL…**Tree Island Steel Ltd**…$2.05….3.90%

53.(56)..TNT.UN..**True North Comm R..**$5.97....10%
U
50.(NEW)..UFC...**Urbanfund Corp**...$0.65....4.62%
21.(19)..USF.UN..**US Financials Incom**..$5.47..9.14%
V
41.(66)..VET...**Vermillion Energy**....$5.61....0.00%
W
49.(46)..WJX......**Wajax Corp......**$9.89....10%
41.(44)..WFC..**Wall Financial Corp**..$18.50..11%
20.(20)..WBE..**WestBond Enterprises**..$0.31..3.23%
24..(38)..WEF..**Western Forest Produc..**$1.06..0%
51.(NEW)..WTE..**Westshore Termin**..$17.02..3.76%
47.(50)..WCP..**Whitecap Resources Inc**..$2.22..8%
36.(57)..WIR.U..**WPT Industrial RE..**$13.50..5.63%
19.(NEW)..WIR.UN..**WPT Industrial**..$18.13..5.81%
XYZ
29.(NEW)..Y..**Yellow Pages Ltd**......$8.10..5.43%

CHAPTER 22
CANADIAN STOCKS BY DIVIDEND %

In Chapter 22 the high dividend stocks are sorted by descending dividend percent. This is useful when you are trying to find a safe stock paying a higher dividend to offset the lower dividend of a stock you may have added to your portfolio. All those stocks with a score over 50 have been highlighted. Several high scoring stocks are paying a dividend under 6%.

The way the score is constructed, it not unusual for a company paying a dividend of less than 3% to have a score in the sixties, even in the seventies. Many companies can be financially strong but not paying a high enough dividend to interest someone looking for a high, safe dividend yield.

In the USA charts stocks paying 6% or more were selected. The difference between the US and Canadian dividend stocks is how few stocks you have in Canada paying a dividend over 6% to choose from. To get enough stocks to consider for Canadian portfolios I dropped the Canadian limit down to those paying a dividend of 3.5% or more.

There are “experts” who advise that you should diversify your portfolio by including stocks from several countries The income tax advantages given to Canadians receiving dividends from only Canadian stocks needs to be compared to US government tax hold backs and currency exchange costs if Canadian's invest in US stocks. The NYSE lists hundreds of foreign corporations.

It is interesting that several large Canadian corporations increased their dividend payouts during the COVID-19 recession. The only other country where this occurred was China which was the first to go into this recession and first to come out.

All the projected losses that those relying on dividend payments would suffer has not come to pass. This is apparently due to blue-chip Canadian companies being financially strong coming into 2020. The strength in dividend payments was not carried over to Canadian share prices. They down 17% in the Fall of 2020 from where they were in February.

The 6 large Canadian banks that operate coast-to-coast through a network of thousands of branches dominate the Canadian blue-chips. A good example would be TD with almost as many branches in the USA as they have in Canada. TD is listed on both the TSX and the NYSE.

Unlike the UK and other countries, the Canadian government did not prohibit the banks from paying dividends during the pandemic. They did prohibit the banks from increasing dividends, buying back their shares and increasing executive salaries. The government wanted the banks to grow their reserves.. The chances of the Canadian banks cutting dividends in the future is small. Some of these banks have been paying increasing dividends without interruptions for far more than 100 years.

<SCORE>
2020.(2019)..Symbol..Company..$Price..Dividend%

26.(57)..ESI..Ensign Energy..$0.73..**32.88%**
36.(33)..SXP..Supremex Inc….$1.13..**23%**
43.(36)..CRWN..Crown Capital Par..$3.26..**18%**
30.(38)..AFCC..Automotive Finco …$1.29..**16%**
34..(36)..SBC..Brompton Split Banc ..$8.20..**15%**
32..(20)..TXT.UN..Top 10 Split Trust…$1.48..**15%**
26.(31)..MKZ.UN..Mackenzie Mas….$0.82...**14%**
48..(25)..EIT.UN...Canoe EIT Inco….$9.11….**13%**
9.(NEW)..ENS..E Split Corp…..$11.88…**13%**
13..(9)..GDV...Global Dividend Gro….$9.39...**13%**
46.(50)..SRT.UN..Slate Retail REIT…$9.27….**13%**
34.(NEW)..BRE.Bridgemarq Real E..$11.70….**12%**
58.(59)...BPY.UN..Brookfield Pro….$15.02….**12%**
20.(28)..ELC...Elysee Develop….$0.34…..**12%**
37.(41)..PIC.A..Premium Inc…$3.37….**12%**
43.(25)..SRT.U..Slate Retail R…$6.94….**12%**
!3.(21)..DS..Dividend Select 15 $6.23....**11.10%**
31.(36)..CHE.UN....Chemtrade Log…$5.44…**11%**
29.(43)..CHW...Chesswood Group .$3.87….**11%**
44.(New)..FCD.UN...Firm Capital ..$4.70….**11%**
35.(22)..MFR.UN…Manulife Float..$6.05…**11%**
42.(52)..MKP…McCan Mortgage C..$12.83..**11%**
27.(NEW)..NWX…Newport Explor...$0.36...**11%**
35.(NEW)..PSI…Parson Systems ..$6.84….**11%**
49.(57)..SOT.UN…Slate Office R...$3.62….**11%**
41.(44)..WFC.Wall Financial Corp….$18.50….**11%**
44.(59)..FCD..Firm Capital Property...$4.70..**10.64%**
10%
50.(54)..BTB.UN..BTB Real Estate ...$3.10..**10%**
42.(36)..CWX..CanWel Building Mate…$5.02..**10%**
39.(26)..ENI.UN..Energy Income...$1.20..**10%**
44.(47)..MR.UN..Melcor REIT…$3.50..**10%**
29.(58)..MRT..Morguard REIT…….$4.97..**10%**
57.(64)..NXR.UN..Nexus Real Estat…$1.54..**10%**
52.(62)..PRV.UN..Pro Real Estate…..$4.62..**10%**
69.(64)..REI.UN..Riocan REIT….$14.76..**10%**

53.(56)..TNT.UN..True North .....$5.97..**10%**
49.(46)..WJX..Wajax Corp.........$9.89..**10%**
34.(26)..BGI.UN..Brookfield Glob..$6.24..**9.50%**
52.(28)..MID.UN..Mint Income ...$5.05..**9.50%**
46.(NEW)..CJR.B..Corus Entertai.....$2.56..**9.38%**
47.(39)..SPS.A..Spotscene Group ..$3.25..**9.23%**
17.(17)..PRM..Big Pharma Split...$13.44..**9.21%**
39.(34)..FAP..Aberdeen Asia-Pacific ..$2.94..**9.18%**
67.(59)..SRU.UN..Smartcentres R...$20.10..**9.17%**
21.(19)..USF.UN..US Financials I...$5.47..**9.14%**
60.(54)..KEY..Keyera Corp.........$21.03..**9.13%**
44.(58)..AD..Alaris Royalty Corp......$12.95..**9%**
31.(40)..BCF..Builders Capital Mortg...$8.60..**9%**
38.(59)..HRR.UN..Automotive Proper....$9.06..**9%**
65.(NEW)...CNU..CNODC Ltd.........$156.40...**9%**
30.(47)..SIA...Sienna Senior Living Inc..$10.32..**9%**
9%
49.(61)..UFS..Domtar Corp............$29.70...**8.90%**
26.(23)..MCS..McChip Resources Inc...$0.45..**8.89%**
63.(47)..CUF.UN..Cominar REIT......,$8.14..**8.85%**
54.(48)..OLY..Olympia Financial G...$32.00..**8.63%**
48.(NEW)..HGI.UN..Global Telecom..$8.40..**8.57%**
35.(32)..EXE....Extendicare Inc........$5.64..**8.51%**
13.(30)..DRA.UN...Dream Hard Asset..$4.82...**8.30%**
49.(49)..PLZ.UN..Plaza Retail REIT.......$3.37..**8.31%**
61.(55)..AI...Atrium Mortgage Inves....$10.95..**8.22%**
20.(19)..CDD.UN...Core Can ......$4.07..**8.19%**
49.(51)..FC...Firm Capital...$11.47..**8.16%**
52.(21)..CIQ.UN..Canadian High Inc..$5.90..**8.14%**
59.(NEW)..HBL.UN..Brand Leaders ...$10.05..**8%**
54.(61)..EIF...Exchange Income Corp...$26.94..**8%**
36.(36)..FSZ..Fiera Capital Corp..$10.24..**8%**
49.(51)..FC...Firm Capital Mortgage ..$11.47..**8%**
65.(67)..PPL..Pembina Pipeline Corp...$32.95..**8%**
49.(49)..RUS...Russel Metals Inc....$18.50..**8%**
56.(44)..TF..Timbercreek Financial...$8.26..**8%**

47.(50)..WCP..Whitecap Resources Inc..$2.22..**8%**
8%
49.(51)..ADN..Acadian Timber Corp..$14.52....**7.99%**
70.(60)...ENB..Enbridge Inc……….$40.70….**7.96%**
55.(26)..MBK.UN..Manulife US Regio$6.48….**7.70%**
52.(25)..RBN.UN..Blue Ribbon Inc...$6.27….**7.66%**
31.(27)..GMP...GMP Capital Inc..$1.32…**7.58%**
60.(62)..POW..Power Corporation ..$23.72….**7.53%**
60.(52)..GWO..Great-West Lifeco…$24.27...**7.51%**
26.(40)..RSI..Rogers Sugar Inc…..$4.80….**7.50%**
53.(47)..NWH.UN..Northwest Health…..$10.72..**7.46%**
48.(40)..FDI...Findev Inc…..………$0.41....**7.32%**
72.(70)..CNQ..Canadian Natural Res.$23.93….**7.10%**
59.(62)..CPX..Capital Power Corp…$27.38….**7.01%**
47.(61)..HR.UN..H&R REIT……..…$9.57….**7%**
56.(50)..IGM..IGM Financial Inc….$33.49….**7%**
7%
52.(33)..HRR.UN..Australian REIT …..$9.44..**6.99%**
47.(55)..AX.UN..Artis REIT…...$7.82….**6.91%**
52.(57)..PZA..Pizza Pizza Royalty…..$8.17....**6.91%**
51.(52)..BEK.B..Becker Milk Co….$11.68....**6.85%**
49.(59)..CRR.UN..Crombie REIT..$13.07….**6.81%**
52.(43)..RCO.UN..Middlefield Can G..$9.81….**6.63%**
44.(52)..FN..First National Financial ..$29.46….**6.62%**
72.(72)..MIC..Genworth MI Canada $33.09…..**6.53%**
60.(57)..DIR.UN..Dream Industrial ....$10….**6.51%**
62.(New)..FCR.UN...First Capital .$13.22….**6.51%**
64.(68)..SLF..Sun Life Financial ..$48.96….**6.49%**
37.(27)..BDT..Bird Construction Inc..$6.05….**6.45%**
67.(73)..CM..Can Imperial Bank of Com..$91.12….**6.41%**
54.(47)...AGF.B..AGF Management…$5.02….**6.37%**
66.(74)..BNS...Bank of Nova Scotia.$56.88….**6.33%**
38.(43)..CSH.UN...Chartwell Retire...$9.36….**6.30%**
49.(NEW)..MAL...Magellan Aero….$6.67….**6.30%**
52.(47)..GEI..Gibson Energy Inc.….$21.95….**6.20%**
34.(NEW)..TPX.B..Molson Coors…$48.75….**6.15%**

68.(58)..ALA...AltaGas Ltd.........$16.65....**6.13%**
32.(19)..RAY.B..Stingray Group .....$4.89....**6.13%**
45.(.52)..RNW..TransAlta Renew...$15.36....**6.12%**
35.(35)..KPT..KP Tissue Inc....$11.85....**6.08%**
37.(49)..SPB...Superior Plus Gro....$11.86....**6.07%**
37.(27)..RAY.A...Stingray Group I....$4.95....**6.06%**
59.(69)..BCE...BCE Inc.............$56.77....**6%**
59.(56)..BIP.UN...Brookfield Infrastru.$55.71....**6%**
43.(42)..XTC..Exco Technologies......$6.46....**6%**
69.(67)..MFC...Manulife Financial ...$17.93....**6%**
33.(41)..NEXA..Nexa Resources......$6.29....**6.00%**
6%
54.(46)..TCL.A..Transcontinental....$15.10....**5.97%**
44.(NEW)..ORC.B..Orca Exploration ..$5.50....**5.96%**
58.(62)..PIF..Polaris Infrastructu..$14.32....**5.96%**
39.(47)...TCL.B..Transcontinental ....$15.10....**5.96%**
66.(74)..BMO..Bank of Montreal.......$72.02....**5.89%**
34.(NEW)..TPX.A..Molson Coors Cana.$48.00....**5.84%**
61.(63)..LB..Laurentian Bank of Can.....$27.51....**5.82%**
19.(NEW)..WIR.UN..WPT Industrial ...$18.13....**5.81%**
72.(NEW)..TRP..TC Energy Corp...$55.94....**5.79%**
39.(39)..CSW.B..Corby Spirit and Wine ..$13.87....**5.77%**
48.(57)..CRT.UN..CT REIT.......$13.87....**5.68%**
36.(57)..WIR.U..WPT Industrial REIT..$13.50....**5.63%**
52.(32)...CHP.UN..Choice Properties .$13.28....**5.57%**
46.(58)..NFI..NFI Group Inc.............$15.35....**5.54%**
45.(NEW)...APY..Anglo Pacific Group...$2.83....**5.44%**
29.(NEW)..Y...Yellow Pages Ltd........$8.10....**5.43%**
33.(NEW)..CNE..Canacol Energy Ltd...$3.86....**5.39%**
45.(46)...ITP...Intertape Polymer Group...$15.22...**5.38%**
50.(NEW)...FCA.UN..Firm Capital Am....$6.00...**5.37%**
70.(75)..TRP..Transcanada Energy......$61.00..**5.31%**
35.(55)..MBN..MBN Corp................$6.07....**5.27%**
72.(74)..TD..The Toronto-Dominon Ban..$59.82....**5.27%**
41.(46)..HPS.A..Hammond Power Soluti..$6.47....**5.26%**
58.(NEW)..IAG..IA Financial Corp...$45.87....**5.15%**

24.(27)..INP..Input Capital Corp….$0.78….**5.13%**
65.(NEW)..CWB..Canadian Western Ba.$22.88….**5.07%**
57.(68)..T..Telus Corp…………..…...$23.05….**5.05%**
41.(NEW)..TII..Terra Firma Capital ….$23.05….**5.05%**
63.(57)..CU..Canadian Utilities Ltd.….$34.55..**5.04%**
39.(40)..CSW.A...Corby Spirit and W…$15.90….**5.03%**
27.(NEW)..TWM..Tidewater Midstream..$0.80….**5.00%**
5%
47.(65)..ARX..ARC Resources ….4.82…**4.98%**
55.(50)..CU.X..Canadian Utilities Ltd…$34.99….**4.98%**
67.(64)...MRG.UN...Morguard North ..$14.18….**4.93%**
61.(56)...SJR.B..Shaw Communicati.$24.16….**4.90%**
60.(63)...D.UN...Dream Office…$20.44….**4.89%**
45.(44)..ISV...Information Services…$16.50….**4.85%**
42.(43)..FRU..Freehold Royalties…$3.73….**4.83%**
43.(38)..SJR.A..Shaw Communicatio…..$24.50....**4.83%**
49.(54)..SMU.UN..Summit Industr REI...$11.26....**4.80%**
33.(NEW)..SFC..Sagicor Financial Co.$6.65….**4.78%**
51.(NEW)..ALC..Algoma Central ….$10.06..**4.77%**
57.(59)..AQN...Algonquin Power & Utilit..$17.55..**4.77%**
38.(19)..MMP.UN..Precious Metals and Min.$2.52..**4.76%**
49.(49)..KEG.UN...The Keg Royalties I….$8.85..**4.75%**
45.(NEW)..FRO.UN..Fronsac REIT…$0.54...**4.73%**
16.(24)..HOM.U..BSR REIT………..$10.96..**4.69%**
59.(62)..NVU.UN..Northview Apa REIT...$34.96...**4.66%**
76.(76)..RY..Royal Bank of Canada…...$93.08..**4.64%**
18.(16)..HOM.UN...BSR REIT……….$14.36...**4.63%**
39.(NEW)..NEO..Neo Performance Mater..$8.66..**4.62%**
50.(NEW)..UFC..Urbanfund Corp………$0.65....**4.62%**
66.(64)..NA..National Bank of Cana…$62.09….**4.57%**
43.(44)..CUP.U...Caribbean Utilities ...$15.56...**4.52%**
37.(42)..CMG..Computer Modelling Group.$4.63...**4.48%**
54.(57)..BEP.UN..Brookfield Renew Pa...$66.91...**4.44%**
54.(55)..ACO.Y...Atco Ltd…………..$39.00….**4.46%**
45.(50)..NWC..The North West Co Inc..$30.00....**4.40%**
62.(65)..EMA..Emera Inc…………..$56.20….**4.36%**

44.(NEW)..ADN..Aecon Group Inc…..$14.76….**4.34%**
53.(NEW)...FTT..Fining International In..$19.11….**4.29%**
36.(NEW)..KBL..K-Bro Linen Inc….$27.75….**4.29%**
48.(53)..AW.UN..A&W Revenue Royalty.$28.10....**4.27%**
53.(51)..MRD..Melcor Development Ltd…$7.70….**4.16%**
59.(62)..ACO.X..Atco Ltd………………$41.71….**4.17%**
53.(62)..IPL..Inter Pipeline Ltd……….....$11.81….**4.06%**
73.(NEW)..AP.UN..Allied Prop REIT…..$40.96….**4.03%**
45.(NEW)..GDL..Goodfellow Inc……$4.99….**4.01%**
24.(23)..CLR..Clearwater Seafoods Inc….$5.70….**4%**
20.(22)..GMN..GobiMin Inc……………...$0.26….**4%**
40.(34)..H..Hydro One Ltd………………..27.73….**4%**
4%
49.(53)..CIX..CI Financial Corp………..$18.09….**3.98%**
60.(69)..GRT.UN..Granite REIT……….$73.76….**3.94%**
34.(31)..ERE.UN..European Reside REI..$4.11….**3.93%**
51.(NEW)..FFH.U..Fairfax Financial Ho...$254.74..**3.93%**
17.(21)..TSL..Tree Island Steel Ltd…...$2.05….**3.90%**
60.(NEW)..CTC.A..Canadian Tire Corpo 117.08...**3.89%**
10.(9)..RE..RE Royalties Ltd……………$1.03…**3.88%**
58.(NEW)..LIF..Labrador Iron Ore Ro...$25.88….**3.86%**
57.(71)..SU..Suncor Energy Inc…..….$21.95….**3.83%**
60.(NEW)..IMO..Imperial Oil Ltd…..$22.76…**3.82%**
59.(56)..KMP.UN..Killam Apart REIT…$17.21….**3.81%**
57.(50)..FCA.U..Firm Capital Am Realty...$6.21..**3.80%**
67.(NEW)..QSR...Restaurant Brands Inter...$54.17..**3.80%**
51.(NEW)..WTE..Westshore Terminal….$17.02…**3.76%**
29.(NEW).SYZ..Sylogist Ltd…………$11.73….**3.75%**
65.(NEW)..RCI.B..Rogers Communicatio.$53.59...**3.73%**
63.(NEW)..TOU…Tourmaline Oil Co…$12.84....**3.73%**
34.(NEW)..QSP.UN..Restaurant Brands ….$75.33..**3.70%**
36.(46)..LNF...Leon's Furniture Lt….$13.50….**3.56%**
40.(30)..CEE...Centamin PLC………..$3.20….**3.49%**
56.(NEW)..PKI..Parkland Corporation ..$34.77....**3.49%**
67.(NEW)..MG...Magna Internation Inc..$61.91….**3.48%**
30.(NEW)..ERF...Enerplus Corp……$3.44….**3.49%**

74.(70)..FTS..Fortis Inc……………..$54.75….**3.49%**
38.(NEW)..GBT...BMTC Group Inc….$8.10….**3.46%**
57.(64)..NPI..Northland Power Inc……..$36.04….**3.33%**
46.(48)..INE...Innergex Renewable Ene...$22.00….**3.27%**
20.(20)..WBE..WestBond Enterprises....$0.31….**3.23%**
34.(43)..ACD..Accord Financial Corp...$6.55….**3.10%**
3%
40.(49)..ET…Evertz Technologies ...$13.29....**2.71%**
39.(57)..AFN..AG Growth……………$27.20….**2.21%**
28.(48)..RME...Rocky Mountain Dealer….$4.35....**1.38%**
31.(NEW)..MX..Methanex Corp…….$26.15….**0.76%**

CHAPTER 23

CANADIAN STOCKS BY STOCK PRICE

Chapter 23 is sorted in descending order by stock price. You may have a certain amount available.to buy a stock. This sort can help you find a stock in the price range you are looking for.

It is not too surprising that those stocks with the highest price score over 50. However, the highest priced stocks are not necessarily the ones paying the highest dividends.

It surprised me that there were a number of stocks that cost less than $5 a share that scored over 50. There is even one scoring under a dollar that scores 50. Such low-priced scores may indicate a bargain with the potential for a good capital gain.

It is also interesting to see which shares costing over $25 a share score under 50.

Most of the stocks paying more than a 3.5% dividend are under $10 a share.

All scores over 50 have been highlighted in this sort Before buying a share always re-score the stock and do a Google search to see if any serious negatives have been reported since the scores in the book were calculated. The stocks in this list are stable but doing this final check is wise..

<SCORE>
2020.(2019)..Symbol..Company………$Price..Dividend %

51.(NEW)..FFH.U..Fairfax Financial ….**$254.74**..3.93%
65.(NEW)..CNU...CNODC Ltd.…**$156.40**….9.00%
60.(NEW)...CTC.A..Canadian Tire Corp…**$117.08**..3.89%

$100

76.(76)..RY..Royal Bank of Canada.…**$93.08**….4.64%
67.(73)..CM..Canadian Imperial Bank ….**$91.12**..6.41%
34.(NEW)..QSP.UN..Restaurant Brands Int….**$75.33**..3.70%
60.(69)..GRT..Granite REIT……….**$73.76**….3.94%
66.(74)..BMO..Bank of Montreal…..**$72.02**…5.89%
54.(57)..BEP.UN..Brookfield Renew…**$66.91**….4.44%
66.(64)..NA..National Bank of Cana..**$62.09**….4.57%
67.(NEW)..MG..Magna Interna Inc..**$61.91**….3.48%
70.(75)..TRP..Transcanada Energy…....**$61.00**….5.31%
72.(74)..TD..The Toronto-Dominon Ba..**$59.82**….5.27%
66.(74)..BNS...Bank of Nova Scotia....**$56.88**….6.33%
59.(69)..BCE...BCE Inc……………**$56.77**….6%
62.(65)..EMA..Emera Inc………...**$56.20**….4.36%
72.(NEW)..TRP..TC Energy Corp…..**$55.94**….5.79%
59.(56)..BIP.UN..Brookfield Infrastru…..**$55.70**….6%
74.(70)..FTS..Fortis Inc…………...**$54.75**….3.49%
67.(NEW)..QSR..Restaurant Brands Inter..**$54.17**..3.80%
65.(NEW)..RCI.B..Rogers Communic….**$53.59**..3.73%

$50

64.(68)..SLF..Sun Life Financial Inc..**$48.96**…6.49%
34.(NEW)..PX.B..Molson Coors Can..I**$48.75**…6.15%
34.(NEW)..TPX.A..Molson Coors Can..**$48.00**....5.84%
58.(NEW)..IAG...IA Financial Corp..**$45.87**….5.15%
59.(62)..ACO.X...Atco Lt…………**$41.71**….4.17%
73.(NEW)..AP.UN...Allied PropRE IT..**$40.96**..4.03%
70.(60)..ENB…Enbridge Inc……..**$40.70**….7.96%

$40

54..(55)..ACO.Y..Atco Ltd…….**$39.00**….4.46%
57.(64)..NPI…Northland Power …**$36.04**….3.33%
55.(50)..CU.X…Canadian Utilities ..**$34.99**..4.98%
59.(62)..NVU.UN..Northview REIT..**$34.96**....4.66%
56.(NEW)..PKI..Parkland Corpo….**$34.77**....3.49%
63.(57)..CU...Canadian Utilities …**$34.55**….5.04%
56.(50)..IGM..IGM Financial Inc….**$33.49**….7%
72.(72)..MIC...Genworth MI Can. **$33.09**….6.53%
65.(67)..PPL..Pembina Pipeline Co..**$32.95**….8%
54.(48)..OLY..Olympia Financial Gro.**$32.00**….8.63%
45.(50)..NWC...The North West Co I....**$30.00**....4.40%

$30

49.(61)..UFS….Domtar Corp…...**$29.73**….8.90%
44.(52)..FN…First National Finan..**$29.46**..6.62%
48.(53)..AW.UN..A&W Revenue R.**$28.10**...4.27%
36.(NEW)..KBL…K-Bro Linen Inc...**$27.7**...4.29%
40.(34)..H………Hydro One Ltd…..$**27.73**….4%
61.(63)..LB…Laurentian Bank ....**$27.51**….5.82%
59.(62)..CPX..Capital Power Corp….**$27.38**.7.01%
39.(57)..AFN…AG Growth…….**$27.20**….2.21%
54.(61)..EIF….Exchange Income Corp…**$26.94**..8%
31.(NEW)..MX..Methanex Corp...**$26.15**….0.76%
58.(NEW)..LIF…Labrador Iron Ore ..**$25.88**…3.86%
43.(38)..SJR.A..Shaw Communicati..**$24.50**....4.83%
60.(52)..GWO…Great-West Lifeco…**$24.27**….7.51%
61.(56)..SJR.B…Shaw Communicat..**$24.16**...4.90%
72.(70)..CNQ…Canadian Natural Re..**$23.93**….7.10%
60.(62)..POW...Power Corporation….**$23.72**….7.53%
57.(68)...T…………Telus Corp….**$23.05**….5.05%
41.(NEW)..TII..Terra Firma Capital….**$23.05**….5.05%
65.(NEW)..CWB..Canad West Bank..**$22.88**….5.07%
60.(NEW)..IMO..Imperial Oil Ltd….**$22.76**….3.82%
46.(48).INE..Innergex Renewable Ene..**$22.00**….3.27%
52.(47)..GEI…Gibson Energy Inc…..**$21.95**….6.20%
57.(71)..SU..Suncor Energy Inc….**$21.95**….3.83%

60.(54)..KEY..Keyera Corp……**$21.03**….9.13%
60.(63)..D.UN..Dream Office RE…**$20.44**..4.89%
67.(59)..SRU.UN..Smartcentres RE…**$20.18**...9.17%
$20
53.(NEW)..FTT..Fining Internatio..**$19.11**….4.29%
40.(35)..ZZZ..Sleep Country Canada..**$19.06**...0.00%
41.(44)..WFC..Wall Financial Corp….**$18.50**..11%
49.(49)..RUSRussel Metals Inc……..**$18.50**….8%
19.(NEW)..WIR.UN..WPT Industri…**$18.13**….5.81%
49.(53)...CIX..CI Financial Corp…**$18.09**….3.98%
69.(67)..MFC...Manulife Financial..**$17.93**….6%
57.(59)..AQN..Algonquin Power ..**$17.55**….4.77%
59.(56)..KMP.UN...Killam Apartm..**$17.21**….3.81%
51.(NEW)..WTE..Westshore Term...**$17.02**…3.76%
68.(58)...ALA...AltaGas Ltd………**$16.65**….6.13%
45.(44)…ISV...Information Servi…**$16.50**….4.85%
39..(40)...CSW.A...Corby Spirit a…**$15.90**….5.03%
43.(44)..CUP.U..Caribbean Utilit....**$15.56**….4.52%
45.(.52)..RNW..TransAlta Renewa..**$15.36**….6.12%
46.(58)..NFI...NFI Group Inc……...**$15.35**....5.54%
45.(46)...ITP...Intertape Polymer…**$15.22**…5.38%
54.(46)..TCL.A..Transcontinental...**$15.10**....5.97%
39.(47)..TCL.B...Transcontinental...**$15.10**....5.96%
58.(59)..BPY.UN..Brookfield Prop..**$15.02**….12%
$15
44.(NEW)..ADN..Aecon Group ..**$14.76**….4.34%
69.(64)..REI.UN..Riocan REIT…**$14.76**….10%
49.(51)..ADN..Acadian Timber ...**$14.52**….7.99%
18.(16)..HOM.UN..BSR REIT….**$14.36**….4.63%
58.(62)..PIF...Polaris Infrastruct…**$14.32**….5.96%
67.(64)..MRG.UN..Morguard No..**$14.18**….4.93%
39.(39)..CSW.B..Corby Spirit a….**$13.87**….5.77%
48.(57)..CRT.UN..CT REIT…….**$13.87**....5.68%
36.(46)..LNF..Leon’s Furniture….**$13.50**….3.56%
36.(57)..WIR.U..WPT Industrial..**$13.50**....5.63%
17.(17)..PRM..Big Pharma Split …**$13.44**…..9.21%

40.(49)..ET..Evertz Technologie...**$13.29**....2.71%
52.(32)..CHP.UN...Choice Propert..**$13.28**....5.57%
62.(New)..FCR.UN...First Capital ...**$13.22**....6.51%
49.(59)..CRR.UN...Crombie REIT...**$13.07**....6.81%
44.(58)..AD..Alaris Royalty Corp...**$12.95**....9%
63.(NEW)..TOU..Tourmaline Oil ...**$12.84**....3.73%
42.(52)..MKP...McCan Mortgage ...**$12.83**....11%
9..(NEW)..ENS...E Split Corp........**$11.88**....13%
37.(49)..SPB...Superior Plus Group....**$11.86**....6.07%
35.(35)..KPT...KP Tissue Inc..........**$11.85**....6.08%
53.(62)..IPL...Inter Pipeline Ltd........**$11.81**....4.06%
29.(NEW)..SYZ....Sylogist Ltd.......**$11.73**....3.75%
34.(NEW)..BRE...Bridgemarq Real...**$11.70**....12%
51.(52)..BEK.B..Becker Milk Comp...**$11.68**....6.85%
49.(51)..FC......Firm Capital...........**$11.47**....8.16%
49.(51)..FC.....Firm Capital Mortg....**$11.47**....8%
49.(54)..SMU.UN...Summit Industrial..**$11.26**....4.80%
16.(24)..HOM.U...BSR REIT..........**$10.96**....4.69%
61.(55)..AI..Atrium Mortgage Invest..**$10.95**....8.22%
60.(57)..DIR.UN...Dream Industrial ..**$10.76**...6.51%
53.(47)..NWH.UN..Northwest Health...**$10.72**...7.46%
30.(47)..SIA...Sienna Senior Living ..**$10.32**....9%
36.(36)..FSZ..Fiera Capital Corp......**$10.24**....8%
51.(NEW)..ALC..Algoma Central ....**$10.06**....4.77%
59.(NEW)..HBL.UN..Brand Leaders..**$10.05**....8%

$10

52.(43)..RCO.UN..Middlefield Can G..**$9.81**....6.63%
47.(61)..HR.UN...H&R REIT...........**$9.57**....7%
52.(33)..HRR.UN...Australian REIT ....**$9.44**....6.99%
13.(9)...GDV...Global Dividend Growt...**$9.39**....13%
38.(43)...CSH.UN...Chartwell Retireme..**$9.36**...6.30%
46.(50)..SRT.UN..Slate Retail REIT......**$9.27**....13%
48.(25)..EIT.UN...Canoe EIT Income Fu...**$9.11**....13%
38.(59)..HRR.UN..Automotive Property....**$9.06**....9%

$9

49.(49)..KEG.UN..The Keg Royalties In....**$8.80**....4.75%

39.(NEW)...NEO..Neo Performance Mate.**$8.66**....*4.62%*
31.(40)..BCF..Builders Capital Mortgage C...**$8.60**....9%
31.(52)..CGX.........Cineplex.............**$8.41**....0.00%
48.(NEW)..HGI.UN..Global Telecom & U..**$8.40**..8.57%
56.(44)..TF.......Timbercreek Financial.........**$8.26**....8%
34.(36)..SBC....Brompton Split Banc Corp....**$8.20**....15%
52.(57)..PZA...Pizza Pizza Royalty Corp...**$8.17**....6.91%
63.(47)..CUF.UN...Cominar REIT............**$8.14**....8.85%
38.(NEW)..GBT...BMTC Group I...**$8.10**....3.46%
29.(NEW)..Y.......Yellow Pages Ltd........**$8.10**....5.43%
$8
47.(55)..AX.UN..Artis REIT.................**$7.82**...6.91%
53.(51)..MRD...Melcor Developmen......**$7.70**....4.16%
38.(48)..BPF.UN..Boston Pizza Royalt....**$7.13**....0.00%
$7
43.(25)..SRT.U...Slate Retail REIT...**$6.94**....12%
35.(NEW)...PSI..Parson Systems Inc..**$6.84**....11%
49.(NEW)..MAL..Magellan Aerospace..**$6.67**....6.30%
33.(NEW)..SFC..Sagicor Financial Co..**$6.65**....4.78%
34.(43)..ACD...Accord Financial Corp..**$6.55**....3.10%
55.(26)..MBK.UN...Manulife US Region..**$6.48**....7.70%
41.(46)..HPS.A..Hammond Power Solu.**$6.47**....5.26%
43.(42)..XTC..Exco Technologies Ltd.....**$6.46**.....6%
33.(41)..NEXA..Nexa Resources.........**$6.29**....6.00%
52.(25)..RBN.UN..Blue Ribbon Income .**$6.27**....7.66%
34.(26)..BGI.UN..Brookfield Global Inf...**$6.24**...9.50%
13.(21)..DS..Dividend Select 15 Corp....... **$6.23**...11%
57.(50)..FCA.U..Firm Capital American..**$6.21**...3.80%
35.(55)..MBN..MBN Corp.................**$6.07**....5.27%
35.(22)..MFR.UN..Manulife Floating Rate..**$6.05**....11%
37.(27)..BDT..Bird Construction Inc.........**$6.05**....6.45%
50.(NEW)..FCA.UN..Firm Capital Ameri..**$6.00**....5.37%
$6
53.(56)..TNT.UN..True North Comm RE.**$5.97**....10%
52.(21)..CIQ.UN..Canadian High Income.. **$5.90**....8.14%
24.(23)..CLR..Clearwater Seafoods Inc....**$5.70**....4%

35.(32)..EXE..Extendicare Inc..............**$5.64.**...8.51%
41.(66)..VET......Vermillion Energy...**$5.61**....0.00%
44.(NEW)..ORC.B..Orca Exploration.. **$5.50**....5.96%
21.(19)..USF.UN..US Financials Income..**$5.47**....9.14%
31.(36)..CHE.UN..Chemtrade Logistics ...**$5.44**....11%
52.(28)..MID.UN..Mint Income Fund....**$5.05**....9.50%
42.(36)..CWX..CanWel Building Mate..**$5.02**....10%
54.(47)..AGF.B..AGF Management Ltd..**$5.02**...6.37%
$5
45.(NEW)..GDL.Goodfellow Inc...**$4.99**...4.01%
29.(58)...MRT.UN..Morguard REI...**$4.97**....10%
37.(27)..RAY.A...Stingray Group ....**$4.95**....6.06%
32.(19)..RAY.B..Stingray Group In..**$4.89**....6.13%
13.(30)..DRA.UN..Dream Hard A.....**$4.82**......8.30%
47.(65)..ARX..ARC Resources Ltd...**$4.82**...4.98%
26.(40)..RSI..Rogers Sugar Inc.......**$4.80**....7.50%
4.(New)..FCD.UN..Firm Capital ...**$4.70**...11%
44.(59)..FCD..Firm Capital Property..**$4.70..**10.64%
52.(62)..PRV.UN..Pro Real Estate In..**$4.62**..10%
37.(42)..CMG..Computer Modelling ..**$4.63**..4.48%
28.(48)..RME..Rocky Mountain Dealer...**$4.35**..1.38%
34.(31)..ERE.UN..European Residential..**$4.11**..3.93%
20.(19)..CDD.UN..Core Canadian Divid..**$4.07**..8.19%
$4
29.(43)..CHW...Chesswood Group L....**$3.87**....11%
42.(43)..FRU..Freehold Royalties Ltd...**$3.73**....4.83%
33.(NEW)..CNE..Canacol Energy Ltd...**$3.86**....5.39%
49.(57)..SOT.UN...Slate Office REIT....**$3.62**....11%
44.(47)..Mr.UN..Melcor REIT............**$3.50**....10%
30.(NEW)..ERF..Enerplus Corp.........**$3.44**....3.49%
37.(41)..PIC.A..Premium Income Corp...**$3.37**....12%
49.(49)..PLZ..Plaza Retail REIT.............**$3.37**....8.31%
43.(36)..CRWN..Crown Capital Partners ..**$3.26**....18%
47.(39)..SPS.A..Spotscene Group Inc.......**$3.25**.....9.23%
40.(30)...CEE..Centamin PLC...............**$3.20**....3.49%
50.(54)..BTB.UN..BTB Real Estate Inve....**$3.10**....10%

26.(53)..IVQ...Invesque Inc………………**$3.00**….0.00%
$3
39.(34)...FAP..Aberdeen Asia-Pacific In….**$2.94**….9.18%
45.(NEW)..APY..Anglo Pacific Group..**$2.83**….5.44%
31.(33)...SWP..Swiss Water Decaf coffee…**$2.68**….0.00%
46.(NEW)..CJR.B...Corus Entertainmen…**$2.56**…..9.38%
38.(19)..MMP.UN..Precious Metals and ..**$2.52**….4.76%
47.(50)..WCP….Whitecap Resources Inc… ..**$2.22**….8%
17.(21).TSL…Tree Island Steel Ltd……….**$2.05**…3.90%
$2
31.(47)..TOG..TORC Oil & Gas Ltd…**$1.72**…0.00%
32.(20)..TXT.UN..Top 10 Split Trust…**$1.48**….15%
31.(27)..GMP...GMP Capital Inc…………**$1.32**…7.58%
39.(26)..ENI.UN..Energy Income Fund…**$1.20**….10.00%
36.(33)..SXP..Supremex Inc……………**$1.13**…23%
30.(38)..AFCC..Automotive Finco Corp..**$1.29**….16%
24.(38)...WEF..Western Forest Products….**$1.06**….0%
10.(9)...RE…RE Royalties Ltd………**$1.03**….3.88%
$1

26.(31)..MKZ.UN..Mackenzie Master..**$0.82**….14%
27.(NEW)..TWM..Tidewater Midstrea..**$0.80**….5.00%
24.(27)..INP..Input Capital Corp……….**$0.78**….5.13%
17.(51)..TGL...TransGlobe Energy ……**$0.78**….0%
26.(57)..ESI..Ensign Energy……………**$0.73**…32.88%
50.(NEW)..UFC..Urbanfund Corp………**$0.65**....4.62%
45.(NEW)..FRO.UN..Fronsac REIT…….**$0.54**….4.73%
26.(23)..MCS...McChip Resources Inc……**$0.45**….8.89%
48.(40)..FDI…Findev Inc…………………**$0.41**…..7.32%
27.(NEW)..NWX...Newport Exploration ….**$0.36**….11%
2.(28)..ELC..Elysee Development Corp…...**$0.34**….12%
20.(20)..WBE..WestBond Enterprises……..**$0.31**….3.23%
20.(22)..GMN..GobiMin Inc………………..**$0.26**….4%

CHAPTER 24

THE LAST WORD

1. COSTS : OVERVIEW

My job for 40 years was designing commercial risk information scoring systems for banks, wholesalers, manufacturers, and insurance companies. A scoring system I created was at a time when the experts in consumer credit scoring were doubtful a risk score could be developed for businesses.

Companies are not humans. The experts doubted that companies could have "character" and behave for decades in a consistent, habitual way like people . To establish credibility in my commercial score, I needed to prove that companies do have characters and do behave consistently.

In 1991, to test my scoring system, I approached the, Canadian Imperial Bank of Commerce and asked if they would test it. The bank had hundreds of thousands of commercial customers. If the score worked, it could quickly and inexpensively identify their high risk customers so they could reduce their exposure to bad debt losses. Scoring reduction could improve their profits and speed up cash flows.

The bank identified 3,000 companies that they had written off to bad debt over the previous three years. Their losses amounted to hundreds of millions of dollars. I matched their records to the last three years of historic risk information in our data base of two million Canadian companies and gave them back their records with our scores attached.

After their analysis of all the data they responded that the scoring was "amazingly accurate" in being able to predict which companies would become bad debts. I had proven that you can risk score businesses, just as you can risk score consumers. That scoring system is still used to make hundreds of thousand of commercial risk decisions every year.

In 2000, after I lost $300,000 in a mutual fund (which an investment adviser had placed my life savings) I remembered that commercial scoring system. I decided to treat investing in stocks as just another form of corporate risk and design a scoring system to grade stocks from the most to the least desirable to add to my portfolio. This was done for my own investing purposes and it was only in 2019 when I was asked to help another investor who had lost hundreds of thousands of dollars that I decided it could be made available to others.

Like most new investors, I had paid little attention to my portfolio when I had given responsibility for its management to an investment advisor. I naively believed that being in the hands of a "professional" that my life savings was safe. Infrequently, I would look at the total portfolio amount in the monthly statements. It seemed to be growing. Knowing in what the mutual fund was invested seemed unnecessary. I really did not know how to determine if my investments were good or bad.

While I understood that I was paying to have my portfolio managed, I had no idea what it was costing me, nor did I think that I needed to care. My advisor had told me that the management fee that would be deducted from my portfolio would be so small that he would be surprised if I even notice it. He was right, I had not noticed the thousands of dollars I was being charged each year. It was well hidden.

I hope that this book has helped open your eyes to the importance of managing your portfolio and knowing exactly what you are invested in and why you are invested in it. However, carefully investing your money is only the first step in becoming financially independent. The next step is determining if you are spending your dividend money frugally.

Your investment discipline is wasted if you spending habits deplete your income and portfolio faster than you can replenish it. Most people think that having a million dollars will make all their financial challenges disappear. Unfortunately, when you have a million dollars you soon come to recognize that a million dollars translates out to a steady dividend income of $60,000, if you wisely invest that million dollars. If you start to spend the million dollars of capital in your portfolio your reliable dividend income will shrink. There is an old expression that rings true, "You can't have your cake and eat too".

The following are the cost realities you must consider if you wish to live well off your investments for the rest of your life:

2. COSTS : CREDIT

If you have credit card debt and are paying 22% interest on the outstanding balance, it makes little sense to be putt your money into the stock market to earn a 6% dividend until that credit card debt is paid off. Your objective is to achieve financial independence, and this means being debt free.

Credit cards are convenient, useful tools as long as they cost you nothing to acquire them and you are prepared to pay off your balances every two weeks to make sure you never pay interest. The bank will still make money. They are charging the vendors who accept credits card a small charge every time you use a card. Do not let credit costs eat away at your cash resources.

3. COSTS : AUTO

A well-made dependable car can provide you with reliable service for ten years or more. Before purchasing do a Google search. Which cars have the best ratings for reliability and low operating costs. As soon as a new car leaves the dealers lot it loses 30% of its value. It is possible to find a used car a year old with the original manufacturer's warranties still on it. Do not be impatient in your search for such a car.

If possible, pay cash for the car. However, interest rates are so low that it makes sense to finance the car if you are receiving 6% on your investments and only paying 1% on an extended car loan. Leasing is designed to make you buy a car every 3 years. If you intend to buy with the intent of owning a car much longer, you will end up paying more than if you finance the car.

Do not skimp on things like undercoating and regular maintenance. These costs are minor compared to what neglect of the car will cost you.

In going in to make an offer on a car, do you homework. Set your "walk away" price. It is the job of the salesman who is selling the car to get as much for it as he can. He will high ball you with the price he gives to suckers. You respond with a price below your "walk away" price. He will look astonished at such a price and say he can not go that low. He will give you another price. You give him your "walk away price" and tell him this is the best you can do. As he tries to get you to come higher, you stand up, thank him for his time and turn to leave. At this point he may come down to your price. If not tell him to phone you if he changes his mind. Go to another dealership with a similar car and use the same approach.

It is usually best to buy cars at the end of the month. Sales representatives have monthly quotas. They get more desperate to close sales as the end of the month is approaching.

Shop around for car insurance. Hundreds of dollars can be saved. Several insurance brokers have on-line services where they can check dozens of insurance companies for the best rate in a few minutes.

4. COSTS : ACCOMODATION

Houses greatly appreciate over several decades if they are in the right location. You want to buy more house than you need and to pay off the mortgage as quickly as you can. A paid off house is an insurance policy to tap into if unforeseen disasters occur. You can sell it and downsize to a smaller house if you have a need for capital. You can always mortgage a house. When you retire it will greatly increase your retirement savings if you want to sell it and simplify your life. You can live in a fully paid large comfortable house for a fraction of what renting a house or apartment would cost.

5. COSTS : ENTERTAINMENT

Fortunes can be spent at expensive restaurants, drinking fine wines, sipping exquisite liquors, and engaging in other entertaining distractions. These are luxuries. If your objective is to achieve financial independence, then the hundreds or the thousands of dollars spent every month on luxuries are not helping you to achieve your goal. Unfortunately, you can often convince yourself that these luxuries are necessities for your happiness or mental health.

6. COSTS : VACATION

Once you achieve financial independence, the frantic quest of taking one- or two-week vacation breaks disappears. You may want to go away for 3 months in the winter and spend it on a warm tropical island living in a very nice 2 bedroom, 2 bathroom condominium with a car and internet. it can be done for what many people will spend on a 2 week cruise.

Package tours are nice, but you are paying significantly more than what you can arrange easily on your own through different internet websites dealing directly with the property owners. The reviews by previous renters can generally be relied on.

Buying a vacation home is hard to justify if maintenance, taxes, and security are a drain on your cash flow. The amount of time you will be able to spend in the vacation property is limited and makes the time versus cost equation hard to justify. You may also be limiting your flexibility to visit new, interesting destinations.

If you must borrow money to go on a vacation, then this is an indication that you can not afford the luxury of going away on a vacation. Find a vacation that you can afford. Be creative.

7. COSTS : CONSUMPTION

You must eat and drink. What you eat and drink impacts both your health and your pocketbook. If you are throwing away food, this should make you think about your spending. Frozen fruit and vegetables are just as healthy as fresh. You only need to take enough out of the package as you need for your meal. Bread can be frozen and thawed when needed. Cooking your own meals instead of buying prepared meals can shrinkyour consumption costs

8. COSTS: SOCIAL

A social cost is one where you feel obligated to spend money in a social situation. Perhaps it is a wedding present, a birthday present, a charity, or a donation to a cause. Are you being selfish in not attending the wedding or birthday party of a distant relative or friend you have not seen in decades?

Every day you receive communications from charities that tug at your heart. They are requesting money to save abandoned dogs, crippled children, shelters for homeless people, etc. If you gave lavishly to all of them, you would soon be impoverished. You have not given everything away, so you are already being selective.

You first obligation is to your immediate family. If after assisting them and there is money left over then you can selectively decide where you might donate it. There is nothing wrong with saying, *"Sorry, as much as I understand there is a need, all the money I have set aside has been allocated. Thanks for contacting me. Goodbye"*

9. COSTS : ACCOUNTING COSTS

A good accountant can save you more than he costs. He can advise you on how to save on taxes and make sure that the tax people never question your financial returns. Good accountants are not inexpensive. Shop around. See if you can relate to the accountant. Explain your financial situation. If the accountant is referred to you, that is one step in engaging them.

For your accountant's sanity and your own, learn to keep good records with backup documentation. I file all receipts by month in plastic sleeves in a 3-ring binder . All bank statements and stock trading documents are in 3 ring binders sorted by month. It takes an hour every month to update these binders. I can usually find any required receipt within a minute. 7 years of these binders are stored for easy retrieval.

10. COSTS: EMERGENCY COST

As much as I see the benefit of having every unallocated dollar invested in stocks that will pay a dividend, I do keep a stash of cash available as an emergency back up. I move this sizable sum to which ever bank is paying the best "introductory" special saving account interest. I am currently getting 2.5% interest on it. Normally savings accounts are paying less than 0.50%.

I never want to be in a position that I would have to sell any of my stocks to generate enough money to live on. Nor do I want to have to borrow money to pay for unpredicted repairs or replacements.

The reality is that no matter how you try to protect yourself from any unforeseen challenge to your financial resources, you can never totally predict what surprises life is going to throw at you. All you can rely on is your flexibility, creativity, experience, and survival instinct. Thus, being unnecessarily defensive and not being willing to take reasoned, logical, informed chances in growing your portfolio is almost as bad as being a speculative investor chasing dreams of millions in questionable penny stocks.

CHAPTR 25

INDEX

CH = Chapter Number ,Q = Question Number,

T= Topic Number

The following phrases and words are highlighted in the book to make it easy for those buying both the printed book and the E-book to find items.

CHAPTER 26

OTHER BOOKS

BY

IAN DUNCAN MACDONALD

(1)

INCOME AND WEALTH FROM SELF-DIRECTED INVESTING

This was Ian MacDonald's first investment book. It relates how an 80-year-old widow worried about outliving her savings approached Ian and asked him for help. She had assisted him in a venture, and he was pleased to help her.

After reviewing her finances, he was appalled to see the poor quality of her investments and how a major bank's financial advisor had been siphoning almost twenty-thousand dollars a year out of her portfolio. That portfolio had shrunk by many hundred thousand dollars under his active management.

Over several months, Ian taught her how to manage her own portfolio. The first thing he showed her was the stock scoring software he had develop for his own use almost 20 years ago. How the scores were calculated opened her eyes to how all the important investment information that she needed to make good investment decisions was easily accessible via the internet.

She took back control her portfolio from the advisor. Quickly she was able to double her monthly income. The portfolio regained much of what had been lost. Pleased to be in total control of her investments, she pleaded with Ian to write a book detailing everything that he had taught her. She felt such a book would help others intimidated by the investment industry to gain full control over their life savings just as she had done.

Despite her age, she was computer literate. Much of Ian's instructions had been via e-mail. The hundreds of questions and answers had been saved. They served as the base for Ian's first investment book.

To help those, who had never invested, to find financially strong dividend stocks, Ian created charts containing lists of the hundreds of companies paying dividends greater than 3.5%. For easy, fast, reference the lists were sorted by dividend percent, stock price, stock score and alphabetically. Since he was Canadian, he used stocks traded on the Toronto Stock Exchange.

Much to Ian's surprise the book was purchased by investors all over the world. Quickly it became evident that he had to bring out a second book to meet the demands of investors who wanted to buy stocks traded on the New York Stock Exchange and the NASDAQ. Within a year he had written his latest investment book, *"BETTER SAFER DIVIDEND INVESTING*". It contains charts on all US common stocks paying dividends of 6% or more and more than 100 questions from investors that he had responded to since the first book was released.

INCOME AND WEALTH FROM SELF-DIRECTED INVESTING can be purchased from Amazon. Go to:

https://www.amazon.ca/INCOME-AND-WEALTH-FROM-SELF-DIRECTED INVESTING-IAN-DUNCAN-MACDONALD/dp/199919800X

Now for something different. You may enjoy Ian MacDonald's

NOVELS

(2)

BEWARE THE ABANDONED.

It is a strange story about a New Mexico based capitalist sect that recruits clever, abandoned children off the world's streets. They turn them into successful capitalists. The sect is then rewarded with a percentage of their graduates' income and wealth.

The action takes place in Paris, Las Vegas, Philadelphia and Delaware. Both the mob and the FBI are seeking the sect's graduate who forcefully retrieved the millions the mob stole from him. Can murders be justified if they help the sect save thousand of abandoned children who might die in the streets? You may have a hard time putting this novel down.

BEWARE THE ABANDONED can be purchased from Amazon. Go to:

https://www.amazon.ca/BEWARE-ABANDONED-IAN-DUNCAN-MACDONALD/dp/0991931793

---

(3)

USING DROUGHT USA,

Rob Lyons, a Secretary of State employee, is assigned to solving the South West's drought by getting separatist in Quebec and Alberta to step aside, while the US invades Ontario and diverts its waters to the Colorado River. It is an election year. The president wants to win votes in California, New Mexico, Arizona and Nevada. A greedy lobbyist, a native chief out for revenge and a love interest make this a page turner.

USING DROUGHT USA can be purchased from Amazon. Go to:

https://www.amazon.ca/USING-DROUGHT-USA-DUNCAN-MACDONALD/dp/0991931769

---

(4)

DUEL,

Rob Lyons, a Secretary of State employee, is sent to St Matts, an island in the Caribbean, to prevent the People's Republic of China from leasing an abandoned British naval base. This base would confirm China's dominance in the region, to the detriment of the USA. Assassination, a threat of nuclear war, an evacuation and a romance make this an interesting, thoughtful read.

DUEL can be purchased from Amazon. Go to:

https://www.amazon.ca/DUEL-Threatening-Massive-Nuclear.../dp/0991931750

CHAPTER 27

Biography

Ian Duncan MacDonald

Born in the mining town of Sudbury, Ontario, Canada. Ian financed his education at McMaster University as a laborer working in a mine and the smelter of the International Nickel Company.

When he graduated in 1967, he took the first job he was offered. It was an entry level job as a credit reporter with the large international commercial risk information company, Dun & Bradstreet Inc. He enjoyed meeting with hundreds of business owners to learn how they managed to survive in a tough competitive world.

At D&B he was given more and more responsibility. His first executive job was as General Manager of their Marketing Services Division in 1970. His last job there, was General Sales Manager. In this position he was responsible for the sales, advertising, and marketing of all 4 divisions of the company and a sales team of 100 sales representatives in 15 offices serving 10,000 corporations across Canada. Turning down a transfer to the head office in New York, he sought greener pastures in 1976.

For the next year and a half, he was responsible for building two start-up subsidiaries for a large European conglomerate. Simultaneously, he was General Manager of Screening Systems International Limited and President of Intercontinental Collections Limited.

A year later when an opportunity arose at Creditel of Canada Limited, he seized it. Within a few years he was a Senior Vice President of their Credit Reporting Division.

In 1996, having achieved great success, Creditel was acquired by Equifax Inc. They were a large international risk data company eager to acquire Creditel's 14,500 customers and the new technology Ian had developed. He joined Equifax as a Vice president and stayed with them until 2005.

Having achieved financial independence, he left Equifax in 2005 to do exactly what he wanted to do for the rest of his life. This involved launching Informus Inc to handle the marketing of his art, books, and consulting services.

All his life he has been an artist. Over 1,300 of his paintings, photographs and digital are can be viewed and bought through his distributor fineartamerica.com.

Since his business life had required him to spend hours everyday writing, it was an easy transition to now start writing fiction and nonfiction books. All five of his books are distributed by amazon.com.

His wife (who is his books primary editor and Vice President of Informus Inc) has made this life's journey easier and richer. He had met her on his first day at McMaster University in 1964. They enjoy their three children and two grandchildren who all live close to them in Toronto.

THE END

(what questions or topics do you want Ian to address in his next book? Send Ian an email imacd@informus.ca)

Printed in Great Britain
by Amazon

65289330R00221